An Epic, Historic, Aviation Adventure

Dr. Duke Thomas, Nieuport 28 and Sopwith Triplane WWI Ace, is pursued by bounty hunters as he struggles to survive war-torn European and Egyptian skies against the best of the Red Baron's Flying Circus.

He explores three continents, sails three oceans, flies combat in French and desert skies, and fights overwhelming Calvary forces as the Spanish Flu pandemic rages, while deciphering antiquity's greatest 2,300 year old mystery.

He follows clues left by Caesar and Cleopatra, Ptolemy, and Alexander the Great, which lead him to a source of riches and power that could change the known world!

Readers' Comments

"Dr. Duke Thomas is the Indiana Jones of the SKY!" **KS**

"A thrilling, nonstop page turner! Romance, battle, antiquity and adrenaline! Can't wait for the nautical sequel of this epic trilogy!" **MBN**

"An historical adventure in the best Wilbur Smith, James Rollins, and Clive Cussler style!" **K**

Sky Raider

Thomas Upson

Second Edition ©September 2023
Sky Raider
©2022 by Thomas Upson
Illustrations and cover art by Brandon Delles
Map illustration by S. Lohr, SeaStory Press

Printed in the United States of America
ISBN 978-1-936818-62-4

SeaStory Press
1508 Seminary St. #2
Key West. Florida 33040
www.seastorypress.com

DEDICATION

This novel is dedicated to
my parents Emily and Jerry, who guided me with love and
helped motivate me to pursue my dreams, and my grandmother
Boompa, who taught me the value of laughter and to respect
being a member of the Thomas family.

"Duty then is the sublimest word in the English language. You should do your duty in all things. You can never hope to do more, you should never wish to do less."

General Robert E. Lee

CHAPTER 1 • BLOODY APRIL

Lieutenant Duke Thomas smiled. He was glad to be alive after another aerial battle. It was April 1917, and he was beginning his third month in France on the Western Front in the "War to End all Wars."

He leaned back on his bunk in the bleak, chilly officer's barracks on the windswept Chateau St. James airfield and wrote about his latest successful flight. It was a hard-fought aerial victory over a bright orange and black German Albatros Biplane fighter. He added it in his diary, already filled with momentous entries and drawings from the last year of his life.

It had been a close struggle until the German pilot turned too hard, impatiently trying to get on Duke's tail. He fell into a spin, which Duke took advantage of by slipping his sleek Nieuport 28 Biplane behind his opponent's tail. He fired his twin Vickers .303 machine guns until his victim's plane fell in flames to the muddy trenches over a mile below. Duke was again drenched in sweat as he drew in his diary. He captured on paper the pilot's wide eyes as they looked directly into his while he pushed himself out of the fire-engulfed plane, flinging himself free of the burning craft. He fell, screaming to his death.

It seemed like only yesterday, to Duke, that he sat mesmerized, watching the Savannah River escape to the Atlantic. He snuggled up with his lady, Vivian O'Hara, and they relaxed into the rhythm of the brassy blues music that seeped out of the Cotton Exchange on River Street in historic Savannah. His family had lived there since the founding of Georgia in 1733.

It was a whole new world in January 1917, and as one of only a few trained American pilots, Duke was due to leave in the morning for France to serve as a Lafayette Escadrille fighter pilot.

He was holding the love of his 25th year closely, and he struggled with the fact he would soon be in combat. His mind warned him that fate was a dangerous hunter, but his heart said: *"She is the most beautiful, loving, passionate lady I have ever known, and I can't live another day without her!"*

Impulsively, he pulled her close and kissed her deeply, and after a deep breath, exclaimed, "Viv! Will you marry me and make me the happiest man in the world? We can go to Christ Church right now where my parents were married and tie the knot with Father O'Flanagan!"

Viv, a very responsible 21-year-old, uncharacteristically flung her 5-foot-6-inch slender, blond-haired frame into his embrace and screamed, "YES!"

All that seemed like a lifetime ago to Duke as he focused on the cold morning breeze that moved the mist off the narrow pasture-like airfield at Chateau St. James, France. The humid, spring cold and impending tension of another combat patrol brought him back to reality as he struggled into his bear-skin flying suit. His plane was fully fueled and loaded with ammunition. He was ready for his dawn patrol as flight commander on what would become a fateful April day.

Duke waved to his personal mechanic, Sergeant Fred Jones, a former automobile mechanic who once worked at Peachtree Garage in Atlanta, Georgia, who helped strap him into his lethal Nieuport Biplane fighter.

The Nieuport Biplane was a light, nimble fighter plane and fully loaded weighed just 1235 pounds. Even with its LeRhone 160hp, 9-cylinder rotary engine, the top speed was only 123 mph, but that didn't worry Duke today. It was a work of beauty with wood-crafted ribs for the wings and fuselage, covered in cotton fabric. The famous Sioux Indian Chieftain, Sitting Bull, was painted on each side of the fuselage, standing out against the camouflage green and blue. Even the wingtips spoke of grace and art with their smooth, symmetrical shape and airfoil that contributed to the agility and performance of this fighter. The upper wing was prone to shedding its cotton fabric covering in high-speed dives, *but that was better than being shot down or burned alive if the new faster German Albatros Biplane fighters got on your tail,* he thought.

MY MOUNT!

Duke gently rubbed the twin Vickers machine guns that fired through the propeller, thanks to Dutch engineer and aircraft designer Anthony Fokker who invented the synchronizing gear, which only allowed the guns to fire when the prop was out of the way. The allies had quickly adopted it based on a captured German Fokker E-1 monoplane.

Fred yelled, "Contact!"

And Duke replied, "Contact!"

He switched on the ignition magnetos. Fred then began his dance-like manual turning of the prop by throwing his right leg into the air and pulling the 8-foot wooden prop with his hands clockwise in front of the engine while smiling at Duke. This instantly created a rough engine cough as the rotary excitedly fired to life. At the same time, the prop disappeared into a brown whirl as the LeRhone angrily spat castor oil and smoke in spurts of rough kicking and popping.

As Duke waited for the engine to stop bucking roughly, it reminded him of his favorite high-strung horse back on the Georgia family plantation. He realized that the Escadrille, represented by the Sioux Indian Chief brightly painted on his blue and green fuselage, was America's sharp end of the spear, fighting against the evil of the Kaiser and the Red Baron's Flying Circus on this lethal part of the front.

It would only be a matter of months until the full force of America would join the fight, he knew. But until then, the price was steep—as had been proven this bloody April when the Red Baron's Flying Circus had decimated his fellow aviators and friends all along the Western Front.

Yesterday was bad, and he had seen one of his best friends, Jimmy Franklin, barely survive an enemy encounter with six red, black, and white Albatros Biplanes of the Flying Circus over the bitterly contested ancient French city of St. Quentin.

The aggressive Flying Circus fighters also sent two of his squadron mates to their deaths. Jimmy received a head wound and was now clinging to life at the military hospital in Paris. But Duke now told himself every morning: "Today is life, tomorrow never comes!" It brought back memories of carefree undergraduate days in Herculaneum, Crete, when he had unearthed, as a Harvard archaeology student, a sarcophagus that had inscribed in Latin that very mantra.

While in Crete working on his thesis with his Harvard archeology and ancient languages class in 1914, he had discovered a 1900-year-old Roman tomb during the dig, and while unearthing it, he had carefully transcribed that very Latin inscription and incorporated it into his life. It created quite a stir when the contents of the tomb revealed a Roman Governor whose skeletal remains were decked out in full regalia. Mysteriously, an oversized ancient Greek coin of Alexander the Great with a large diamond eye was dangling from his skull on a gold chain. A matching gold box, intricately engraved with a large lion beside a cliff-side spring and a peregrine falcon diving into a flock of ducks, was clasped in his right skeletal hand.

Duke had carefully pulled it from the clenched fist, which showed signs of advanced arthritic changes and old healed fractures of two of his phalanges, which led Duke to realize this Governor had led a hard-fought life and was not a rich, pampered aristocrat.

When he carefully worked the ancient lock with his dissection pick, and the lid sprang open, he found the gold box contained several Egyptian scrolls, which he copied and still kept with him, along with the diamond-eyed coin. He was now a Ph.D. in archeology and ancient languages, but these scrolls proved to be coded into some type of cipher which, to date, he couldn't bend to his understanding.

Little did he know what power that experience, that gold box, that coin, and that quote would give him during the brutal battles of the world war that lay ahead. The war would destroy life, maim bodies, and twist minds out of recognition and function.

He realized that each day depended on leaving every bit of the past behind, except for the combat skills he learned as the squadron struggled to survive and fight another day!

His LeRhone rotary engine roared angrily like an enraged lion as it warmed to full function while the ground crew strained to hold the tail. Duke was ready to pay back the enemy for the savage mauling his squadron had suffered yesterday. Today, he inherited the flight leader streamers from his dead fellow southerner, Sonny Jones, who died in a fiery streak of horror yesterday. Duke had watched as Sonny accepted his fate and, after saluting his friend, put his 1911 Colt .45 to his temple and pulled the trigger rather than burn alive in his Nieuport Biplane.

Duke repeated his power statement: "We will prevail despite all odds!" This had been a favorite of his grandfather, who served in Major General Nathanial Bedford Forrest's undefeated Confederate Cavalry brigade during the dark days of the War of Northern Aggression from 1861-65. He always carried his grandfather's original wrist breaker cavalry saber in the Nieuport Biplane's tight confines as a reminder and as a weapon if shot down!

Duke looked left and saw Lieutenant Frank Wilson of Texas with his element of two Nieuport 28s. To his right, another dear friend, Lieutenant John Patton of an old proud family from Charleston, South Carolina, sat mounted in his cockpit with the grin of a bloodthirsty pirate on his lips. He was in charge of two new replacement pilots. All were new to the dangerous canyons of the lethal sky but anxious to prove their courage and eager to represent America in these foreign skies.

After each man gave Duke a thumbs up, they advanced their blip-switch throttles and raced loosely down the runway. They looked like a ragged gaggle of Canadian geese wobbling into the dawn-streaked sky, spewing a trail of castor oil from their roaring rotary engines.

They climbed nimbly to over three miles above the abused

front line, which was etched with dark brown, pitted earth and snake-like trenches as far as the eye could see. Black puffs and angry air bounced the Nieuport Biplanes around the sky like butterflies. The Imperial German anti-aircraft gunners began to range them while they crossed into enemy-controlled skies. Quickly, Duke pulled farther skyward, and the squadron safely cleared the first gauntlet of death from the anti-aircraft guns. He strained his eyes, looking for the black specks which would signal his mortal enemy.

Despite the cold and intense fatigue he felt at this thin hypoxic altitude, a distinct flash from the sun directly overhead warned Duke of enemy fighters. He rocked his wings and pointed sunward just in time to warn his wingman as the first German red Albatros D III Biplane fighter aircraft's deadly *"ak ak ak ak"* of twin Spandau machine-gun fire cut down Frank's mount. Duke pulled back hard on his stick. His vision went from fuzzy to black due to the intense gravitational forces (Gs) that pulled the blood from his head.

He still heard the *"ak ak ak ak"* of enemy machine-gun fire behind him and felt the sting of supersonic air pass close to his left ear. Suddenly, Duke felt a burning sensation in his left shoulder. As he relaxed the stick pressure which released him from the G forces, his vision returned from black to tunnel-like. He saw the horror around him while two other Nieuports tumbled earthward, trailing smoke and fire. He screamed at Ares, the Greek God of War, to guide him.

The machine guns of a red German Albatros Biplane, with a black skull and crossbones, hammered away at John slightly below him. Duke half-rolled hard left and pulled back on the joystick, which controlled his fighter plane's vertical position. Once again, he lost all but his central vision to the intense G forces as he performed this split-S maneuver and fell unseen behind the German.

Duke rested his right glove-encased finger on his joystick-mounted trigger while lining up the German Albatros in his oversized metal gunsight in front of his windscreen. When the crosshairs of his machine gun sight lined up with the enemy, he pulled hard on the trigger. Steady three-second bursts of Vickers machine-gun fire poured into the death-dealing red enemy's plane, now growing in his windscreen. It erupted in flames as Duke's tracer rounds found the engine.

He watched in horror as the leather-clad German Imperial pilot became surrounded by flames. The Generals on both sides of the trenches thought their pilots would jump to safety instead of fighting to the death. They refused to issue them parachutes. Without a parachute, the German pilot climbed out onto the left wing walk beside the fuselage, avoiding the worst of the fiery inferno. This caused the Albatros to drop its left wing and begin a slow, inevitable death spiral. The German pilot desperately reached into the cockpit to try and control his plane by grabbing the joystick.

Suddenly, the chivalry of the sky combined with his Southern honor overwhelmed Duke. He slowly maneuvered his nimble Nieuport 28 fighter closer and closer. He hoped to save the pilot and reach the flaming coffin before it disintegrated or exploded, taking them both to their graves. It was an unheard-of risk that Duke had never considered until this very moment.

His right wing was almost touching the trailing edge of the German Albatros's rapidly burning fuselage. Duke quickly matched the speed and left-turning spiral with his Nieuport 28 and yelled, "Hurry up, climb on!"

The pilot did not hear him.

The Imperial German pilot, his calm blue eyes blazing, reached backward, his body forming the shape of a cross. He was suspended for a moment between the fighters. His thick leather fur-lined glove grabbed the right wooden strut that supported each of the two wings of Duke's Nieuport fighter. Duke's right wing immediately dropped, and it took every ounce of his strength to hold a partially level attitude.

The German slowly crawled toward the wing root and safety while Duke rolled down and away to the right. It was not one second too soon. The remainder of the Albatros exploded to a fine mist while violently rocking the Nieuport!

"Hold on!" yelled Duke as the shockwave rolled over his aircraft.

By this time, all of Duke's squadron had disappeared. Had they been destroyed or damaged? Were they headed back toward home? Duke was low on fuel. One and a half hours of combat time facing life and death struggles in the canyons of the sky seemed like minutes instead of hours.

Duke turned for home but saw a menacing flight of three enemy aircraft approaching him from above. His heart sank as he saw the Imperial black crosses embossed on their wings! They quickly formed a solid arrow-shaped formation around him since he couldn't maneuver with his German passenger glued to his right wing. He anxiously looked over to the flight leader who had joined formation with him on his right in a solid blood-red Albatros D III Biplane.

Duke was shocked as he saw the invincible Red Baron himself with a shining blue and gold medal flashing under his white silk scarf. He lifted his oil-soaked goggles, nodded his head, and briskly saluted. Then, his two wingmen in Albatros Biplanes, one a solid plum purple and the other a checkered red and black, did the same. Duke was amazed that the most famous fighter pilot in the world with fifty-two confirmed victories thus far would spare him. With proud tears in his eyes, he tightly returned the salute. The three German fighters escorted him to the front lines and then peeled away, returning to German territory.

Duke's engine, now dangerously low on fuel, began to run rough. He only had a few more miles to the Chateau St. James airfield, but he was now at treetop level. His German hitchhiker was very pale and losing his grip. Duke reached over the leather cockpit rail and grabbed his arm just in time to prevent his fall to certain death as he faded into unconsciousness.

Grimly, Duke flew on as his right arm began to burn with pain from holding the helpless pilot on the wing walk. His other hand played between stick and throttle while his toes danced on the rudder bar, trying to keep the little Nieuport Biplane straight and level, on course, and airborne! Finally, the airfield materialized. Duke cut the engine ignition with the magnetos and glided in, using his one available arm for a flawless landing just when he needed it the most!

CHAPTER 2 • The Blue Max

Duke leaned his head back onto the leather headrest and looked skyward after rolling to a stop by the maintenance hangar and shutting down. After a deep breath, Duke closed his eyes and said to himself, "That was too close!"

Reality suddenly reached his auditory canals as loud moans from the German pilot shook the cotton fabric-covered Nieuport above the ringing from the deafening engine noise in his ears. Duke quickly unbuckled and gently lowered the semi-conscious pilot to the ground while the field medical staff trundled over with the medical lorry behind some ornery mules. Duke noticed the pilot had burns around his face and a scalp laceration that turned his blond hair dark red with blood. He unwound his white silk scarf, beautifully monogrammed by his mother with DT, and tightly wound it around the scalp laceration. Immediately, the bleeding slowed.

The pilot was about his age but shorter and very well dressed in the finest cashmere-lined leather. Around his neck, he wore a bright blue and gold medal: the Pour Le Merit, also known as the Blue Max. It was Germany's highest award for valor. Slowly, the piercing blue eyes opened. In excellent Oxford-accented English, the pilot spoke.

"My name is Lieutenant Max Wagner, cousin of Manfred von Richthofen, who is called the Red Baron, and I want to thank you for saving my life." As he tried to extend his hand, he dropped back into unconsciousness while the medics loaded him into the field ambulance.

Duke took a deep breath and looked at the remnants of his flight and was shocked. Only three of the original seven had returned. All were damaged, including his tail, which miraculously held together after the Albatros exploded.

John walked over to him, smiled, and said, "Man, that was the best flying and shooting I have ever seen! Thanks for saving my bacon! I owe you another round!"

Duke laughed and said, "Make it two rounds and let's get those new SPAD Biplanes that are in all the French squadrons now. Without them, we don't stand a chance against the Germans! Did anyone see what happened to Frank or our other missing pilots?"

"One of the new guys from Thomasville, Georgia, named Chipper Bragg, said he saw Frank come down intact in a field without his prop turning, but there is no word on the others. Who is the Hun you saved?" said John.

"Lieutenant Max Wagner, evidently very talented and with a lot of kills, or he wouldn't wear the Blue Max and get an escort from the Red Baron himself!" said Duke.

Duke told John about the escort to the front lines. "If they can get my Nieuport patched up, I'm going to make a run to try and find Frank before dark. Can you get the coordinates for me?" said Duke.

"Sure, but the old man is pissed, and he is already sending for you!" replied John.

"Frank could be injured, and I'm damn sure not going to leave a mate behind! He's saved my bacon before, and I owe him!" Duke responded.

Just then, an orderly arrived and yelled, "Lieutenant, the Major says to report to his office now!"

The squadron commander, Major David Vann DSO, was

red-faced as he pounded the desk. His massive gut almost knocked over a half-empty bottle of McAllen single malt scotch. Duke stood at attention and admired the dark wood-paneled office of the ancient Chateau, rumored to have been a favorite hunting lodge for King Louis VII.

The Major berated him voraciously for losing most of his attacking flight. Finally, the Major took a deep breath, grabbed two crystal-etched scotch glasses, and poured them both a sizable dose of the dark-brown, smoky whisky.

"So, what happened?" he asked.

Duke took a lingering swallow of the dark scotch as he visualized the horror of the day and slowly began.

"The Red Baron's Flying Circus jumped us from above from out of the sun over our assigned patrol area near Vimy. We were at max service ceiling in those worn-out Nieuports, but we fought like demons against the bastards! We lost two aircraft in the first pass. The higher firepower from the Albatros III's twin Spandau machine guns was no match against our Vickers guns. I was able to flame one that was on John's tail. Luckily, I saved the Hun from burning alive, and he is in our field clinic now. We need replacement aircraft immediately, and the SPAD fighter would turn the tables in our favor!"

"Damn you, Duke! You know that as American pilots flying for the Lafayette Escadrille, we are last on the list for new replacement fighter aircraft. We have to make do until the full force of America arrives. By the way, there is a large bloodstain on your left shoulder. Go report to the medical clinic immediately!"

Duke looked down and suddenly felt the pain, pumping in time with his heart. The adrenaline of combat had suppressed it until now.

"Sir, I have a downed pilot who could be wounded. I need to return for him in my Nieuport. I won't risk any other aircraft.

Lt. Frank Wilson is an experienced pilot, and we need him!"

"Absolutely not, Lieutenant! Now get out of my sight, and you're off the duty roster until a full court-martial convenes to explain how you lost four of my aircraft but somehow came back with a German? "

Duke was livid. He was shocked that the desk-jockey Commanding Officer, who wasn't even a pilot but a worn-out, grossly overweight cavalry officer, could clip his wings!

No matter, he thought, *if the Germans can't shoot me down, I won't let him either!*

He walked to the hospital and watched the nurse, Kimberly Stamper, peel away his ruined flying uniform. He worried about his friend Frank. The French doctor walked over and began examining him. After cleaning the wound with alcohol, he announced that the bullet had passed cleanly through, just below his collar bone without damaging his left lung. However, his collar bone was fractured. He would not be able to return to duty for two to three weeks due to infection risk.

As Duke waited for Nurse Stamper to finish bandaging and splinting his left arm, he noticed the German pilot was in the next bed. His scalp was tightly bandaged, and he had white ointment on the right side of his burned face.

"Good afternoon, Lieutenant Thomas. Glad to see you're OK after saving my life this morning."

"You're looking a lot better than last time I saw you, Lt. Wagner!"

"Sounds like the good doctor wants to give me another transfusion and then transfer me to the base prison in a couple of days. He said my scalp needed 25 stitches, and the facial burns were second degree, so I should heal without scarring. Maybe I won't scare any of my girlfriends and hopefully not my wife!"

"Your English is excellent," laughed Duke.

"For what my parents paid to send me to Oxford, I would hope so! I have a history and ancient languages degree," responded Max.

"What was your main area of interest?" asked Duke with sudden academic curiosity.

"Ancient Greek and Egyptian hieroglyphics, both focused on the early Roman era in Linguistics, but my passion is Alexander the Great. I was fortunate to earn my Ph.D. and write my thesis while studying the Rosetta stone and Macedonian history at the British Museum in London. Oh, what I wouldn't do for a pint of ale right now!"

"You and me both!" smiled Duke.

"Seems we have a lot in common. I'm an archeologist in the real world and earned my Ph.D. from Harvard last year. But I have had a fit trying to translate some fragmentary documents I found on a dig in Crete a few years ago," Duke said.

Duke filled Max in on his findings of the ancient Roman tomb with the coin of Alexander the Great and the gold box containing the papyrus fragments he had copied but was unable to translate. He even showed Max the coin, which he always wore for luck.

"What era did you say the Roman Governor was entombed?" asked Lt. Wagner.

"During or slightly after Julius Caesar's reign," responded Duke.

Suddenly, Max's blue eyes shone like freshly cut sapphire as he related one of the greatest mysteries of antiquity: the final resting place and tomb of Alexander the Great.

He explained that legend states it is the wealthiest burial place of all time, even making the tomb of Alexander the Great's fa-

15

ther, King Phillip of Macedon, seem like that of a pauper. Alexander was buried with all the greatest riches and treasures of Babylon, which he had conquered after defeating King Darius III of Persia in 331BC. He then led his Greek forces to conquest after conquest across the known world, amassing even more wealth. The Persians had been the greatest power of the ancient world before Alexander's time and had even conquered Jerusalem. Babylon was their capital and one of the seven ancient wonders of the world with its hanging gardens and uncounted riches.

Max also related the ancient legend, first prophesied by the Oracle of Siwa, that whoever possessed Alexander's armor of gold, his body, and the tomb could never be defeated in battle! Just as Alexander had conquered the known world without significant defeat and was ready to continue his campaign until death by poisoning stole him in Babylon in 323BC at only thirty-two years of age.

Duke's mouth now was hanging open, and he wondered if the morphine was still impacting his brain or Max's. But he recognized that these legends of Alexander were the same as those he heard during his studies at Harvard.

Duke realized he was lucid, as was Max.

He whispered, "I have a copy of the papyrus fragments with me if you would be interested in looking them over?"

Max nearly fell out of bed with enthusiasm. Duke said he would have his orderly bring them by later, but now he had to recover a friend who was downed this morning in their engagement.

Max asked for Frank's aircraft markings and looked away as he said that he did see his aircraft go down, but it was not out of control or engulfed in fire, although the engine was smoking and the prop wasn't turning. He related the position as slightly West of Vimy, where there were fields without much shelling damage available for a safe landing.

"I must warn you, Lieutenant, this area is heavily patrolled by a cavalry unit Captain Alfred von Manstein commands. He comes from the same ancient Prussian family tree that I do. Our families have fought side by side for our homeland since before Peter the Great, as we do now."

"I respect your warning, Lt. Wagner, but I must once again roll the dice of chance to help save my friend, as I'm sure you would do as well."

Duke stood up to leave and felt his left arm begin to throb and stiffen as he walked out of the medical tent.

"Wait!" shouted Max as he quickly wrote a message in German on a spare dressing package beside his bed and placed his shining blue and gold Pour le Merite (Blue Max) medal inside.

"I look forward to you returning this to me and meeting your friend. Good luck!"

"Thanks, Lt. Wagner! By the way, how did you earn this medal?"

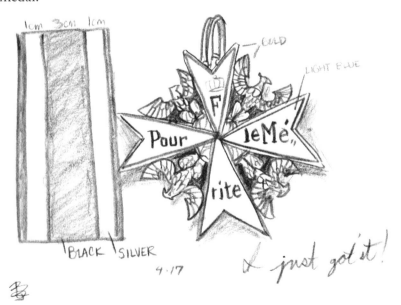

Max hesitated and then said, "Not a month ago, the Kaiser

himself presented it to me after achieving my twenty-fourth victory, and I'm happy to say none of them were American planes."

The day was waning, and Duke pushed quickly toward the maintenance hangar, trying not to attract any attention with his arm in a sling.

"Fred, is my bird patched up and ready to go?"

"Lieutenant, we need all night and maybe most of this week! The rudder post and the horizontal stabilizer need to be replaced! I can't believe you made it back with what was left holding your tail together, especially with your extra baggage," scowled Fred.

"Damn!" said Duke, but as he looked into the corner of the hanger, he saw the Commanding Officer's (CO's) rarely used DH1 Biplane, which was a pusher-style model with the engine behind the pilot pushing the tub-shaped oversized two-seater with its 70hp Renault V8 engine. The CO's plane was equipped with one forward-mounted Lewis .303 machine gun for the front seat pilot. It was designed by Geoffrey de Havilland and was state-of-the-art, front-line equipment when it first came to service in 1916. It was now badly outclassed by the Germans due to its anemic speed of 80 mph.

"Fred, is the CO's plane fueled and armed?" inquired Duke.

"Yes, sir, but his pilot just told me they were going to Paris this weekend for another... meeting?" said Fred with a snicker.

"Don't ask me anything else! Just roll it out and be quick about it. That's an order!" yelled Duke.

"Yes, sir!" replied Fred with a crooked grin. "This wouldn't have anything to do with Lt. Wilson, would it, sir?"

"Time is money, and speed is life. Get a move on it, Fred!" yelled Duke as he winked at Fred.

He grabbed his flight gear, including his saber, but didn't even try to pull on his worn calf-skin leather flight jacket. He slipped it over his left shoulder after pulling his right arm into the sleeve. Duke knew he would have to fly low and fast if he had any chance of getting Frank out before dark.

As he climbed aboard, Duke called his orderly over and whispered for him to confidentially deliver his worn leather brief-case, which contained the papyrus copies, to Lt. Wagner in the hospital.

There were no seat belts or parachutes to attach, so Duke quickly yelled, "Contact!"

"Contact!" replied Fred as he danced with the prop and swung it to a brown blur. The engine happily coughed to life.

Duke couldn't wait for the engine to warm. He immediately gave full power to the beastly craft. It bounced down the runway like an ostrich trying to take off, just as the Commanding Officer came tumbling out of his office, red-faced and screaming to the heavens!

Duke used his uninjured arm to handle the stick, which controlled pitch (up and down) and bank (left and right), while his feet danced on the rudder bars controlling yaw (left and right). His injured left arm was in a position to handle the blip switch that controlled his throttle and speed.

He climbed quickly to just above tree level and headed east. The prevailing late-spring winds pushed him to the front once again. For the third time that day, he gambled with death while crossing the trenches, however, this time at a much lower, more dangerous altitude. Not only was he targeted by German anti-air-craft, but he was so low, the trench soldiers fired at him with their Lugers! If he survived the Germans, a court-martial, and maybe a firing squad, then a transfer to the trenches could await him.

"I can't worry about what I can't control," Duke told him-self. He pushed all fear and negative thoughts into the cold twilight slipstream. He remembered that he flew to release his mind from the tyranny of earthly things!

He focused all his dwindling strength on dodging fire from every quarter as he flashed across the front, only seeing a few holes materialize in the wings despite the thunderous reception he received. Mercifully, he was through the front line, and the dank fetid smell of death from the unburied bodies in no man's land was soon behind him.

Duke took a deep breath as he adjusted course on his wobbling compass toward the area around Vimy where he hoped to find Frank. He strained his eyes, looking above his DH1 Biplane in hopes no German fighters were hunting this late in the day.

He boldly raced the dying rays of the sun, speeding off into the east on his course, hoping to ride a fraction of their speed of light as he admired the orange and pink glow from the bases of the elephantine cumulus clouds in the distance.

He pulled the trigger on the Lewis gun for a test burst and was gratified to smell the cordite as the rapid explosive shells echoed in his ears. He looked down to see he was crossing over a large field with a dark brown twisted shape in the middle. He kicked the left rudder and dropped his left wing in a tight bank to get a closer look. That's when he saw Sitting Bull, the Sioux Chief and emblem of the squadron, looking straight up at him from the fuselage of the Nieuport 28 Biplane and a huddled shape waving a white and red shirt at him.

It was Frank, and he was alive! Duke banked hard enough at the edge of the field for his vision to start to tunnel from the positive G forces, but he still saw muzzle flashes coming from the tree line. Before attempting a dangerous landing in this rough field, he quickly lined up for a burst of steady fire from his Lewis machine gun. He knew this wouldn't stop them for long as he reduced his power and set up to land beside Frank. He bounced so hard on landing, he thought his gear was going to shear off in the rough, uneven field, but everything held together as he rolled to a stop beside the wreckage. He left the engine running as he jumped out to see why Frank wasn't moving quickly to the DH1?

"Frank, are you hurt?" cried Duke over the hissing engine and distant rifle fire.

"Hey, Duke! Get the hell out of here. I'm hit pretty bad in the leg, so I'm only going to get you killed!" replied Frank.

"No way, buddy, grab my good arm!" yelled Duke.

And by working together, they climbed up onto the biplane's wing, and with a hard push from Duke's good arm, Frank dropped into the cockpit.

Duke was exhausted, but he looked back and saw a lone cavalry officer at full gallop almost on top of the aircraft, and he ducked just in time to save his head.

Duke reached into the pilot's cockpit, pulled his razor-sharp Confederate saber from its sheath, and turned to face the second charge with gusto.

The German Captain raised his sword between his eyes, and Duke returned the challenge, likewise raising his sword as Knights had done for over a thousand years. The German officer plunged ahead at full gallop while Duke protected his wounded left arm by standing close to the DH1. It was certain death unless he could roll at just the right instant under the German's beautiful white charger and cut the saddle leather or hamstring, thereby dropping the German Captain to the ground and defeating him.

Duke's breath was coming hard, and he remembered all the swordplay he had with his grandfather, who always told him never to broadcast his intentions, and instead to stand tall, breathe deeply to relax, and to go for the killing blow instead of a long duel.

He felt empowered as he remembered his tall, lean grandfather, Captain Robert Thomas, who rode with Confederate General Nathanial Bedford Forrest in the Civil War and was never defeated.

Duke's sword arm was uninjured and strong from regular practice at the Chateau with the French Cavalry officers that often visited. He smiled at oncoming death with the confidence of a lion ready to bring down her prey!

As the beautiful white charger pounded the field and was almost on top of Duke, the German Captain shouted, "Huzza!" But he broadcast his death stroke a moment too soon. Duke dodged the hissing saber stroke and simultaneously rolled under and sliced the giant white mount's hamstring. The horse immediately collapsed, throwing the Captain to the ground. He lost his sword, brass spiked helmet, and had the wind knocked out of him. Duke stood over him, ready to complete the coup de grace.

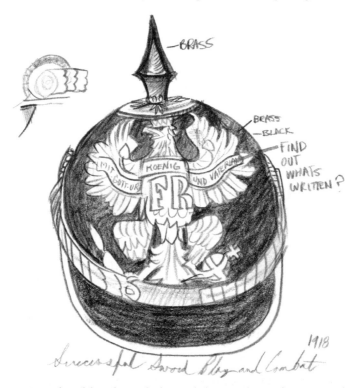

But his blood cooled, and he took a chance and said, "Good evening, Captain von Manstein." The Captain looked pale and then shocked as Duke removed his Luger to prevent further bloodshed.

"I hope you are not badly hurt?" said Duke.

"No, and how did you know my name?" said the Captain with a heavy Bavarian accent as he stiffly stood up, sadly eyeing his wounded charger.

"Who are you?" said the still-shocked officer.

Duke reached into his calf-skin leather flight jacket and gave the Captain the Pour le Merite and the message from Max.

The troops were slowly advancing from the woods but were not shooting for fear of hitting their commander.

After he read the message, von Manstein said, "I was told by Captain Manfred von Richthofen, who is a close friend, that a brave American pilot had saved another close friend, Max. I am so relieved to know he is in the hospital expected to make a full recovery!"

"Max asked in this note that if circumstances permit, I am to allow you to return with his Blue Max. Since you have defeated me with honor and have not broken our parley with firearms, I am now your prisoner, and you have captured my sword and tied my hands with this truce. Therefore, as a matter of honor, I will not pursue our engagement, but my troops will continue their duty. I only request that you not engage them or inflict casualties. What you do beyond that is out of my control, but please put my horse out of his misery."

Duke used the Captain's Luger and performed the coup de grace on the beautiful animal and quickly climbed aboard the idling DH1, but before leaving, he returned the Captain's sword and said, "You may need this if we meet again."

They both smiled, as warriors do, in anticipation of future combat!

Duke gave the DH1 Biplane all the good news the engine could produce and was able to clear the trees, surviving sporadic small-arms fire from the oncoming ground troops.

Frank was now unconscious, tightly wedged in the front seat, so he didn't experience the horror of another low-level front-line crossing. It was near pitch-black as the overloaded DH1 Biplane crossed the lines with what seemed to be endless arrays of multicolored fireworks of death from the many guns in the enemy trenches surrounding them.

Just before the last trenches, a loud bang seemed to tear out one of the rotary engine's cylinders and part of the prop; the DH-1Biplane now was barely in the air and vibrating violently!

Duke saw the red and white cross of a French medical field hospital behind the lines. He aimed for a nearby open field with no lights beside it, plowing into an abyss of darkness.

CHAPTER 3 • ATHENA

It was Thanksgiving 1915, and Duke savored the late fall in Savannah. He stretched out next to the fire on the large, soft leather lounger to enjoy his strong black coffee. His father, Dr. Jonathan Thomas III, handed his shotgun to the waiting game manager.

He was a busy General Surgeon. There were gray streaks in his blond hair, just like his son's. He had completed his surgical residency at Harvard and stood just two inches shy of Duke's six feet four inches but was now a lot thicker in the waist. He joined his oldest son by the crackling morning fire after adding some Irish whiskey, instead of cream, to his steaming mug of Turkish coffee.

The smell of bacon coming from the plantation's kitchen made their stomachs groan. They looked forward to the heavy breakfast, which made the frosty morning more welcoming before the duck hunt.

This was a family tradition. Passed down from father to son since the 25,000 acres of Peru Plantation were granted by King George in appreciation of his forefather's service. Jonathan Thomas Senior was a decorated Royal Naval captain and served as ship's Captain to bring his family to Georgia with General Oglethorpe and help form the last American colony in 1733. They landed on a high bluff up the Savannah River, several miles from the Atlantic coast, and named the city Savannah. It was the capital of the vibrant 13th colony, which wisely forbade barristers from being citizens as part of its charter, and was named Georgia in honor of King George, who sponsored the colony. The new colony of Georgia was also a buffer from the Spanish in Florida, who attempted to make raids into South Carolina and Charleston.

When Duke and his agile father scouted the flooded rice fields beside the salt marsh last evening, the mallards were thick. Both men smiled in anticipation of the upcoming morning hunt.

Duke also hoped to use his Peregrine falcon to hunt some more of the smaller isolated ponds during his holiday. This was Duke's favorite way to hunt, which he had learned as a 12-year-old apprentice from his friend and neighbor, Bob White. He had passed on to Duke this ancient sport of kings, which continued to be practiced unchanged from the original techniques published in *The Book of Falconry or Hawking* from 1575 by George Tuberville.

Just yesterday, Duke had taken his fierce Peregrine falcon, Killer, out to a pond close to Peru's main antebellum house. After gently removing her hood and releasing her from his left calf-leather gloved fist, he watched as she climbed like a rocket until she was only a speck high above him.

YELLOW

Killer!

Then he and his Chocolate Labrador named Georgia Girl (GG for short) rushed through the brush around the pond and flushed a gaggle of mallards into flight. The ducks sped away, whistling with speed, and climbed over the open pasture beside the pond. Duke watched in awe as Killer folded into the shape of an arrowhead and dove at over 200mph into the flock, where a puff of feathers, followed by two more, brought three fat mallard ducks tumbling to earth.

The last to fall was followed by Duke's majestic Peregrine falcon, who quickly landed on her kill and spread her wings, mantling over the inert green-head mallard. She began to pluck feathers and dig into the tender breast. Duke and GG had already quickly picked up the other two mallards and placed them in the battered leather game pouch hanging from his shoulder, which also had fresh pre-cut strips of venison heart that Duke now put on his leather-gloved fist.

He slowly made it to Killer and offered her the first strip, which she eagerly took after jumping from the kill to Duke's gloved left hand. He then pushed some leaves over the duck and slipped the big green-head mallard, unnoticed by Killer as she picked at the tender venison heart, into the game bag so she didn't feel like Duke had robbed her. GG carefully kept her distance after learning from previous experience not to get too close to Killer, or she would foot her, leaving her with a bloody, painful nose.

Hunting was a release and a break for Duke, who had done well as he applied his quick mind to his studies in archeology and ancient languages at Harvard. He was now writing his thesis based on Caesar's campaigns and his findings from excavations in Crete over the past two digging seasons. Duke took a deep breath as he relaxed, enjoying his long-awaited holiday in Georgia.

"Duke, how is school going?" his dad asked. He added a thick lump of salted butter to the bowl of stone-ground grits the long-time family cook, Miss Isabelle, had generously served him beside his plate of eggs, toast, and sizzling bacon. The sumptuous aroma filled the room, churning both men's stomachs.

"Making good progress on my thesis, and unless something comes up, I may have my Ph.D. before your May birthday! My work is focused on Julius Caesar and his conquest of Egypt after his success in Spain and Gaul. At that time, he was fifty-two, your age Dad, and he had been in nearly constant combat for eleven years.

"He had conquered the whole of Italy, Gaul, Spain, parts of Greece, and was about to reach the pinnacle of his career by overcoming Egypt with only two depleted legions totaling 3200 men, a third of their previous strength, and 800 horses. Little did he expect to meet the love of his life, Cleopatra VII, then 21 years old, who was acting as co-Pharaoh with her younger brother, Ptolemy XIII.

"She was presented to Caesar after rolling out of a rug in which she had been smuggled into his presence to avoid her brother's evil intentions. As reported by Plutarch, 'This romantic ruse totally captivated Caesar's heart, and he was utterly captivated by her grace and charm.'

"She and her thirteen-year-old brother, Ptolemy XIII—descended from the Ptolemaic dynasty of Macedonia, Greece—were in conflict trying to establish the sole rule of Egypt. Their ancestor, the first Ptolemy and one of Alexander's most loyal friends and best General, had governed the country as Pharaoh after Alexander the Great died in 323 BC in Babylon. His dynasty continued to rule almost 300 years later.

"But by the end of the Egyptian campaign, Caesar culminated it all with one of the most famous quotes of ancient time, 'Veni, Vidi, Vici!' *I came, I saw, I conquered!* Territory, loyalty, and the lovely Cleopatra!" said Duke with the excitement of a warrior.

"Sounds like how I talked your mother into marrying me!" said Duke's dad as father and son laughed loudly together.

"What an excellent field of study. This will make another doctor in the family, and that would be a hell of a birthday gift, son! I'm very proud of you!" praised Duke's dad. He added, "And as a reward for your outstanding accomplishment, your mother and I want to send you to Americus to earn your pilot's license in those Curtis Jenny Biplanes you have talked so much about since you got a ride in one last year!"

They both laughed in the joy of the moment as Duke rushed to embrace his father for this unexpected gift. "Wow, thanks Dad!" shouted Duke in heartfelt joy at this surprise.

Just then, his mom, Anne, walked in with his younger brother, Robby, in tow.

"Well, what did I miss?" smiled his mom.

"Good morning, honey! I was just telling Duke how I talked you into marrying me." His dad smiled as they both stood up. Duke quickly walked around and pulled out his mom's chair as she gently reached up and kissed her son on the cheek.

"Dad also told me about your gift of flying lessons once I finish my Ph.D.! Thanks, Mom!" said Duke, as he knew who really came up with the idea.

"You're welcome, darling. We're so proud of you and love you so much! Be happy and chase your dreams, honey," said his mom as they embraced.

"Hey, Robby," said Duke.

"Can I go hunting, Dad? Please!" shouted the stocky eleven-year-old.

"This is your brother's turn. Remember, he has been working hard in Boston and hasn't had a chance to go all year."

"OK, I guess," croaked Robby as he shot a quick smile at Duke. "Just leave me a few for next time."

Duke laughed and gave him a quick wink. "Don't worry, buddy. You know I'm not as good a wing shot as you are."

They all laughed since Duke was not only a good shot but was on the Harvard skeet team and hoped to make the Olympics next summer.

Breakfast flew by, and they jumped on the horses the game-keepers had ready outside and then raced by the early dawn light to the hunting area. They each laughed at the old competition between father and son on the fast, high-strung horses.

"Whoever is last, cleans the birds!" yelled Duke as he leaned forward, pushing his trusty charger forward along the well-worn path.

But his dad knew the shortcut better, and by the time Duke arrived, his dad was smiling, drinking coffee, and said, "I was about to give up on you!"

They both laughed loudly as Phillip, the ancient game manager, handed Duke a steaming mug, and the waiting field staff took the reins of his mount. Then he wisely said, "Y'all better head out to the blind. Them ducks ain't gonna wait much longer!" while handing the hunters their trusty double-barreled L. C. Smith 20-gauge shotguns.

By the time they climbed into the blind in the flooded rice field, the first light was just breaking through the giant live oaks that surrounded the east side. The gray Spanish moss looked like icicles hanging from the outstretched arms of the ancient trees, many of which predated the Thomas family's arrival. Duke's faithful retriever, GG, looked up at the sky in anticipation and shivered in excitement. They all waited happily for the whistling sound of the first flights of ducks to arrive. The air smelled of salt from the adjacent marshes and pine from the thousands of acres of virgin longleaf pine that stood silent watch over the higher ground of the seaside plantation, just as they had done for over 200 hundred years.

Cotton looked like snow as it covered the fields in white and stood ready for harvest. The prized Sea Island cotton, scattered between the rice fields by the marsh and the longleaf pines farther inland, was the cash crop that kept the plantation running successfully. But peace, and the ancient rhythm of plantation life by the Atlantic ocean, hung lazily over the crisp air of a well-run working plantation.

"How is everything going with your surgery practice, Dad?"

"I'm blessed with a lot more work than I can do, and I'm looking for another partner to join us," his dad answered. Duke could see the dark rings of fatigue under his eyes despite the early morning hour.

Suddenly, a flight of teal screamed by making the whistling sound they both loved, followed by the sound of gentle splashes as they landed in the decoys. Phillip, the game manager, had nicely laid out the decoy spread in the shape of a V with a missing spot in the beginning that lured in the ducks.

Then, a big flight of mallards appeared to the east, and Duke grabbed his trusty duck call and sounded out, "*quack, quack, quaaack.*" It sounded so real, his father smiled, and the flight cupped up, diving in straight for the decoys.

As they streaked in closer to the water whistling right over the decoys, his dad said, "Let's take 'em!"

Suddenly, the whole blind seemed to shake as they both unloaded their double-barrel shotguns and five green-head mallards folded into the water: two on the right where his father stood and three on the left from Duke's well-placed shots. He had waited for just a second after his dad's first blast, which flared the flight, and was able to line up two birds with his first shot and one with his second.

"Bird!" shouted Duke, and GG sprang into the water like a torpedo headed for a battleship.

They smiled at each other as they quickly reloaded their shotguns and watched more flights headed their way.

"Nice double, my boy!" praised Duke's father.

Suddenly, the blind began shaking and pounding despite neither man firing his gun. Bright flashes of light and clumps of dirt began pelting Duke. *What was happening?!*

He opened his eyes and found that he was not in a Georgia duck blind but in a field hospital in France, which was being shaken by artillery fire falling very close. A nurse covered him with her body as the world seemed to dissolve around him, with shapes floating in and out of focus and screams pounding his tympanic membranes. His head felt like it was about to explode with pressure, and when he reached up to grab it with his uninjured right arm, he felt a bulky wet bandage tightly wound about his scalp.

As his eyes began to focus, he realized how calm and beautiful the deep green eyes of his nurse looked, and he started to relax under her protective embrace. She realized he was conscious and whispered, "It will be over soon. The Germans are shelling the area in preparation for the spring offensive that we all know is coming any day. The doctor didn't want to move you before you woke up because of your scalp laceration. I'm glad he didn't. You are American?"

Her French accent was so beautiful, and the scent of her rose perfume lingered over him as he realized her Celtic, earthy beauty was so enchanting that he couldn't speak for a moment. Her cheeks were the color of a red sunrise, and her warm embrace did little to hide her generous soft bosom, which she somehow squeezed into her thin, white hospital gown, causing a growing sensation in his groin.

When they both realized the shelling had been over for a while, they disconnected and blushed deeply.

"Please forgive me," croaked Duke. "My name is Duke

Thomas, and yes, I'm an American flying with the Lafayette Escadrille. Unfortunately, I'm not really sure why I'm here since the last I remember was crossing the trenches with my fellow pilot, Frank. Of course! Frank! Where is my friend?" exclaimed Duke.

"He is stable but will need transport to Paris for more recovery and surgery on his fractured leg," the nurse calmly responded.

"I'm sorry. It just all suddenly came flooding back. He was wounded, so it is such a relief to know he is OK. Can you please tell me your name? "

"Juliette," said the beautiful nurse as she straightened her white apron and pushed her red thick curly hair onto her shoulders. She looked like the goddess Athena as her smile radiated through the tent and seemed to lighten the deep headache which still pounded at Duke. She was at least five feet ten inches tall and carried herself like a debutante with her tiny waist and buxom figure.

She realized how wracked with pain his expression was, and after cleaning off the debris from his bed, reached down to quickly pull the sheet and expose his thigh to give him a morphine injection. She couldn't help but see his full manhood and blushed while they shared a brief embarrassing smile, and she quickly re-covered him.

"They will be transporting you to Paris for better treatment because your shoulder wound is already showing signs of infection," Juliette said quietly while looking toward the doctor who called for her from across the ward.

As the morphine began to seep through his bones and ease the headache, Duke's warming smile spread across his face, and he reached up gently, grasping her hand, and said, "Thank you. I mean, Merci!"

"You are the most beautiful, compassionate woman I have

ever met. Perhaps you will give me the honor of repaying you with dinner when we both are next in Paris?"

"Well, Lt. Thomas, I think that is the morphine speaking, but if you remember my name, Juliette Moet, then you can find me at 14 Rue Herold, and perhaps we will have le dîner."

"Au revoir!" she said with a wink and disappeared into the maze of white and green of the medical ward in the front-line field hospital as Duke drifted off to a dream-filled sleep.

CHAPTER 4 • Harvard

He pulled heroically to full extension with the coxie's steady beat of "stroke-stroke-stroke" in the key position of the eight-man rowing shell as the regatta's final race of the season approached the finish line. Duke was the captain of Harvard's rowing team, and each man was giving it all he had. The crowd was cheering along the banks of the Charles River, and his crew strained to catch the Yale Varsity Eight, which was only feet ahead. Suddenly, his left shoulder seemed to tear, and the oar dropped out of his hands, pulling the shell into the side of the Yale Eight and throwing all rowers into the chilly water of the Charles River.

"Lt. Thomas!" he heard, and as he opened his eyes to a wet sponge soaking his face, he realized it was the hospital orderly whipping away the feverish sweat which soaked his face and body.

He was fighting the infection in his left shoulder that had finally started to abate, but he was still very weak and frustrated as he slowly recovered in the Val-de-Grace, Paris hospital.

Frank had made excellent progress and was in the post-operative ward, expected to make a full recovery.

Major Vann had been in to check on the men just yesterday and informed Duke he was being recommended for the Distinguished Service Order (DSO) medal for attaining his fifth victory over Lt. Wagner, and he was made an Officer of the French Legion of Honor for saving Lt. Frank Wilson.

Frank had seen the encounter with Captain von Manstein

and told the Major of his heroic stand and success in saving their lives in the field.

The medical staff had explained to Major Vann that Lt. Wilson would have died had it not been for Duke's heroics in rescuing him and transporting him to the field hospital.

The Major then said, "You should face a court-martial for disobeying my direct order and destroying my DH1. You will not be allowed to return to my Escadrille!

"If your lucky success in rescuing Lt. Wilson were not such a morale booster, I would not support your medal recommendations by Lt. Wilson and my junior staff."

He went on to say, "Since the United States declared war on Germany, every pilot will eventually be needed for the front, but since that will take a while, I am transferring you, if or when you recover, to the worst possible posting! The Egyptian desert and the British Expeditionary Flying service. Oh, and by the way, I sent your mechanic, now Private Jones, to the front!"

Major Vann smiled at the wisdom of his ruthless decisions and walked out before Duke could absorb this horrendous news as he closed his eyes, trying to ease the throbbing pain in his shoulder.

"A British unit in the deserts of Egypt?" repeated Duke quietly in his feverish state.

Then, suddenly, he opened his eyes and a smile broke across his pale and sweat-drenched face.

"The Oasis of Siwa!" he yelled.

The orderly came quickly to his bedside and said, "Sir, you are delirious from fever."

"No," replied Duke.

"I'm one step closer to solving the greatest riddle of all time. Finding the tomb of Alexander the Great," and he fell into a deep sleep.

"Je ne comprends pas," *I don't understand*, laughed the orderly. "Americans!"

CHAPTER 5 • THE DESERT

Duke spent his sick leave in Paris, reporting daily to the wound-dressing outpatient wing of Pitie-Salpetriere University Hospital. He began the vigorous stretches and exercises the French rehabilitation staff advised him would help strengthen his shoulder.

He had only a week left to complete his recovery and report to the Flight Surgeon to pass his physical, or he would be sent to the front, per Major Vann's latest orders. There he would join his mechanic, Fred Jones, if he was still alive, as he was already in the hottest part of the front.

The infected bullet wound had eroded part of Duke's shoulder blade and severely weakened his shoulder girdle, so it was very difficult to fully lift his left arm, which was also very weak, although his grip remained strong. The therapy was helping, but Duke knew it would take months, not just a week, to recover fully.

He could hardly believe it was July 1917, and he was in the most beautiful city he had ever seen, besides Savannah. But he could find no peace or rest due to his chronic pain and nightmares about the termination of his last flight. He had done everything his heart and Southern honor had told him to do. Now, instead of receiving praise and promotion, he was seeing his talented, loyal mechanic condemned to death in a muddy trench.

The last month seemed like a nightmare as he felt the tears of frustration growing in his eyes as he worried about Fred, and he felt fully responsible for his transfer to The Third Battle of Ypres.

He crushed his hands together in anger and yelled the Major's name skyward in vain! Then, after he took a deep breath to clear his mind, *her* beautiful face seemed to appear before him as he took several more deep breaths with his eyes still closed. Juliette! He suddenly remembered her address, and her angelic figure appeared in his mind!

Duke left his small apartment and flagged a coach. He quickly disappeared amongst the throngs of Parisians and soldiers on leave, crowding the Champs–Elysees. The driver expertly found his way, past the Arch de Triumph, to Rue Herold.

"Au revoir, Monsieur, just a little on the left," said the driver as he hurried away for his next fare after dropping Duke at the corner.

It was a warm evening with scents of lavender and rose in the air. As if in a minefield, Duke stepped carefully along the narrow cobblestoned street packed with neat, small upscale apartments filling every inch of the old historic section of Paris. Then, number 14 appeared on the left. It was much larger than the surrounding structures and seemed hidden in the ancient mimosa vines that coated the front of the building's stone walls.

Duke took a deep breath, gently lifted the brass handle shaped like a fleur de lis, and knocked against the door, sending deep vibrating metallic thuds throughout the ancient, oversized door and building. Almost instantly, a butler in starched white attire opened the door and ushered him inside.

"Uhm, I'm Lieutenant Thomas here to see Miss Juliette... Uh-uhm, she took care of me at the field hospital just last month and gave me her address to call on her so that I could thank her for saving my life. I'm sure you must get many patients coming by to thank her," Duke said.

He felt sweat start to form on his forehead and his headache begin to throb, but at least it was out!

"Monsieur, we have never had anyone of your description or condition come to this old family home with a similar request, but I will be happy to present your card to Mademoiselle when she returns from the hospital later this evening. Perhaps you can return tomorrow?"

Duke gazed around the high, dark wood-paneled ceilings, enjoying the fresh-cut roses on the mantle, and admired the beautiful full-size Greek marble sculpture of Mercury in front of the marble staircase. It was an old and elegant home, yet relaxing.

Duke quickly realized Juliette had helped him once, and perhaps she was his only hope of returning to flying, in addition to being the most beautiful nurse he had ever seen.

He didn't have a calling card but borrowed a notecard from the butler and wrote, *"Your humble servant, Lt. Duke Thomas, requests the honor of your company at Café de la Paix this evening to repay my debt to you, the skilled and beautiful nurse, Miss Juliette, who saved my life. I will wait as long as possible and will return tomorrow evening and the next, if necessary, to await your presence."* He signed his name with a flourish.

As he handed the card to the butler, Duke asked, "Monsieur, kindly tell me her last name." The butler smiled and pointed to the large painting of Marshall Ney on horseback in full military attire atop the adjacent library's oversized fireplace.

"This is her great grandfather, and her name is Juliette Ney Bibesco Anthoine Moet. I will give her your note when she arrives. Au revoir, Lieutenant." And the butler quickly escorted him to the door.

Duke bowed and said, "Thank you very much. Au Revoir, monsieur," and left the exquisite entry hall of the old majestic home.

He couldn't help thinking how his grandfather's commander, General Forrest, and Juliette's great grandfather, Marshall Ney, would have had a lot to talk about, especially good cavalry horses, victories, and lost causes.

Duke knew that Napoleon nicknamed Marshall Ney "le Brave des Braves." The bravest of the brave because he never renounced his Emperor, Napoleon, even after he was tried for treason and faced a firing squad in 1815. Duke remained thankful; his grandfather wasn't shot by a firing squad.

General Frost   1918

Duke made his way to the quaint but popular Café de la Paix. It wasn't too far from Juliette's home, and he had seen it on the carriage ride. It was now almost dark, and he ordered a bottle of 1912 Dom Perignon with a fresh baguette and cheese. His hopes were high that she would show up tonight.

As he ordered, he realized this was the best way to spend his extra combat pay. He admired the beautiful cafe in the dimmed evening lights and absorbed the romantic string music drifting down the street. The cool evening air surrounded him and allowed him to slowly relax into the twilight for the first time in weeks. Duke wondered why he finally felt relaxed and safe without flashbacks of his last crash and near-death experience and decided maybe it was because he was close to the one who had saved him from death.

"Lieutenant, Lieutenant!!" an angelic voice suddenly exclaimed.

Duke's eyes opened from his momentary daydream, and he thought he must have truly found heaven.

There, in front of him, stood the most beautiful, exotic, sensual woman he had ever seen. She was in a flowing white silk dress that accentuated her large bosom and tight waist, and was so sheer it was as if nothing covered those majestic curves. She was smiling at him, and suddenly he realized as he smelled the faint scent of roses and saw her long curly red hair and emerald green eyes, it was Juliette, and he really was in heaven!

She walked closer to him in three-inch white heels that brought her moist red lips to his chin as he stood to his full six feet four inches so that he could embrace her and kiss each of her rose-scented cheeks.

"It's wonderful to see you, Juliette. Thanks for coming so I could repay you for saving my life!"

Duke tried to keep from falling because his head was spinning from such beauty and poise.

"It is my honor to visit with such a brave airman who is helping to save our country from the German tyranny. To be honest, I have been thinking of you and wondering how your recovery and treatment have been going."

She blushed and went on, "In all sincerity, I was hoping you would remember me and my address."

Duke recognized an English girl's school accent and smiled at her sweetness.

"I will never forget you for many reasons, but now is the time to celebrate our reunion in Paris! How is Dom Perignon?" Duke asked.

"It is my absolute favorite and happens to be my family's label," winked Juliette.

The night began with a loud pop and a cork that disappeared into the darkness. The table became a warren of words as they quickly caught up with each other.

She explained her mother's side of the family and their long history in France back to Louis XIIII and her famous great grandfather. Then she described how her father's family had started the Moet and Chandon champagne house in Epigney on the Marne river and how pleased she was with his choice of champagne.

She was an only child, she said, and her parents were away at their sugar cane plantation in the West Indies, avoiding the wartime shortages while working to increase the supply of sugar and rum for the French military. She had attended boarding school in London until the war began, and she became a nurse last year to help heal the men trying to save France.

"Duke, I almost forgot to tell you that your mechanic came by shortly after your transfer. He left this briefcase at the field hospital and said it was private *and urgent*. He also said he was assigned to front-line service! He was quite sad but otherwise looked good," said Juliette.

Duke peaked in the briefcase and saw his scrolls with additional translation and documents from Lt Wagner. Duke wondered if he had actually translated them. Then, he quickly closed the battered case and smiled at the beautiful goddess sipping champagne beside him.

Juliette continued, "Fred said the German pilot gave it to him the night before he escaped."

"What?" exclaimed Duke. "Did he get recaptured?"

"Not according to Fred, who said no one saw or heard from him again until a cable came through stating he was credited with shooting down two British FE2s."

"Juliette, this briefcase you gave me is so important. It will help me at my next posting in Egypt, if I can only pass the flight physical next week. I need more time for healing, but Major Vann has it in for me since I rescued Frank and crashed his personal party plane in the process. If I fail the physical, then it's off to the hottest part of the front as a trench soldier!"

She looked like she had just seen a ghost as all this information settled in, and Duke wished he had controlled himself and not told her everything so suddenly.

Then, just like the new dawn, she lit up and said, "Show me your arm and shoulder!" Duke went through his range of motion and exercises while she watched with a scowl on her face.

"No, no, no! No wonder you aren't healing well. Those are the wrong therapeutic exercises for your wounded shoulder!" She stood up behind him and began massaging and moving his shoulder and arm in a series of extensions and flexions, which immediately felt better and produced more strength and motion.

"Wow, that feels so much better, and I can see how this can work! Oh, my angel! " Duke said.

He pulled her tightly to his chest and lightly kissed her.

It was wartime, he thought, *and feelings had to be acted on while time and life allowed*. He was reminded of the lesson he learned while working on the Roman tomb's excavations: "Today is life, tomorrow never comes."

To his surprise and shock, Juliette pulled him tightly to her body, and they kissed again. Duke was breathing so hard, she had only to rub her hips against him lightly, and he was her slave.

Duke quickly deposited the last of his francs on the table as they ran hand in hand from the Café, finally reaching her house where they slipped in through the maids' entrance and down into the cellar.

"It is so late, no one will come down again tonight, and we can enjoy another bottle and snuggle in these blankets. I want to know all about you!" said Juliette.

As they talked non-stop late into the night, one after another Dom Perignon corks popped and bounced off the cellar bottles with a hiss. They took turns pouring the bubbling liquid into each other's open mouths, laughing infectiously and feeling a deep connection. Could it truly be "love at first sight"?

Duke's passion mounted as he tried to control his feelings, but soon he began to gently remove her clothing, with her encouragement, desperately trying not to tear the sheer silk white dress. He repeatedly tried to remove the clasps of the perfectly fitted white leather diamond-encrusted heels and then decided they looked too good on her long slim legs and left them on. The bubbles flowed into Juliette's mouth and bathed her body in a coating of golden bubbles. The moonlight flowing through the cellar window gave her an angelic glow. He savored the taste of the Dom Perignon as it mixed with her essence, and looked into her emerald green eyes, and realized he had found his lifetime love. He was living fully in the moment but in a dream-like state with the Amazonian woman of his dreams!

"Take me now, mon amour!" screamed Juliette. "Je me peux pas attendre une seconde de plus!"

"Are you sure, my love?" Duke said. He was in an agony of pleasure and could barely control his voice. "But I must also tell you something," Duke begged.

But Juliette was busy pulling off the last of his uniform and he lost touch with time and space as he released the passion of his love.

They clung to each other, covered in sweat, champagne, and the juices of love. Their sleep was free of nightmares and full of hope, fulfillment, love, and a life together. Duke had found his angel, his muse, his goddess, his lifetime love, but when he awoke to the bright sunlight pouring through the cellar window, he realized something was unfinished.

Juliette clung to his chest, asleep with a beautiful smile on her face and a body so perfect that it needed to be held tightly and protected against all the evil in the world. A world at war raged around them as they found shelter and love in this wine cavern, but Duke still had to face the truth: he was married to another woman. Vivian was from another continent, another time, another place, another reality! It tore at his heart and soul as he stared at the cellar walls while Juliette slept the deep sleep of happiness, fatigue, and love. What could he do?

Suddenly, it all became clear. Duke needed to live in the moment. As the inscription in Crete screamed out from two thousand years ago, time and life were fleeting gifts to be enjoyed now, not later when death closed all men's eyes. Duke decided in the peace of the cellar not to destroy this special and very brief time they had together. Soon he would head back to the hell of death in the sky, or even worse, as Fred was facing, death in the trenches.

The life expectancy of a new pilot on the front was now less than three weeks, and even the London times called April 1917 "Bloody April" due to the Red Baron's powerful Flying Circus. Duke had watched dear friend after dear friend take off with him, never to return, and he had seen many others fall apart internally and then turn into a shell of what they used to be from daily death and non-stop combat. Duke rarely slept and had recurrent nightmares of falling to his death in a flaming coffin, which only last night had briefly left him.

Duke knew nothing of what he would face in Egypt, but deep inside, he felt it was somehow the place he needed to be and the time he needed to be there. He had less than a week to heal, and with Juliette's help, he knew he could get strong enough to pass not only physically but also mentally! She was his angel, and they would enjoy every minute of the time left in Paris with no regrets or guilt!

This was their time, and as Duke was looking at her beautiful face, her green eyes suddenly appeared with a smile to match his. "Bonjour, mon amour." Their lips touched, and they fell into each other's arms and began eagerly again, right where they had stopped their passion just hours ago.

They worked together with Juliette's new therapeutic exercises to prepare Duke's partially-healed shoulder with stretching, massage, mobilization, and endless lovemaking every day and night. Somehow, miraculously, Juliette helped him to improve enough to pass the flight physical! The flight surgeon barely looked at Duke. Instead, he chattered away in French with ravishing Juliette before signing off on the medical form and sending them away with a wink to Juliette.

The loving couple quickly exited Pitie-Salpetriere Hospital and rushed into the warm wave of summer heat, which matched the desire growing inside each of them as they stopped at Café de la Paix for champagne.

They slipped into their favorite back corner table. They embraced, completely oblivious to their surroundings. Their lips joined and time slipped away until the sweating champagne brought them back to the disappearing summer twilight. They each savored the beginning of Duke's last night in Paris as the cold liquid bubbled down their throats. Duke slipped his hand up Juliette's left thigh to her equally wet lips. She moaned like a snow leopard enjoying her latest kill!

She slowly spread her legs, pushing her heels straight out from under the table as Duke' kissed her. She grabbed him and pulled him closer as she released a moan of pleasure, thrusting her hips forward and toppled the table, turning the empty bottle of Dom Perignon and champagne flutes into a blur of flying glass. They made a hasty exit as Duke tossed a 50 franc note onto the chair.

Early the next morning, Duke awoke in their cellar of passion, covered in dried sweat. With deep sadness in his heart, he slowly pulled his military uniform out of his stuffed duffel bag. Juliette's gaze lingered a moment too long, and he was unable to withstand her final assault. "Take me, Duke, like the man you are, and we will go to heaven!"

"Mon amour!" shouted Juliette as Duke could wait no longer and spent his passion so loudly it shook the bottles in the cellar. They collapsed into each other's arms, reveling in love from the most passionate ecstasy either had ever experienced.

They lay bathed in sweat, breathing deeply and kissing as Duke pulled her close to his slick body and said, "I have never experienced such love. Please wait for me."

Juliette said with deep passion, "I will wait and come to you, my love, no matter how long or far away you may be."

Duke looked at his Rolex, realizing he could miss the train if he didn't hurry. He jumped into his traveling uniform. Juliette pulled on a tight blue silk shirt and black pants with her black leather riding boots. Duke grabbed his duffel bag, and they then rushed hand-in-hand to Paris-Gare-de-Lyon for his train to Marseille. As they arrived, the train was just pulling out. Duke kissed Juliette deeply, then luckily reached the last car at a full run, throwing his gear on board before swinging up on the rail and looking back for Juliette.

"Je t'aime, Duke!" cried Juliette as Duke squinted through the steam of the moving train.

"I love you too!" Duke yelled. He hoped she could hear him above the shrill whistle and cries of the conductor.

Their eyes locked as an affirmation of these feelings stronger than words could ever express and that they both felt with every beat of their hearts and souls.

They both knew this couldn't be the end; it was only the beginning as Duke rolled down the tracks and watched Juliette rubbing her womb knowingly until the steam and distance blocked her after they shared a final expectant smile and blown kiss.

CHAPTER 6 • EGYPT

The slow-moving tramp steamer, *Leviathan,* had been in service well beyond its useful life. She groaned under the pounding of the Mediterranean swells. Day after broiling day passed in the officers' mess and quarters. The occasional summer storms, although intense, cooled the crew and military passengers briefly but worried the officers immensely as the steamer seemed to list beyond recoverable limits. At the same time, it relentlessly edged closer and closer to the port of Alexandria, Egypt.

Duke had been assigned to the Egyptian Expeditionary Force, a British Empire military formation now under General Edmund Allenby, who needed more pilots to support his maneuver style of warfare. Duke was to report to Cairo, Egypt, for his new aviation assignment.

Duke's mind finally began to return to reality as the smell of Africa washed over the steamer, and they passed Crete, barely visible in the far northern horizon after his third night at sea. He was madly in love with Juliette in a way that had never existed before, and the intensity of the separation left his heart and body full of longing. His heart ached with loneliness and passion instead of fatigue.

He was miserable, and he was married to Vivian, whom he also loved, but it was different. She wrote him narrative-style letters weekly of all that was going on in Savannah as America mobilized, trained, and began sending men to war in Europe. Savannah was abuzz with rumors of spies, U-boats, new rationing of sugar and other essential commodities, and the intensity of her latest letter was surprising.

River Street, she said, was packed with soldiers, and Duke's parents worked harder than ever to help plant more crops and heal more of the sick as more and more troops passed through this strategic port.

America was now at war with Germany, as was Duke's heart between the passionate love he felt for the earthy, Celtic, primal beauty of Juliette and the committed, church-sealed, lifelong loyalty of Vivian.

Finally, as he watched Crete slip by, he realized that time would solve these battles of life and death with Germany and passion vs. responsibility in love. But first, he had to survive his next assignment and the bloodbath of a world at war.

That night, after a long evening squall, Duke retired to his small quarters he shared with Lt. Flight Officer Tom Holmes. Once inside, he pulled the last of his meager belongings from his duffel bag, and the neglected briefcase dropped out.

His mind flashed back to when he asked German Imperial Pilot, Lt. Wagner, to translate the copied ancient Roman/Greek mysterious manuscript. It was now almost three months ago, and Duke realized he hadn't even looked at the results.

He gingerly opened the battered but secure calf leather briefcase and gently removed his most valuable belongings. He spread them carefully on the small reading table. The little whale oil lamp dimly flickered a pale-yellow glow, which was enough to confirm the translation was complete and printed on his crisp new stationery monogrammed with DT. Duke eagerly squinted into the deepening evening as he embraced each word that jumped off the parchment, and his mouth dropped open in utter astonishment as it began to register.

It described not the Roman Governor of Crete's last will and testament as he had long expected, but instead, his mission on behalf of Julius Caesar, which was so magnificent in its results that he was appointed Governor for life and his family given hereditary rights to a considerable portion of the island!

The translation also revealed that Governor Marcus Antonius Tiberius was one of the richest men in the world at the time of his death! Duke gasped at this honor and wondered what he could have done to earn such unimaginable wealth and esteem?

Suddenly, just as the alarm bells sounded, Tom burst in, shouting that a U-boat was sighted. Duke stashed the important translation and ran to his battle station on deck.

They spent the rest of the next hour scanning for the tell-tale white plume from a torpedo's wake as the small destroyer escort hammered the sea with depth charge after depth charge. Thankfully, neither man saw any sign of white wake, and, after further false alarms, they finally moved to the officer's mess for coffee a couple of hours later.

"I could use a spot of whiskey!" bellowed Tom.

"I think a whole bottle would be better," Duke exclaimed.

They roared with laughter, relieved they survived. They enjoyed the compadre of two soldiers who faced daily death while in combat, sent there by foolish politicians and monarchs who never set foot on the battlefield.

They knew millions had died already, and millions more would soon follow, some on the multiple fronts of the world war, others due to starvation, exposure, and most unpredictable of all, rampant disease, especially the new disease called the Spanish flu, which would ultimately infect about a third of the world population and kill fifty million people.

Tom Holmes was from Edinburgh, which he described proudly as Scotland's capital, in the county of Midlothian on the Firth of Fourth's southern shore, and his family had proudly served in all major British Empire campaigns since before Waterloo. He spoke with a strong brogue, and when he decided to do something, his determination was unstoppable.

He also had four German planes to his credit from the Western Front in the Marne sector and was also assigned to General Allenby. He had been flying the Sopwith Camel Biplane, which was already famous for its brilliant design by Tommy Sopwith but had a vicious reputation for torque due to the short-coupled rotary engine. However, according to Tom, that's what made it so nimble and effective in combat.

What a small flyer

He couldn't wait to take down number five and earn the title "Flying Ace!" He often poked fun at Duke as the senior pilot and ace.

Tom was married to his lifelong sweetheart, Alice, who was expecting their first child any day.

CHAPTER 7 • Tiberius

After two cups of the worst black coffee on the whole journey, Duke was calm enough to head back down to continue reading the translation of Governor Tiberius's journey to becoming the Cornelius Vanderbilt of two thousand years ago! He opened the translation and was so transfixed, he didn't hear Tom return.

Duke picked up the translation again from where he stopped during the U-boat scare. He was in awe that he was reading for the first time a document that was over 2000 years old and created before Christ's birth.

> I was a young man once and served in Caesar's best legion, the glorious 13th. I was always thrust into the most critical parts of any battle. During the Gaul, Germania, and Britain campaigns, I became a Centurion ultimately assigned to Caesar's elite personal bodyguard and shock troops due to my success and leadership, turning defeat into victory. I then became the commander of the Praetorian Guard and a close advisor and confidant of Caesar. We fought together during our final campaign: The Siege of Alexandria. I was at Caesar's side throughout the battle, including the critical moment best described by Plutarch: "The enemy tried to cut off his fleet; he was forced to repel the danger by using fire, and this spread from the dockyards and destroyed the great

library."

As Caesar tried to win the close battle, Cleopatra, who had become his lover, stormed into our war room which overlooked the worst of the fighting. She screamed, "Caesar! The library is in flames! It must be stopped!"

"My darling, I need every man, or the battle is lost and Egypt will be destroyed, not just the library!" replied Caesar.

Cleopatra stood, legs in a wide stance, arms folded across her chest, turning her piercing green eyes directly on Caesar and screamed, "I will go alone if I have to, but I must try!"

Suddenly, Caesar knew he was outmaneuvered and turned to me, his most trusted and capable Praetorian Commander, proven in all our campaigns together.

"Commander Marcus Tiberius, take my personal bodyguard and follow Queen Cleopatra to the library and save what you can as she knows the most critical papyrus and books."

"My Caesar, you will be unprotected if I leave on this mission!" I screamed in frustration.

"I have been fighting all my life, and these Ptolemaic forces are hotly engaged elsewhere! I think I can survive briefly without your protection. You have one hour, and then we must counter-attack to save our fleet. That is all, and be quick about it, my friend!"

I rushed behind the personal guard and followed Queen Cleopatra to the library. We followed her into the depths, gasping on the thick smoke as we made our way to the far western corner of the room, only to find it fully engulfed in flames.

She yelled, "Commander Tiberius, you must save Pharaoh's special documents!" as she unlocked a hidden doorway only to find it full of smoke. She passed out and was taken out to fresh air by two of my guard members.

I pushed ahead through the thick smoke, coughing on the foul air, and found a chest marked in Latin: "Pharaoh's eyes only; all others face blindness and eternal suffering."

I grabbed the hot chest and felt the brass straps burn through my leather combat vest and shirt, burning my hands and skin, but I held on with pure determination and got out just as the building collapsed in flames behind me. I fell to the ground, gasping for air, and coughed until my head and eyes cleared and the burning pain on my arms and chest calmed.

The Queen was gone, and most of my men were already fighting to save the fleet since a full hour had already passed. I secured the chest in Caesar's galleon and immediately joined the battle that raged long into the night. Ptolemaic forces fell one after another to my razor-sharp short sword, which whistled and cleaved until blood soaked my burned battle garments and soothed the pain of my burned body. Finally, the Egyptian survivors melted away in fear and exhaustion.

With the first light of morning, I was with Caesar on his galleon. The sight was glorious for Caesar as all remaining enemies were in full retreat or heavily engaged with many casualties inflicted by our troops.

Caesar threw his red robe to the ground, looked skyward with arms outstretched, and yelled like a man possessed: "Veni! Vidi! Vici!"

With a huge smile and twinkle in his eye, Caesar said, "Marcus, see what all the fuss is about over that chest and then brief me. Of course, Cleopatra will want it all back! But we get a first look!"

Caesar collapsed in his chair and grabbed a gold pitcher full of the best Cretan wine and drank to control his thirst and trembling hands. It had been a battle so closely contested that even now, he wondered how he had strategically succeeded, but history would decide that. Now he vowed to sacrifice a hundred bulls and feast his legions to celebrate the thrilling victory.

We had been at war for over eleven years, beginning with the Gallic war, which Caesar almost lost when Vercingetorix of the Arverni united the Gauls against Rome. Finally, he was defeated at The Battle of Alesia six years later. Then, three years later, Caesar's crossing of the Rubicon with his best legion, the 13th, started the civil war with the simple words, "Let the dice be tossed." It had been a non-stop war since this time for us, and finally, the end was in sight.

What a warrior

That is why Caesar was in Egypt two years later, chasing
down Pompey, his last major Roman threat. Pompey had fled
to Alexandria, Egypt, where Pharaoh Ptolemy XIII murdered
him. But following the delivery of his fellow council's head,
Caesar decided to support beautiful Cleopatra VII's claim to
the throne instead of the murdering Ptolemy XIII. Just one
final battle remained: The Battle of the Nile, which Caesar
would also win and then install his spectacular consort,
Cleopatra, as ruler.

I smiled as Caesar poured my golden chalice to overflowing,
and we laughed with the joy of those free to enjoy another
day of life in a world full of death.

"Your wish is my command, mighty Caesar!" I smiled, and we
drank deeply until the blood-red wine flowed down our soiled
battle tunics.

59

"I couldn't have succeeded without your elite guard and leadership, my friend!" yelled Caesar.

He refilled my chalice and took another gulp from the spectacular golden pitcher. It had an image engraved on its sides, depicting Minotaur impaling a Persian soldier. We smiled and drank as the last smoke from the Library of Alexandria wafted through the open hatches of the fortified galleon. As I looked toward the dying embers of the library, even my military mind wondered if it was worth it.

The history, art, treasures, inventions, and truths of the ancient world were gone! Only the single chest of Pharaoh's documents remained. What could be so important that Cleopatra instructed this, of all treasures, be saved?

I slammed my chalice to the table and embraced my oldest and truest friend and commander, "My Lord, I will discover the mystery of this chest and report all to you within a fortnight!"

Caesar smiled, exclaiming, "My loyal commander, I wait with anticipation for your report. I hope you will have these answers within three days, and meanwhile, I go to fight our final naval battle against these barbarians on the Nile! The Praetorian Guard will remain here with you to distract the Egyptian naval galleys from the impending battle."

"Yes, my lord," I saluted as we embraced, and I exclaimed, "for Rome and Caesar!"

CHAPTER 8 • PTOLEMY

Duke continued reading Marcus's death bed revelations, which he hoped would explain one of the greatest mysteries of all time. He felt transported back to Roman times as he read.

After secretly transporting the chest covered with a rug to the Egyptian palace, I deployed my elite but exhausted Praetorian Guard around the outside to convince any spies that Caesar remained in residence. I then ensconced myself in a private wing of the second floor to begin my search of the only remaining historically significant object saved from the Alexandria library.

I instructed the palace slaves to feed my men and provide a double serving of wine to a third of the Guard at a time. I then began my research of the contents of the ancient chest.

I examined the lock and realized no one had ever opened it. While kneeling, I broke it with the hilt of my short stabbing sword—with great difficulty.

Then I started to massage the chest open while I reread the curse which said, "For Pharaoh's eyes only; all others face blindness and eternal suffering."

I grabbed a glass of vinegar from the table beside the chest to help neutralize any toxins I might encounter when it opened. After pouring it on my robe, which I then wrapped around my face, I forced open the ancient chest.

Suddenly, a coil sprung as quick and deadly as an Asp directly toward my covered face. It sprayed a white powder across my wet robe, which I flung aside before running from the room.

Slowly, the white residue dissipated as the twilight and final rays of the sun pierced the evening air in what I now realized was the antechamber of the throne room. I dared not waste any more time because Caesar devoured time, and there wasn't any to spare. The immensity of the contents of the chest demand that I cautiously return to my mission.

I opened all the windows and doors while carefully making my way back to the chest, and what awaited my eyes, I will never forget!

An ancient and partially crumbling stone tablet fragment was visible behind several rolls of papyrus. No wonder the bloody chest was so heavy. As I looked closer, I recognized the Hebrew letters and began to investigate the mystery that would dominate the rest of my life. Chiseled deep into the stone fragment behind the numeral 'VI' was engraved: "Thou shalt not Kill."

I remembered the Jews who had repeated the same words over and over during their Sabbath in the slums of Rome where I had barely survived childhood. They had protected and fed me when no Roman would even look at the urchin of a child orphan covered in rags who would beg, borrow, steal, or somehow find food, just trying to live another day. I learned Hebrew from these close-knit people and respect for their and other religions. Somehow I survived until I was big enough to lie my way into the army as a common soldier, at what I claimed was my thirteenth year of age.

I rose through the ranks to become a Centurion. Then when I saved Caesar during his defeat at the Battle of Gergovia in Gaul, after Vercingetorix's brilliant campaign decimated the rest of his bodyguards and cavalry, I realized God had something special in mind for my life.

I was appointed the new Praetorian Guard commander by Caesar and immediately rebuilt and retrained this hand-picked elite unit. I chose the best men from my legion and from amongst the prisoners, who would otherwise be sent to the Arena in Rome as gladiators if they weren't executed first. The Gauls were the best warriors who had ever engaged the Roman legions. With their Celtic body tattoos, massive physical size, and otherworldly war cries combined with no fear of death, they were nearly invincible. These troops had been unbeatable with their current leader, Vercengetrix, until the Battle of Alesia.

Caesar's brilliant use of siege works and tactical movement encircled Vercingetorix, who almost broke out to join his massive relieving army, which would have spelled inevitable defeat for Rome. However, at the weakest point of encirclement and at the most critical moment of the battle, Caesar and I engaged the Gauls as they were almost through. Thanks to my Praetorian guard's supreme effort and sacrifice, we stopped the breakthrough and defeated the Gauls, barely, and with heavy losses.

I was elevated to Caesar's closest confidant and commander after being rewarded with an estate in Southern Italy. Unfortunately, I have never seen it since I haven't left Caesar's side during the last years of non-stop battles.

I smiled at these memories as I worked my way through the chest and slowly realized the magnitude of what confronted me.

I then called my second in command, Brutus Quintus, who was one of the Gallic warriors I had saved to join my guard unit and had more than once saved me from certain death.

"Brutus, I must have complete security and be undisturbed until I complete this mission for Caesar! Do not let anyone near this palace and keep a 24-hour guard at all times. There are spies and renegade Ptolemaic soldiers everywhere! I will let you know when I'm done. Until then, have my food and drink screened for poison and delivered by your hand only!" ordered Marcus.

"Yes, Commander!" replied Brutus.

After placing the stone tablet fragment with the sixth commandment on the floor, I removed many more rolls of signed and detailed papyrus and animal skins with treaties, agreements, ledgers, and titles over the next two days. Finally, I realized only one other object rested at the bottom of the chest.

I carefully leaned over, suspecting another booby trap, and gently lifted the heavy object, covered in deeply aged leather, to eye level. Night had fallen on the second day of my non-stop exploration of the chest, and the jackals and wolves howled in the distance as they circled and then feasted on human remains from the ongoing battle. Reverently, I lifted the package to the torch to see what mysterious object emerged, and I gently peeled the leather away.

The leather was so brittle, it cracked and fell away in pieces until, shining in my hands, was a gold Phrygian helmet of classic Greek design! It was magnificent in its luster, beauty, and design but showed multiple signs of battle damage, especially a deep forehead-to-cheek guard sword gash and multiple dents on the crown.

My curiosity grew, wondering if perhaps this was Ptolemy's battle helmet with which he had traveled and conquered the known world with Alexander the Great? Then I turned to examine the back of the masterpiece and, with my eyes widely open, read aloud the three words perfectly engraved in the inlaid silver: "ALEXANDER OF MACEDON."

But how could this be? Caesar and I had visited the Tomb of Alexander close to the same docks where the galleys were originally tied. We had seen the sarcophagus, and even this helmet, but with no battle scars, behind the viewing gallery open to visiting dignitaries. The monument had an inscription that explained Alexander the Great was laid to rest there by the original Ptolemy I, who had been his childhood friend, classmate, bodyguard, and eventually one of his most powerful Generals - all before Alexander's death almost three hundred years ago.

Ptolemy orchestrated the capture of Alexander's sarcophagus and all the treasures contained in the elaborate funeral procession and giant hearse/carriage. This procession was taking his body from Babylon back to his Macedonian home and the burial place of Argead Kings at the direction of Perdiccas, to whom Alexander had given his signet ring to maintain the empire on his deathbed. Meanwhile, Ptolemy had wisely taken his loyal troops to Egypt, where he had established a separate independent kingdom.

The hearse, built in the shape of a box, was about twelve feet wide and eighteen feet long with a barrel-like roof, all covered in gold with precious stones. Inside the hearse's rear door, golden lions sat on each side, their heads turned to watch all who entered. The hearse was so massive and heavy, it took forty-four horses to pull it. Each had a golden crown and bells. Engineers and road crews had to smooth the path.

Ptolemy led a squadron of his best cavalry to masterfully hijack the procession and take Alexander's mummified body and treasure to Memphis, Egypt. After two years of preparation, the brilliant General Ptolemy had outfoxed and outmaneuvered Perdiccas and was taking Alexander, his king and friend, to the continent he had made a blood oath to bury him in.

He had defeated the Greek troops of General Perdiccas with a surprise morning attack out of the desert's dunes as he and Alexander had done together in many previous battles against the Persians. He had inflicted minimal casualties and released the men to return to Babylon under a flag of truce in hopes no further bloodshed would be necessary between the previous comrades.

However, this was not to be the case. The legend that whoever possessed Alexander's body and armor would never be defeated in battle was soon proven to be true as Ptolemy defeated the Greek armies sent to recover the body and take Egypt from him. He continued to expand his empire until his death about forty years later. He left his Ptolemaic dynasty intact to the current day with his progeny, Ptolemy XIII, still a pharaoh, and soon his sister Cleopatra would take over this role. He had also left a brilliant weapon secretly hidden for his lineage so they would never be defeated!

But Caesar was about to change that.

I gently placed the heavy golden helmet, brightly glittering in the torchlight, on the empty table and looked back into the chest. Suddenly I saw it: one final document hidden under the helmet.

A sealed papyrus scroll.

I gingerly lifted the scroll and saw it was stamped with Ptolemy I's signet ring, the wax seal still unbroken!

I wondered if I should get Caesar's permission to break the seal but then realized I already had it. So, with trembling hands and my razor-sharp engraved dagger, I gently parted the seal, and the scroll rolled open, thankfully without crumbling.

It was hand-written in Latin and signed by Ptolemy I.

"As I approach the return to my ancestors, it is with great satisfaction that I write this for the eyes of a future pharaoh of my lineage in his time of greatest need.

"My eyes grow dim, and my hand falters as I truthfully record the greatest weapons which are secure and secretly located within the realm of Egypt. It required the greatest deception that remains to this day in all the world. It was done to honor my great King, previous Pharaoh, and God: Alexander, whom I followed and served faithfully both in life and as you will see, even after his death." So began the document shakily written in Ptolemy's hand.

"I was Alexander's head bodyguard seven years before his death when he expressed a desire to consult the oracle of Zeus-Ammon at the Siwa Oasis. According to legend, Perseus, Heracles, and countless others consulted this oracle. Now it was fitting for the new Pharaoh and God, Alexander, to do the same.

"He needed to confirm his divine parentage and status as a god. He was also preparing for his Asian campaign and needed guidance on the design and location of Alexandria, his new city on the Nile. Finally, he needed the demons cleared on whether his father's killers had been punished.

"It was a brutal journey of three weeks through the barren desert, marked by near death from thirst as our guides became lost in the terrible South Khamsin wind, but thirsty and exhausted, we finally arrived. Alexander immediately entered the temple alone to consult the oracle.

"When he departed the temple hours later, his face shone brightly like the reflection of the sun! He seemed rejuvenated and told me in confidence that he had learned secret matters, and his path forward was clear! He also told me in the event of his death, the oracle instructed that he was to be buried here or his achievements would be forgotten.

"He said the Oracle prophesied that whoever possessed his

glorious gold battle armor and tomb after his death would never be defeated in battle.

"He then pulled out his gold-hilted short sword. After removing his battle-scarred golden helmet with his name in silver flashing in the sunlight, he cut his forehead and instructed me to do the same.

"As the blood dripped over our brows, we smiled and touched our heads together, mingling each other's blood, and I swore this secret oath to Zeus: 'This prophecy would be our secret to our last breath and that I, Ptolemy, would fulfill it or suffer the curse of Zeus!'"

This parchment was almost three hundred years old, but the writing was as clear as this morning's sunrise. I looked up at the immense room and high marble-encased ceiling and took a deep breath. Could this be true?

Ptolemy continued, "We conquered the known world together, and I became a General during these long campaigns. When Alexander lay on his deathbed in Babylon, he pulled me close when we were alone, discussing the next battle plans, and he said, 'My friend, I will not recover. I have only one request, that you should fulfill your oath that we shared those seven years ago at the Oasis of Siwa!'

"As I choked back tears, I croaked, 'Yes, my lord,' and stumbled from the throne room in agony! I would never see my King, Pharaoh, and friend alive again.

"He died that night, and I left for Egypt with my loyal forces where I have ruled and expanded this kingdom for over forty years."

Ptolemy's writing became more irregular and shorter. It was apparent he was struggling with the papyrus as he left instructions for his descendants and future pharaohs in the event of a severe crisis.

"Now, my Pharaoh and blood, I must hurry as my time rapidly passes.

"Yes, I fulfilled my oath! I captured Alexander's body and his hearse filled with untold treasures from Babylon, Jerusalem, and the known world. It was taken first to Memphis, Egypt, where I had his armor and sarcophagus duplicated by the best artisans in Egypt in complete secrecy. These artisans were then relocated with their families to join an expedition searching for the source of the Nile and were soon lost with the rest of that team. Dead men tell no tales.

"The replica sarcophagus and armor were moved to Alexandria with great ceremony, while at the same time, I sent my most elite cavalry squadron under total darkness and secrecy to the Oasis of Siwa with the real body, burial hearse, and treasure. Here, they prepared the final resting place and tomb for Alexander in the place that Alexander and I had chosen together many years before in complete secrecy.

"It was screened from the Oasis by distance and a rocky escarpment that fell into a ravine along an ancient creekbed lined by steep cliffs! It was a hidden garden of serenity, quiet, and peace, with a small stream pouring from the base of a huge desert cliff. We spent two nights here as friends, enjoying the fresh gazelle we dispatched by spear on hard horseback hunts. This helped us recondition and provision for our return to found the new city of Alexandria.

"We immediately realized we weren't alone our first night as the cliffs echoed to the heart-piercing roar of a dominant male lion on the prowl. We built a large fire with the horses short-tethered in the firelight but could not save the remains of our gazelle. We tensely awaited first light, and without a word, each of us mounted our warhorses to find our lion. He was easy to track as the carcass of our gazelle left a bloody trail in the dry sand and rock.

"Unfortunately, he saw us first and launched a vicious attack on Alexander, whose horse was taken down and, with a quick twisting of his head, killed by the largest lion I had ever seen. Alexander grabbed his spear as he was thrown from the horse, but his non-throwing arm was bleeding from a light talon swipe of the great and fearless beast. His leather tunic was torn and exposed his gold chain and coin.

"Alexander was in a war frenzy and bellowed his war cry as he ran straight toward the beast. He raised his lance as the giant killing machine opened his bloody mouth and growled so deeply, I was rooted in place by shock and awe! I watched in a trance as the two mighty killers rushed toward each other, but suddenly, Alexander tripped over a hidden stone, and his spear flew uselessly from his hand. It would surely be his death as the lion leaped and stood as large as a Persian warhorse over my General.

However, the beast hesitated as a flash from the diamond in the coin around Alexander's neck seemed to distract him. Then, from the brush beside the wadi, two lionesses with cubs emerged and circled Alexander, pushing the male away while snarling at me. The cubs jumped on the General, who remained very still, and began sniffing his lion's mane cloak, which he always wore.

"I was stunned! In all our hunts, a lion had never spared a downed hunter, much less protected him! Perhaps this was proof of what the Oracle had just told us all: "Alexander was a God, King, and Pharaoh!" Slowly, the lions walked to the brush, followed reluctantly by the cubs who seemed to be swarming around Alexander and playfully licking him. A loud roar scattered the cubs who bolted to their mothers in the brush.

"Alexander jumped up to pursue the lion pride, but I rode quickly to head him off, jumped off my horse, and embraced him, saying, 'Alexander! The lions even know you are a Pharaoh and God!'

"Immediately above this valley of death, the scream of a Peregrine falcon pierced the air as she dove with blinding speed into a flock of ducks who had been flushed by the passing lion pride. Feathers filled the sky as two large ducks dropped at our feet while the falcon fell with yet another duck in the upper reaches of the cliff. These we ate as I dressed Alexander's lion lacerations.

"'This is an omen, my friend, that victory, despite overwhelming odds, awaits us in the Asian campaign. It confirms my status as a God, immune to the greatest hunter on earth!' said Alexander as we savored the wonderful duck which oozed tasty grease from the rolls of fat in the tender breast.

"We had found the home of the mightiest of all desert hunters, the Peregrine falcon, and the lion, who was the favorite of all creatures to Alexander. That is why he always chose to wear a lion's mane cape.

"We called it the Valley of Death from Earth and Sky and painted the symbols of Horus, the falcon, and the lion as markers for Alexander's burial site, close to where Alexander had been brought to ground. This was to be a sacred site and the final resting place of the world's greatest General, Pharaoh, and God, as I had sworn to my friend when his time came.

"Now, eighteen months after dispatching my best cavalry commander, Captain Lucius, he returned with the glorious news that the entombment had occurred in this very valley without discovery by any Oasis visitors. He received the Oracle's blessing, for which she received a king's ransom to maintain the secrecy. He described the location as close to the site we had inscribed with Horus and the Lion in the Valley of Death from Earth and Sky. He had wisely placed the massive tomb in an unseen crevice in the cliff face after enlarging a hidden cavern that faced the rising sun. He then removed all the traces of the monument. Captain Lucius swore on his life that no one would ever see this site as it was not visible to any other than the Gods, except during the full Blue Khonsu, which occurred only at full moonrise every three years.

"Lucius had lost most of his unit and asked that the remaining men all be allowed time for recovery.

"'My friend and loyal commander, please take my barge to Memphis and spend the next fortnight in recovery at my palace, and then report to me for our next critical engagement,'" I exclaimed as I patted my loyal servant and soldier on his back.

"Unfortunately, as Pharaoh, I know loose lips sink ships or empires. I then sent for my naval commander, Lord Plutanamen.

"'My Lord, see that my ship never reaches Memphis, nor any of its occupants survive the journey!' I cried.

"'But my Pharaoh, your ship is the finest in the fleet and seaworthy in all conditions, and Captain Lucius is the finest cavalry commander in the Army!' he cried, wringing his hands in frustration while lowering his head respectfully.

"'These are my orders, Lord. If you can't do it, then I will send for my Admiral!' I replied.

"'Yes, my Pharaoh, I apologize! Your wish is my command!' cried Plutanamen as he strode quickly from the throne room door with sad tension etched on his aging face.

"I sadly regret those deaths I ordered to this day as I take my final breaths."

CHAPTER 9 • St. Elmo

Duke's head rolled left and right, knocking over his empty coffee cup and awaking him to the violent change in the sea. Was he in Pharaoh's galley on the Nile en route to Memphis and certain death? He couldn't tell. *Wait! Is this a dream?* He looked down at the final page of the translation and realized it was real!

Duke gathered himself and stuffed the precious translation back into his leather briefcase while he reached into his duffle bag and pulled out his last unopened bottle of MacAllen 18-year-old scotch. He had been saving this for his next aerial victory, but now he realized he would need all his wits to survive the war, especially with this unbelievable revelation!

This is what dreams, fortunes, power, and history were made of, and now it sat in front of him for the taking. It would take all his archeology training and talent to find it!

Should he, or even could he do it right, he thought, and then remembered he had graduated from Harvard with his Ph.D. in Archeology at the top of his class! If anyone could do it, it would be him, and a rare smile spread across his sunburned face as his Caribbean blue eyes twinkled in anticipation.

War and death raged all around him! He might not even survive this journey and end up like those loyal cavalry troops that Pharaoh had mercilessly drowned to maintain Alexander's secret! Duke knew he should not worry about what he couldn't control. He took a deep, cleansing breath and let all the tension evaporate.

He poured a glass of the peaty, dark nectar. The smoky aroma engulfed him then gently filled his mouth with the deep, sharp, wonderful oakiness and distant sweetness of sherry from the casks that had nurtured the years of aging of this firewater from the Islay Scotch isles. As rivulets of nectar flowed from palate to gut, he started to relax and embrace this incredible gift that had spilled out from his briefcase and now lived forever in the confines of his cortex.

It was the greatest unsolved archaeological mystery of all time. It included the true final resting place of Alexander, which was lost to history for over two thousand years, and the even older long-lost location of the Ark of the Covenant, which reputedly held power beyond anything currently known to man!

Could it be that his whole life had been leading to this very place? His Ph.D. in Archeology from Harvard, the dig in Crete which uncovered these ancient documents, untranslatable until his last aerial victory and inflight transfer, therefore saving his German foe, von Wagner, who secretly translated them for him. His unexpected discharge from the Western Front and posting to the British Expeditionary Force in Egypt would now put him within range of the Oasis of Siwa.

Was this fate or good karma?

He wasn't motivated by money; his family had more than enough! He didn't crave fame but instead quietly sought peace and happiness. He didn't want power and, in fact, strongly resented anyone with power who used it toward nefarious purposes, like the kings who had started this bloodbath and his last Commanding Officer who had wrongly sent men, including his squadron mates and now his mechanic as well, to certain death.

What did Duke want, and why was he here?

As he worked his way through the glorious but rapidly dwindling bottle of smoky McAllen, he started to realize that he wanted to know the truth of these mysteries!

He had been trained by the best in the academic world to discover and discern these facts.

And if fame, reputation, and fortune followed, he would use this newfound truth for good to help finish this war and prevent another; to find solutions, not problems, and to be a beacon of good to the world and rewrite history so all the world could see the truth.

Was he being idealistic and setting himself up for failure? He knew deep inside that he would find the right path and solution to these riddles. Duke savored the last drops of the burning scotch, slammed the glass down without awakening his bunkmate Tom Holmes, and slipped out the door of the rocking ship.

On reaching the deck, he immediately understood the reason for the ship's motion. A squall line reached as far as he could see in the inky darkness. In the distance, piercing bolts of lightning blew through the billowing clouds before bursting into the sea.

Duke held on tightly while the fresh salt air tinged with saltwater washed the sleep, scotch, and shock of discovery from his eyes.

This was life! He would do all he could to see this mystery through! He looked up to heaven as if for a sign and saw arcs of lightning passing above the ship and showering it with an unworldly glow.

Could it be? St. Elmo's Fire? He had never seen this before, but he had his answer as all sailors considered this a good omen and a sign of the patron saint Erasmus of Formia's protection!

Duke smiled to the heavens and made his way back to his cabin to finish the final pages of the greatest mystery he had ever known. He smiled, grabbed the document with excitement, and was transported again, over 2000 years back in time, as Pharaoh Ptolemy continued his biography and epic tale:

"Every three years during the Blue Khonsu, my beloved brethren, I have visited this sacred site in secret while my retainers slept in the Oasis. On my first visit, when the Oracle least expected, I strangled her. No one else knew the secret of this sacred tomb. If our kingdom and dynasty are ever about to collapse, the exact details of this tomb of untold power are available to you and only you. I placed a capstone with my seal at the base of the Sphinx's right foot, under which a map shows the entrance to the tomb, now known only to you.

My successor and Pharaoh, let no other person ever know of this tomb of unworldly power or ever possess it. If so, our dynasty will end, and you will be cursed as the last of my powerful line!"

CHAPTER 10 • ALEXANDRIA

The *Leviathan* docked two days later in Alexandria to a world of chaos, dust, and noise. Duke and Tom, as Lieutenants, were loaded into a staff car, which whisked them off to General Allenby's headquarters in Cairo for immediate assignment to squadron service. Both were bone tired, thirsty, and ready to get to the squadron to start flying their newly assigned Biplane scouts, but first: military protocol. They finally arrived after a rough, dusty ride to General Headquarters in Cairo and immediately went to see General Allenby. It was August 1917 in Egypt, and even at headquarters, it was oppressively hot, despite slowly turning fans in the high stone-lined General's office.

The men waited patiently until General Allenby, preceded by his cadre of adjuvants, exploded into the room. Tom and Duke jumped to attention. He fixed his discerning gaze on the two officers. He held his bushy eyebrows high, and his long aristocratic forehead was tense.

He said, "Gentlemen, welcome to Egypt. I don't have much time, so let's get started. You two are the best fighter pilots I could steal for my Egyptian Expeditionary Desert Air Force, and you are sorely needed right now."

He looked them up and down. "You are to form a new aviation unit, designated Group 77. Effective immediately, you are both elevated in rank to Captain.

"Captain Thomas, you are Group Commander. Captain Holmes, you are Executive Officer of the 77th, both in the Royal

Flying Corps. You are to assemble a long-range reconnaissance group from existing local aviation assets."

The General paused to make sure they were taking in his orders.

"Your goal is to search out and destroy, or otherwise disrupt, the Senussi insurrection of Arabs loyal to the Turkish and German forces who are creating a rebellion in the Western Desert between El Alamein, Siwa Oasis, and Giza. These heathen tribesmen have sworn allegiance to the Turkish Sultan and, therefore, to Germany, his ally. They are destroying all roads, communication, and supply, threatening my Western flank.

"You are to isolate your unit, by any means necessary, from the many spies who will report your intentions to the rebellious tribesmen by basing as close to the enemy formations as possible. Colonel Balfour, my most capable camel cavalry commander, will have his battalion ready to strike based on your aerial intelligence."

The men were speechless. This was far more adventure and action than they had anticipated this quickly. Duke smiled and winked at Tom with great anticipation.

"I propose a toast to this critical unit and its success!" cried General Allenby as he passed around a smoky-tasting Laphroaig scotch.

The men all downed the dark smoky nectar with relish and felt their spirits rise with the challenge ahead. Its critically necessary results required immediate action. As he finished his scotch, Duke admired the beautiful Purdey double-barrel shotguns that lined the wall behind the General's teak desk and his sleek fly rod leaning against it. As Duke had heard, he was truly a gentleman and sportsman, and Duke felt a connection with him beyond this current assignment. They now had an excellent General with who they were to remain in direct contact as their mission progressed.

The General wished them good hunting as they were then

escorted from his office and through the officers' mess. They passed pool tables and a long bar with batmen dressed in starched whites serving iced glasses of champagne and cocktails to the lounging officers. They reached their dusty vehicle and were thrown into the chaos of Cairo. They didn't even have time for a cold drink!

It felt like a dream as it had happened so fast, and they knew nothing of this place. Thankfully, General Allenby had provided his best supply officer, Colonel George Scott, to direct and execute their supply orders, and he joined them in the crew car.

As they bounced down the road, Colonel Scott said, "Gentlemen, much has been prepared for you. We have a partial squadron of nine FE2 tactical reconnaissance Biplanes and five Sopwith Camel fighters for air superiority and ground support. We also have a Sopwith Triplane, which just arrived last week. All are set up with extra long-range fuel. The RFC pilots with the most experience were told to meet you in the Giza officers' club on the airfield and to be prepared to begin flying operations tomorrow."

They were dropped at the officers' barracks at the Giza airstrip, assigned desert flying gear, given malaria pills, and a cursory medical exam by the British flight surgeon. Then after dropping their gear in the field offices, they headed to the officers' club.

It was typical of all other wartime clubs that Duke and Tom had experienced, with one exception: the Egyptian women who prepared the meals and cleaned were fully dressed and covered from head to toe in black clothing. The pilots and officers were drinking heavily, and the air was thick with smoke. Duke met Lt. Raj Djione from Nepal, a flight commander of the FE2 tactical aircraft, and Duke immediately liked him.

"Namaste," he said.

"Good evening, Captain Thomas. We have been looking forward to meeting you!" yelled Raj over the jazz band in the background playing on the phonograph.

He gently raised his hands into a folded prayer position in front of his chest and bowed his head. Raj then rested his hand on the hilt of his buffalo-horned, deeply curved Khukuri blade attached to his waist.

"Looks like a good knife," said Duke as he stuck his hand out, which Raj grasped, shaking it firmly.

"It is the best. In Nepal, we Ghurka warriors have used them for centuries as special forces troops for the British. When you run out of ammo or your gun jams, this blade is always ready!" Raj said with a confident but ruthless smile on his face.

"I have personally sent six of my enemies to hell with this very blade! And I suggest you get your British-issue Bowie knife as soon as you can! The desert tribes are ruthless and will torture any captured pilots!" noted Raj.

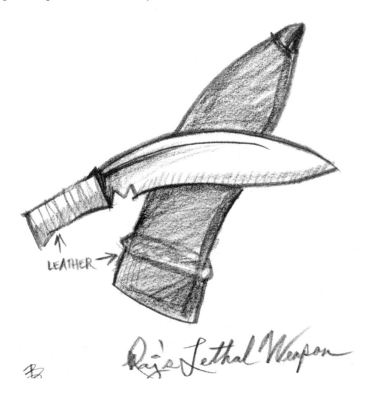

LEATHER →

Raj's Lethal Weapon

The rest of the hand-picked pilots leaned forward to express their greetings and handshakes to both Duke and Tom, while rounds of the best beer available flowed freely. The details of flying in the desert became the primary topic of conversation.

"Don't let Raj bother you!" shouted Capt. Rick O'Brien. "He has a death wish matched by courage and is one of the most skilled pilots and edged-weapon experts I have ever seen. What he says is true. I'm a fellow Nieuport pilot with four victories and am damn glad to meet you. I'm from jolly old London, mate, and I can't wait to get back to my pub and three brats!" shouted Rick with a thick accent above the jazz music.

The pilots were exhausted from non-stop patrols attempting to harass and spot the free-ranging enemy cavalry. Still, they were thankful that due to limited aerial combat from German units, they had no air-to-air losses. It seemed the primary losses were due to mechanical issues, weather, and ground fire.

The group was down to 50% strength and had a huge area to cover to protect General Allenby's flank. Duke put the unit on a temporary stand down for a fortnight to reorganize and train the pilots while re-equipping with the new long-range aircraft.

Duke toasted his new 77th Long Range group, "Gentleman, we have an aggressive enemy at our doorstep, and it is our job to protect General Allenby's flank. If we fail, all of Egypt will fall under German control! Tomorrow we begin training with new aircraft at 0600 in the briefing room. The training and flying will be non-stop and intense, but you are the best, so I look forward to flying and winning with you!"

"Huzzah! Huzzah! Huzzah!" yelled the group in unison while raising their pint glasses to the stars.

Duke said good evening and went straight to his quarters for some overdue sleep and planning.

CHAPTER 11 • Giza

As Duke pushed his men and machines to the edge, cracks in performance, maintenance, and skill became clear. The squadron was unified in purpose and followed Duke's natural leadership in the air and on the ground, but some men were not up to Duke's standards and were reassigned to other area squadrons.

Unfortunately, two Camel Biplane pilots were killed in a mid-air collision, which depleted his resources to absolute minimums as no new replacement pilots or machines would be available. Priority for supply was given to the Western Front, where another major offensive was underway.

He loved the smell, quiet, and coolness of the desert before dawn. He often assisted his lead mechanic, Master Sergeant John Majors of Cork, England, to rework the demanding radial engines for peak performance and range. At his direction, Duke and the other pilots inspected all their .303 Lewis machine gun rounds to help reduce jamming and found the quality to be very poor, requiring over 20% to be discarded. Then, at the morning briefings, Duke assigned patrol routes, leaving altitude to the individual flight leaders.

His pilot cadre's leadership ability and skills had become clear to Duke as he assigned the airworthy and now well-tuned aircraft to each flight leader.

Captain Tom Holmes was the leader of the Camel flight composed of the three remaining Sopwith Camel Biplanes. These were specially modified to carry two 10kg anti-personnel bombs and an enlarged main fuel tank, giving an extra hour of range. Duke had also added a special engine-leaning feature that allowed the engine mixture to be pulled back once at cruise altitude, which, with the extra fuel, more than doubled the lethal Camel's range.

Lt. Raj Djione was Commander of FE2 flight A, composed of four aircraft, and Captain Rick O'Brien was B flight commander, composed of the remaining five FE2s. All were modified to carry only the pilot and no observer with extra fuel in a customized fuel tank placed in the rear seat, which Colonel Scott had provided especially for the Long-Range Group, as well as the 10 kg anti-personnel bombs. This new configuration allowed for extra .303 ammunition for the front-mounted machine gun but left barely enough room for the pilot, who sat in the very front of the bathtub-shaped cockpit with the roaring radial engine mounted behind the rear fuel tank in a pusher configuration.

At the final morning briefing before combat patrols were to begin in three days, Duke said, "Gentleman, you are the best squadron I have ever flown with, and we are ready to strike a blow against the enemy! Today is our last training session, and as usual, I will fly my black Sopwith Tripe as an aggressive enemy and try to disrupt your patrol.

"Be sure to keep your formations tight. Flight leaders, watch your range. We can't afford any more losses in training! Today is our longest mission to date, and we will cross into enemy territory, so keep your eyes moving. We could encounter German fighter patrols."

Duke savored the aroma and taste of his strong, heavily-sugared Turkish coffee with a smile of satisfaction. He sipped it while they waited for the planes to warm up on the flight line. He knew he had molded this squadron into a weapon, carefully customized to defeat the roving enemy forces in their desert element from the least likely area: the sky. There was nothing more feared by man or beast than death from above. Now was the time to prove if it would be as effective as General Allenby needed.

Duke strapped his Sopwith triplane on with the help of Sergeant John Majors, his chief mechanic. The mechanics had stayed up late and painted *Black Death* in white on the side of their Ace commander's aircraft in recognition of his lethal reputation of marksmanship after shooting down his first five opponents with minimal ammunition.

Duke smiled at the fearsome name his crew had created and gave a brisk salute to his ground crew.

"Good hunting, sir!" yelled John as he flashed a thumbs up and jumped off the wing.

Duke felt at one with his favorite aerial mount as he listened to the growing hum of the engine and felt the vibration of the steel-framed fuselage engulf him. He pushed the throttle forward while keeping the special mixture controls fully rich for take-off and led the three flights of his strike force quickly down the sandy desert runway, leaving clouds of dust and the smell of castor oil as the only signs of the squadron's presence at the secret, well-guarded airfield. His Clerget 9Z rotary nine-cylinder 130hp engine hummed in harmony with the fully advanced throttle and jumped quickly into the dense, cool morning air, climbing like a homesick angel.

By the time he reached 15,000 feet, the single synchronized Vickers .303 machine gun had been successfully tested, and the mixture carefully leaned for the thin hypoxic environment. He felt like a hunting Peregrine falcon with a commanding view of the barren desert.

Duke looked west toward the Qattara Depression with the Oasis of Siwa just beyond his visual range, but he could still see the Pyramids of Giza and the Sphinx behind him to the East. He crossed into the contested Western Desert, carefully scanning the sky for enemy aircraft.

The cold, thin, hypoxic air slowly began to dull his senses, but he recognized the signs of altitude sickness and rolled the agile Tripe left and right, shaking the dullness from his body while yelling, "Freedom!" As he dropped his altitude by a thousand feet, he watched his three flights spread out into combat formation over a mile below him.

The flight quickly ate the miles until the outline of the Oasis began to appear at the Libyan border and the point of no return approached. All three flights began their turn to the southeast and the return to Giza. Duke chose this point to make his surprise pass on the trailing A-flight of the aggressive Lt. Raj Djione and flashed under the flight up into a loop just in front of Raj's FE2.

The three covering Sopwith Camels of Capt. Tom Holmes finally saw the mock aerial combat and engaged Duke in a series of passes: looping, rolling, and tumbling through the wild, blue cloudless sky until all had been completely worked over by the nimble Tripe.

They leveled out just feet from the sweltering desert emptiness. Tom looked over at Duke shaking his head in disbelief at the mauling that his flight took by a single expertly flown Tripe. They formed up around their wing commander as he climbed to a cooler altitude, heading back to base, closely watching the last quarter of their fuel quickly disappear. Finally, as the reserve fuel was switched on, there appeared out of the haze ahead the tiny collection of hangers and desert strip on the outskirts of Giza that the 77th Long Range Group called home.

It had been a successful final training mission, and as the crews debriefed with their mechanics on the squawks that needed repair and attention, Duke called the men together.

"Well done, flight! Not a single straggler, but next time, Camel flight, watch for an enemy attack from out of the sun! I don't want to lose any of my group! Now you are all issued a 24-hour leave, so unwind, have fun, and get ready to start the battle when you return. Remember, loose lips sink ships or planes, so keep quiet about our mission."

Duke strolled to his spartan field office, thinking of fuel, ammo, range, and tactics, but then looked skyward and saw the Giza pyramids in the distant haze. Suddenly, he remembered that he had an appointment with destiny!

Could there really be something to find in the shadows of the three famous stone monuments? He remembered the Sphinx and the hidden directions to Alexander's tomb that Ptolemy deposited over two thousand years ago! Could he possibly find this ancient treasure map? Would it even still exist after all this time? Only one way to find out!

Later, after catching up on critical documents, Duke shouted to his driver, Corporal Shaw, "Let's go to the Giza pyramid complex! I still haven't had a chance to see the Sphinx."

CHAPTER 12 • THE SPHINX

Duke enjoyed the ride past the secluded entrance to the airfield, where the Ghurka guards snapped to attention when they recognized their base commander's car. They fired off brisk British special forces salutes as their deadly Khukuri knives flashed in the late afternoon sun. There were advantages to being the Commanding Officer, including the Rolls Royce staff car. It had a large comfortable back seat covered in brown leather. Duke relaxed as the car whisked him out the gate.

Duke drove with the top down and enjoyed the early evening breeze as he cleared his mind of leading the squadron and focused instead on finding the secret map of Ptolemy. He remembered the location was marked with Pharaoh's seal at the right foot of the human-head lion's body: the Sphinx.

The driver, Corporal Shaw, suddenly laid on the horn as a caravan of camels followed by scampering goats blocked the road ahead of them. The Egyptian nomads were deep brown wherever their skin showed. Their smiling, curious brown eyes followed the staff car. Duke waved, and the small, nearly-naked children along with a few of the chattering black-encased women waved back, but the men ominously didn't respond.

Once past the traffic jam, Corporal Shaw exclaimed, "Sorry, Captain, those buggers are a menace to traffic, but I will get you there in no time, sir!" Just as they came around the next turn, they ran into another surprise. Lt. Raj Djione, along with Captains Rick O'Brien and Tom Holmes, sat morosely on the running boards of the other staff car. It had just come from the airfield and sat on the side of the road with a steaming radiator.

"Corporal, pull over and give these men a hand!" shouted Duke.

The staff car pulled over to the now smiling men. Duke invited the flight commanders to join him while the other engine cooled, and they opened his favorite 16-year-old Lagavulin Scotch for some refreshment.

The men were in high spirits after helping top off the radiator. Duke chauffeured them to Shepheard's Hotel in downtown Cairo where he joined them at the long bar for a cold and very dirty martini.

"Raj, how do you think the men will handle operations?" asked Duke.

They sipped on the cooling refreshment while the large ceiling fans chewed the dense evening air and created a comforting breeze in the large open-air, marble-encased bar. The attentive bartender briskly refilled the now empty martini glasses as Rick blurted out, "Captain Thomas, they are like a bunch of tied up English bulldogs ready to tear into the enemy!"

"Rick, we are off duty. Just call me Duke."

"Thank you, sir."

Raj added, "Yes, sir. They are ready, and I'm impressed with the FE2's armament and the amazing range! We haven't fully leaned the mixtures yet, and we are flying more than twice the distance I have ever covered in these wonderful birds. The practice strafing and the bombing of moving targets have turned us into flying death for any enemy guerilla forces!"

"It reminds me of the stories my father and grandfather told me when they served the British as Gurkha special forces," Raj said. "They defeated all enemy forces, often outnumbered, but never overcome. Sometimes they ran out of ammunition and resorted to hand-to-hand combat using their Khukuri razor-sharp blades. Despite severe losses, they never surrendered!"

He reached to his belt and whipped out his shining blade from the black buffalo hide sheath.

The Khukuri blade was sharply curved and reminded Duke of the Greek cavalry short sword, which Alexander's troops carried throughout many victories on their march of conquest to the far reaches of the known world. But it had a unique buffalo hoof shape at the base of the steel blade, which funneled blood off the handle in the heat of combat.

Raj's eyes shone with the fury of impending combat. He stood up and whirled the blade like an extension of his body.

Duke, Tom, and Rick erupted in laughter. The Nepalese warrior quickly sheathed his blade. He was breathing deeply but soon joined the laughter as a General officer made his way to the bar. He ominously approached the men.

"Attention!" shouted a Colonel at the far end of the bar. The men all jumped up as they recognized their commander, General Allenby, was quickly approaching.

"Captain Thomas and his deadly falcons, I presume. Thanks for making so much space for me at the long bar! At ease, men," smiled the capable General.

"Yes, sir! Please join us," replied Duke.

The General ordered a gin and tonic, and the bar settled back down to a general hum of excitement at having their leader amongst them.

"Colonel Balfour, my best cavalry commander, who is ready to support your Western patrols, told me you were here. We decided to come to check on your progress," said the General. He quietly looked into Duke's blue eyes as if searching for reassurance.

"Captain, when do you get to work on finding these rene-gade enemy forces that are pushing closer and closer to Cairo? We are frequently on patrol and, despite an occasional brief engage-ment, have not been able to destroy them! They blend into the desert before we can mass our camel calvary for the decisive killing stroke like your Nepalese friend seems so capable of!" barked the deeply tanned field officer, Colonel Balfour.

Raj smiled as he ordered a Laphroaig Scotch up neat.

Unsure of who might be listening to details of the mission, Duke leaned in close to the two officers seated beside him. He said, "Sir, we begin full operational patrols in 24 hours. I will send daily reports of our progress, and when we make contact, we will try and push the enemy away from the Cairo frontier out into the White Western desert for Colonel Balfour.

"This will put them between his forces at the Faraira and Siwa Oasis for a decisive engagement if we are successful. We are building an emergency airstrip with fuel and supplies just south of Siwa. It can be used for limited short-term operations to support your cavalry troops if needed."

The Colonel smiled in anticipation of the upcoming con-flict. He said, "Well planned, Captain. Keep us up to date on your combat patrols and any contact with the buggers."

"Yes, sir!" replied Duke.

"One last thing," whispered General Allenby. "Intelligence shows the Germans have moved a squadron of their new Fokker DR1 Triplanes to their base just west of El Alamein, which is com-manded by one of their best aces, a Captain von Wagner. Looking at your dossier, it seems you two have met before?"

Duke took a deep breath as memories of their engagement flashed through his mind.

"Yes, sir! I shot him down once before and can do it again!" replied Duke with a smile of confidence that didn't betray the uneasy feeling beginning to well up in his gut.

General Allenby and the Colonel belted the last of their drinks, grabbed their dress hats and cavalry whips, and quickly stood up.

"Thank you, Captain, for your hospitality. Keep me up to date!" exclaimed General Allenby.

The whole bar quickly stood to attention and became silent. The two officers made their way out of the long bar, passing through the oversized, bronze-inlaid dark teak doors.

The two fellow pilots looked at their commander as he smiled and said, "This is going to be more fun than we thought!"

They all laughed with deepening tension as they realized that this would change the odds against them dramatically, despite the relaxing impact of their cocktails. The Germans must have superior intelligence to have deployed the squadron at this critical moment of the Egyptian campaign.

Duke downed his martini and quickly paid cash for all the drinks. Then, despite his fellow pilots' pleas to join them at the neighboring belly dancing establishment, he withdrew to his staff car for a trip to the Sphinx. "It has been a pleasure, gentlemen. Your car will take care of you now, and I have other business. I look forward to our day together tomorrow. See you at our 0600 hours pilot briefing!"

By the time Duke arrived at the Sphinx, it was late and very dark with no moon visible. No light to help with his search for the tell-tale seal at the right limestone foot of the 4500-year-old monolith built during the Old Kingdom of Egypt by the great-grandson of King Khufu.

Corporal Shaw, despite shining the torch and using a spade to expose more of the base of the ancient beast's right foot, could not find any sign of the engraving or 2,000-year-old capstone.

Finally, as the impending dawn began to slip over the Eastern desert, Duke headed to the staff car, which the Corporal had warmed up, ready to return to the base. Duke pulled his trench coat tightly around his exhausted frame since the desert cooled dramatically after dark. He drifted off to a fitful nap, only to awaken as the car stopped in front of the briefing room on the Giza airfield, which was already full of pilots.

Duke grabbed his sugary Turkish coffee from his waiting batman. He inhaled the aroma and enjoyed the roasted thick nectar that kickstarted his morning. He briskly walked to the covered map, which he had prepared the previous evening.

He tore the cover away, showing the map and course depicted for the long-awaited first mission. The mission was based on General Allenby's staff's intelligence on the last known location of the elusive mobile enemy ground and cavalry forces. He had also modified his patrol plans based on Captain von Wagner's elite squadron's new arrival, therefore deciding to keep the squadron together in a wide-sweeping patrol instead of three separate groups.

Max's Mount

This would allow him to maximize his aerial firepower in the event of contact with aerial forces and to provide maximal confidence to the flights who had already heard of the newly-arrived German DR1 Fokker Triplanes made famous by von Wagner's cousin, The Red Baron.

"Good morning. By now, you all have heard of the newly arrived German Triplanes," said Duke.

He wanted to get the pink elephant out while murmurs of discontent erupted from the pilots.

"This only sharpens our resolve to defeat these encroaching ground forces and lets us know how scared they are of our Long-Range Aerial Group!" shouted Duke.

The men erupted in cheers, encouraged by the words of their commander.

Duke began, "Today, we reach out to Siwa Oasis, where secretly, I have prepared an emergency strip with supplies and fuel in the event any of us need it. Please mark this on your charts, which are to be destroyed along with your aircraft in the event of a forced landing in enemy territory! The last sighting of the enemy was just west of the Oasis, and the Fokker Triplanes are based at their airfield in El Alamein, so keep your eyes open. Wingmen, stay close and don't lose focus. FE flights are to stagger in a wide Finger Four configuration, stair-stepping altitudes from four to eight thousand feet. Meanwhile, the Camel flight flies top cover at ten thousand feet, and I fly high cover at twelve thousand feet. Don't forget to lean your mixtures and check your guns. Now to your planes! Good luck, gentlemen," cried Duke.

The men snapped to attention, and he led them out to their already warming aircraft.

CHAPTER 14 • DEATH FROM ABOVE

The first two weeks of long-range missions followed the same general route and routine. Occasional sightings of nomad family groups and caravans struggling through the desert wastes occurred, but there were no enemy sightings.

Duke's squadron efficiency was dwindling due to maintenance, but there were no aircraft or personnel losses due to aerial combat. It was now October, and after another predawn briefing, the crews started the four-hour-long mission with little enthusiasm. The toll of daily missions had reduced the usual complement of thirteen aircraft to nine with only two fighters, including Duke's Sopwith Triplane, to provide top cover due to mechanical problems.

Duke decided to alter the course to the northeast, which brought the squadron closer to the enemy base at El Alamein. Perhaps this would allow them to contact the aggressive enemy insurgents that intelligence reported was close to Qara Oasis, where the Senussi rebels had destroyed a squadron of scouts from Colonel Balfour's regiment just yesterday.

As usual, the flights formed up in loose spread formation to cover the most territory while remaining in visual contact with each other between 5000 and 10,000 feet. The FE bombing scouts were loaded with anti-personnel bombs, and Duke remained at 12,000 feet with Tom as his wingman to provide top cover and protection from German fighters.

The flight was once again uneventful. Duke was lulled into

a state of complacency until the squadron began its turn back to base at the point of no return. Duke saw Lt. Raj's flight make a sudden turn and descend! This was quickly followed by a bomb burst which brought Capt. O'Brien's FE Biplane flight down to just above the desert as Duke saw multiple bomb bursts and small arms and machine gun flashes.

Then, smoke began to drift from multiple areas as it became clear this was a large enemy formation with cavalry, supply wagons, and machine guns. Bright tracer rounds surrounded the FE formations while they returned fire with their nose-mounted Lewis machine guns after dropping all their anti-personnel bombs.

One of the FEs of Raj's flight began to trail smoke and broke off the attack heading for Giza, followed by his wingman. Then Duke saw three specks drop like Peregrine falcons out of the sun and latch onto the tail of the first smoking FE bomber, which exploded under intense twin Spandau German machine-gun fire from the three Fokker Triplanes. Duke dove at full throttle, yelling at the top of his lungs for more speed to save his wounded flight. The second FE turned aggressively into the German fighters but could only fire a few rounds before it caught fire and crashed into the desert in a huge fireball.

As the German Fokker Triplanes turned their attack on the remaining FE bombers, Duke arrived at top speed immediately, sending the trailing Fokker Triplane down in flames. At the same time, Tom fired until the second Triplane began trailing smoke and broke for El Alamein.

Duke thought, *No way,* as he pulled up with his excess speed into a beautiful Immelmann turn, a half loop and half roll, which allowed him to lock onto the tail of the fleeing Fokker. He lined up as the Fokker pilot maneuvered frantically left and right, followed by a dive to the sandy desert floor.

The Fokker hugged the sand dunes and headed toward the fleeing column of troops, trying to evade the stream of lead pouring from Duke's single synchronized Vickers .303 machine gun. Each three-second burst tore more and more fabric and wood from the left wing, and just as the Fokker reached the broken enemy formation, the wing failed, and he rolled into the sand and last irregular column of camels.

Duke continued his firing as he passed through the formation, sending camels, horses, and men falling or fleeing in all directions. It was total devastation with no place to hide for this enemy formation. The last Fokker Triplane was mad as a hornet as he dove into the chaos, attacking the FE2 bombers about a mile away as Duke crushed his throttle fully forward to the firewall, attempting to save his bomber pilots.

But he was too late as one, then two, tumbled to earth in flames before he could catch the Fokker villain. He made an unwise head-on pass with both pilots firing head-to-head, but Duke had only one Vickers gun while the German had two synchronized Spandau machine guns, and he immediately scored hits on Duke's right wing and strut, which began to shake. He barely missed the Fokker as each turned right at the last instant, almost touching, and clearly seeing the smile on the enemy pilot's face as their head flashed by within inches of each other at a combined closing speed of over 250mph!

Duke was in trouble as the vibration increased and the right strut broke off, so he slowed down to prevent the whole wing from failing and sending him to a sandy death. But this slower speed allowed him to pull his turn tighter, which created more positive Gs than he had ever experienced.

His vision began to tunnel as the G forces pulled the blood from his head and eyes until he could only see a small central area in front of his Sopwith Triplane, *Black Death*. He tensed his abdomen and yelled, "Dixie!" as loud as possible to push the blood back from his abdomen and lungs into his head to restore his vision and prevent G-lock. His vision returned just in time to see the Fokker right in front of his gun sight!

He grabbed the trigger and released a long four-second burst of fire, which swept the Fokker's length and ended up in the Oberursel URII 9 cylinder 110 hp rotary engine that immediately began to smoke. He pulled the trigger again to finish the Fokker, but he was out of ammunition, and he pounded on the Vickers barrel in frustration.

The Fokker saw the opening and swung around behind Duke to send him to his grave, but as he flashed by smoking, Duke saw the Skull and Crossbones in black on the red and white fuselage and remembered the same paint scheme from a previous aerial duel. Could it be Captain von Wagner? He would never recognize

Duke in this Sopwith.

Duke closed his eyes and began, "Our Father who art in heaven, hallowed be thy name…." but then he saw the Fokker pull up on his right wing. *Maybe his guns had jammed?* pondered Duke.

The enemy pilot lifted his goggles and removed his helmet; his blond hair and smiling blue eyes revealed Duke's respected adversary, Max von Wagner, who fired off a proud salute, which Duke returned briskly with a smile of relief on his face.

They both looked around and saw a deserted sky and large plumes of smoke farther west where the enemy column had been badly mauled.

It quickly became clear that neither aircraft would make it to their home base or even survive a crash landing in their current battle-damaged condition. Then Duke remembered the emergency field close to Siwa Oasis. It was clearly their only choice as vibrations continued despite Duke's slow speed, and von Wagner was losing altitude steadily due to severe damage to the engine, which was smoking.

Duke signaled for Max von Wagner to follow him as they were very close. He couldn't see the emergency strip, so he circled as more parts flew from the damaged wing, the vibration became constant, and the plane became even harder to control.

Finally! He saw the flat desert runway with a small hut and palm trees at the south end. He chopped his power, and with the best landing of his career, rolled to a stop beside the supply hut.

Max had more difficulty as his engine was now out, and he would have to make a dangerous dead stick landing with no power to help him. He was a glider now and would have to use his altitude to produce enough energy to reach the field and safely land. He had flown gliders during his youth in Bavaria, and it showed as he made a flawless landing and rolled up beside his adversarial brother in arms, Duke.

The two men leaped from their planes, surveying the battle damage to their mounts, and then met inside the supply hut where Duke had already discovered a bottle of Oban Scotch, which he poured freely between the combatants. The air hung still and quiet as they both recovered from the adrenaline-soaked combat that had seen Max von Wagner send down four FE2s with no survivors.

Duke shot down two Triplanes, although one pilot may have survived and escaped with the remains of the enemy column.

Then they had shot each other down! Neither was wounded, but their planes needed much work, and by morning, the area would be full of aircraft searching for survivors, so they had tonight to repair or destroy their mounts and to catch up on life as friends.

They agreed to a truce and to leave the war behind for this one night while helping each other.

Max said, "Duke, you fly that Tripe like a falcon! I couldn't believe you shot me up after I almost shot your wing off, and you knocked down two of my best pilots! I bet your score of victories has really grown!"

"As has yours, my friend! Your reputation precedes you now that you have, by my count, thirty-three allied victories, including my four fine chaps today. God rest their souls," said Duke.

"God rest their souls and those of my pilots. I pray this war ends soon! And your score now stands at eight, including today. Let's drink to a quick end to this madness!" cried Max.

After another round of toasts to the departed pilots of both countries, the friends felt revived enough to scrounge canned bully beef and biscuits with some coffee and reflect on the past months. Max had been promoted to Captain and was one of Germany's leading aces. He had married his childhood sweetheart, Angie, who was expecting their first child early next year. This led to more toasts and cheers to the upcoming new life.

Duke erupted in praise about his passionate love for

Juliette, who continued to write the most erotic letters, heavily rose perfumed, that he answered voraciously. He pondered his marital love of Vivian, and they concluded time would resolve all.

Finally, both men spoke quietly as they started a bigger fire outside to warm up as the desert temperature had dropped precipitously with sunset, and the wind only added to the cold. The firelight reflected on each of their faces.

"We are close enough that I can almost feel it!" said Duke.

"I agree! And I thought we should at least explore a little. I saw a patch of green a few kilometers east of this airstrip with a dried-up creek bed right beside this supply shed that seems to lead back to a little oasis and gorge," added Max.

That and the empty scotch bottle settled the matter. The men decided to walk down to the dry creek bed with two torches from the supply shack and follow their instincts, trying to discover the ancient burial site of Alexander.

A coyote cried in the distance and was immediately joined by a chorus of high-pitched barking laughter as the men looked at each other with concern followed by laughter. What could a coyote do that a bullet hadn't been able to do? The many casualties of the day's battle were miles away, but the predators and scavengers were already hard at work. The desert cut-throats and nomads would soon also be stripping weapons and anything of value from the dead and wounded bodies. The men needed to hurry.

"There are still lions reported in this part of the desert," noted Max.

He patted his Lugar while Duke gently fingered his grandfather's old Colt pistol on his belt.

"I'm more concerned about the nomads who would slit our throat and strip us too. They would especially love your fancy Blue Max!" laughed Duke.

After an hour or so walking through boulders and deep sandy spots along the dried creek bed, they reached the patch of oasis hidden in a gorge with cliffs that stood over a hundred feet and was only visible by air and through a small choke point at the corner of the old creek bed.

It was a beautiful untouched gem in the desert, shielded from the elements with fresh spring water pouring from a cliff's base into a low pool surrounded by date palms, ferns, and other thick vegetation. Tracks of all shapes and sizes surrounded the pool, and the men immediately noticed the giant lion tracks and gazelle, rabbit, coyote, and fox, among many others.

In the bright moonlight, they searched the base of each cliff and wondered at all the cut stone that seemed to lay randomly along the valley floor. Both men shouted, "This is Egyptian-style hand-cut limestone and could have been used as a ramp!"

Now they looked upward to the cliffside, and soon, when the moon was at its zenith, they spotted a strange series of unnatural shadows that produced a shape like a man's head, or was it a lion? No, it was a Sphinx! With Max's help, Duke climbed up on the ledges and fragments of stone to the base of these shadows and yelled to Max, "There's something inscribed at the base of the right foot of the Sphinx's shadow."

Duke turned on his torch, swept away the accumulated sand around the cut stone, and discovered Ptolemy's seal carved into the limestone.

Duke was shocked and lost his grip and tumbled to the ground. He jumped up, wiping away the dust as he yelled, "It's there! Ptolemy's seal. Just like he said in the translation. I thought it was the Sphinx in Giza, but it's the Sphinx's shadow here only visible during the Blue Khonsu, which must be this very night! How could we have been so lucky?"

The men jumped in excitement, and then, just as Alexander and Ptolemy had done in this exact spot over two thousand years ago, they made a blood oath of secrecy and cooperation to keep secret between them whatever was hidden in the cliff. However, they both knew the war waited for no one and no archeological find, no matter how spectacular!

They hustled back to their damaged aircraft while placing brush around the small entrance to the "Valley of Death from Earth and Sky," as Alexander and Ptolemy had named it. It was fortuitous but eerie and mysterious that Duke had found the seal after a day of such death from the sky, and he wondered about death from the earth just as the loudest spine-shaking lion's roar he had ever heard echoed from the valley behind them. Both men broke into a fast pace straight to the dying fire on the emergency strip and made it back in less than forty-five minutes.

After they caught their breath and silently added more wood to the fire, Max began talking about his idyllic academic days of archaeological and language studies at Oxford, which he had completed just before the war started for Germany in 1914. He had hoped to join an expedition and refine his skills in the field. Unfortunately, since his family's centuries-old hotel business was not doing well and the war started, he instead had volunteered for the same cavalry unit as his cousin, Manfred von Richthofen. They both transferred to the air service after the cavalry became useless when the war turned to trench warfare on the outskirts of Paris.

The men shared their love of history, especially the excitement of possibly finding the long-lost Alexander's final resting place and the immense treasure thought to be buried with him. Max's family's condition had worsened as the war raged on, and his meager Captain's pay wasn't helping. He shared his worries of poverty after the war, especially with a new baby on the way. He fantasied that perhaps this treasure would be what his family so desperately needed. Duke wondered later as both men began working on aircraft repairs if Max might become a tomb raider instead of a history maker.

As the repairs quickly progressed, Duke found enough fuel to refill each Triplane tank while Max replaced his damaged fuel line and magneto. Duke found a spare Sopwith Camel strut that seemed a close enough fit and replaced his destroyed aileron with another Camel spare. He patched the wing with spare dope and fabric that he hoped would hold together for the long flight home. If it failed, his bleached bones would never be found.

It had been a day and night like no other, and the men percolated a fresh batch of coffee and sat down to rest just as the first hint of dawn broke to the east. The earth never stood still, especially when momentous times enfolded them, but they absorbed the pink, purple, orange, and finally yellow of the desert sunrise in silent awe.

They agreed to return after the war ended to this very spot and resume the critical work on this mysterious find in complete secrecy.

The remote, but sacred, Oasis of Siwa was only seven miles away but was not visible from this well-camouflaged airstrip, and the caravan route was well south. The risk of discovery was very small, but they needed to leave quickly before search patrols discovered them and the secret valley.

The men embraced, and Duke reached into his leather flight jacket and pulled out Max's original Blue Max medal, which he had given him after saving his life in France. He returned the overall gold medal painted blue with its blue and gold ribbon to his friend and said, "You earned this, not me."

Max said, "Thanks! I never thought I would see it again after my escape, and I sure couldn't afford a replacement now that gold is so expensive. Unfortunately, as you may know, I did kill two sentries getting away, and I think there is now a reward for my recapture, so you may want to keep our time here quiet," Max added with a strange smirk.

Duke was shocked as he hadn't heard this during his recovery in the hospital. He didn't have time to discuss this shocking truth now as the sun was entirely over the horizon, and patrols would arrive any minute.

They each then propped the other's aircraft to a rumbling start by hand, swinging the eight-foot-long, curved wooden props to a blur as the rotary engines happily sprung to life.

As the engines warmed, Duke said, "We now have to become enemies again."

Max responded, "We will never be enemies, my friend! But I do think we are now even. You saved my life, and now I saved yours, so we have no debts between us, only friendship and the future adventure of a lifetime together once this bloody war ends! Let's both try and stay alive, but we must still do our duty for God and country!"

"For God and country!" replied Duke.

With that, both men strapped on their Triplanes. And after a brisk salute, the two birds, one red with black iron crosses and the other black with English roundels, thundered down the runway into the rising sun and back into a world at war, leaving silence and swirling dust at the now silent and abandoned airstrip.

Only one set of eyes watched their departure—the fierce golden eyes of the lioness who intently focused on Duke's black mount.

CHAPTER 15 • Courage of the Early Morning

As Duke climbed to his cruising altitude of fifteen thousand feet, he kept a close eye on his temporary wing repair. He took in the peacefulness of the brisk morning sun and watched as the horizon changed from purple to crimson and finally bright orange. It cleared his head. He felt lucky that flying released his mind from the tyranny of lesser things and allowed him to focus on the here and now, not the problems of life on the ground.

He still didn't know what to do about Vivian and Juliette or how he would handle the archaeological finds post-war, but now, it didn't seem to matter. He flew with the joy of freedom and adventure he had felt since his first flight in Americus, Georgia. In a frail, underpowered training Curtis Jenny Biplane, over the thick, longleaf pines of the endless Georgia horizon that he loved with all his soul.

He and Frank had soloed together in those carefree days and flown low over the corn and cotton fields, often scaring the plow horses as the farmers raised their fists in frustration while they roared over. One day, Duke's engine failed, and he landed nose up in a freshly plowed field beside a dirt road. Thankfully, Frank landed just in time to save him from an angry farmer's pitchfork who chased them as they took off from the rutted road.

They laughed that night at the Windsor Hotel's upstairs bar as they retold the story of Duke's escape to some giggling Southern Belles they snuggled the night away with before returning to the airfield the next morning. *Those were the days*, thought Duke as he flew back toward the safety of the Giza airstrip.

What he did know was that Max had spared his life, just as he had saved his, and they shared one of the greatest secrets in the archaeological world. This was real and would last long after the war when it finally came time to complete their joint discovery, which could change history if all the translations were true! But Duke wondered if he was wrong about Max.

Now that he knew about his desperate financial condition and his status as a war criminal for killing sentries during his escape, Duke felt a deep uneasiness in his heart. First, he had to get back to the Giza airstrip and win this war; then he would decide how to manage Max.

He thought of the men and aircraft he lost yesterday. Yes, they had scored a tremendous victory over the enemy and had destroyed supplies and killed many combatants, but they would reorganize. He had to get word to Colonel Balfour to follow up this success with his calvary and whip out the survivors. But he also had to get air supremacy. To do this, he had to destroy Max's lethal Fokker Triplane squadron before they assaulted the British cavalry.

Then, like many times before while flying, the solution dawned on him: he would take the war to the German's airfield and destroy the squadron on the ground! *I won't have to engage them in aerial combat where they have the advantage over what's left of my squadron. We will hit them out of the sun at the break of dawn when they least expect it.* Then, like the beauty of this morning's sunrise, a peaceful feeling engulfed him.

As he began his descent to the Giza airfield, he said a silent prayer of thanks for successfully making it back to his squadron. He felt the urge to release his fury at the loss of his squadron mates and, despite the repairs, pulled into a loop followed by a barrel roll and then a snap roll.

Then, Duke pulled up into a dangerous vertical climb until he stalled and kicked full right rudder, which allowed the nose to swing down with the added engine torque to a vertical dive, a Hammerhead maneuver. Duke screamed, "Dixie!" to the heavens in pure joy as one maneuver blurred into another, and he felt the G forces pushing and pulling his body, even collapsing his vision.

He pulled harder and harder until he finally reached ground level at maximum airspeed! He then carefully rolled three times as he crossed the field to signify the three victories he had achieved against the loss of his four FE2s. The squadron, warming up to begin a search for survivors, cheered him joyously as he rolled to a stop and shut down the rotary engine in front of his hanger.

The engine hissed and popped at the fuel loss, and the prop finally shuttered to a stop. He reached forward and patted the cowling to thank his Sopwith Triplane that pulled him safely from deep in the desert. Duke then leaned back on the leather headrest and looked up gratefully to the heavens. He had spent yet another of his nine lives. He wondered how many he had left?

The men rushed to the black Sopwith Triplane and lifted him on their shoulders. They immediately took him to the officers' club, their hope and fighting spirit suddenly renewed. As he gathered the survivors around him and saw that all his flight leaders had survived, he ordered drinks all around for the whole squadron. The men relished the strength and skill of their leader.

They solemnly toasted their departed squadron mates with four separate shots of strong whiskey. They raised their glasses three more times for the victories of their commanding officer, who had saved all of their lives.

When the men had settled down, Duke had all non-military personnel leave the club, then banged his fist on the bar. His audience was silent.

"Gentlemen, we scored a major victory on the ground yesterday against the Germans! But the cost was high. Now I have a plan to pay back our departed friends and countrymen! Captain Tom Holmes deserves credit for one of the Huns, so add that one to his score, and now he is officially an ace with five kills!" Duke added.

He was happy to credit his Scottish wingman and friend with the Fokker to motivate himself and the squadron to future joint success.

The men yelled and pounded on the bar and walls until the officers' club felt like it was shaking!

"I have a plan to honor our dead," said Duke as the club became deathly silent and all remembered the faces and lives sacrificed yesterday.

"We will destroy the Germans where they live and breathe with an attack out of the rising sun using every aircraft that we have tomorrow morning at their airfield in El Alamein!" he said.

"I want every aircraft serviceable and flying. Check your ammunition and ordnance so that every round counts. I don't want a single German Triplane, hanger, or building left after our attack. Flight leaders, meet me in my office at 0300 and pilots 0330 for our pre-mission briefing.

"Until then, all personnel are restricted to base! We will call the mission 'hellfire'," said Duke with an unworldly intensity.

He slammed his glass down and headed out the door as the club buzzed with excitement behind him.

He could hear the squadron cheering as he made his way to the communications office to send a telegram to Colonel Balfour to coordinate his attack with the cavalry's advance on the remainder of the enemy.

Tomorrow would make or break the British western front in the Middle East, and he felt the weight of command as he had never experienced before. Duke dictated the telegram and sent his orderly, Sergeant Murphy, out to tell Captain Tom Holmes and maintenance officer Sergeant John Majors to meet him in his office.

The two men arrived looking like hungry lions and ready for anything. Duke briskly returned their salutes and pointed to the two chairs in front of his ancient British desk. His small but comfortable office was spartan. It had the appearance of a Sheik's tent with Arabian carpets covering the sandy unfinished planks and tapestry hanging from all but one wall where a glazed-over window faced the airstrip.

He pulled three cut crystal glasses from the desk's top drawer and carefully poured a peaty 16-year-old Lagavulin Scotch. Duke first toasted Tom's new ace status, followed by their lost comrades, and finally the upcoming mission of retribution. The scotch quickly warmed their bodies and loosened their tongues.

After allowing the leaders to empty their glasses, Duke said, "OK, out with it. How many planes can we have ready for tomorrow morning, and what is the disposition of the men?"

"Sir, we lost four of our best FE2s and pilots yesterday, and one came back barely flyable, which leaves only four in flyable condition! Also, Captain Holmes' Camel is so shot up, it is barely in flying condition!" exclaimed Sergeant Majors. "But don't worry, Captain, my crews are already working nonstop in the hangers. They will get every bird that was down for repairs before this mission, the current damaged ones, and our spares in the air by 0400 tomorrow! If the buggers don't get the job done, I will give up my stripes!"

"And if you do get them all flying, I will add another stripe to your sleeve!" yelled Duke as he poured another round of the dark scotch.

Tom quickly added, "The pilots are hungry to avenge our losses yesterday, and this mission is just the ticket, sir! The only problem I see is that none of the men have any night flying experience, and Lt. Raj Djione is wounded. I just spoke with the flight surgeon in Cairo this morning, and he said Raj shouldn't fly for a week. Of course, Raj didn't listen and left against medical advice. He is already headed to the airfield!"

Duke laughed, "You can't keep that Gurkha warrior down!"

"I agree with you, Tom, about the night flying experience, and we sure can't get any before tonight, can we? There is a bright Blue Moon, which only occurs every three years. This is another sign of our impending success and victory.

"I want you to brief your crews that the moon will light the sky enough for each flight to form a loose formation and to focus on the fire from the exhaust stack of our reliable rotary engines from each aircraft. They can use that flame as the focal point to form up on their wingman," he said.

"We will be at the limit of our range when we attack out of the rising sun. Each flight will have a maximum of fifteen minutes at combat power over the airfield, but every Fokker must be destroyed on the ground before we turn for home.

"We will attack in two waves. I will lead the first wave of FE2s, and Tom, you and the other Camel will lead the second wave of FE2s. Watch out for any anti-aircraft batteries, and if our timing and intelligence are right, the Fokker Triplanes will be lined up and warming up on the flight line just as we hit them! If any aircraft survive the first wave, we will get them on our second pass before they have time to take off and engage us. Remember the emergency strip at Siwa Oasis if any battle damage is too severe to make it back here. After the first pass, I will fly top cover in case any Fokkers get off the ground, and Tom, I need your two Camels to join me as my wingmen after your first pass. Any questions?" said Duke.

"No, sir!" replied the men.

"One last thing, no lights are to be visible on the flight

line, and I want all light bulbs in the mess hall and briefing room replaced with red bulbs to protect our night vision. Also, each pilot is to personally check his ammunition and bomb loads because we don't need any guns jamming on target! Each of our Sopwith fighters will also carry a full load of bombs since we are short on FE's. Drop them on your first pass so you are ready for aerial combat when you pull off the field.

"Now is our chance to regain air superiority and destroy the enemy on the Middle Eastern front! Let's make history, gentlemen!" cried Duke.

The men saluted and quickly left his office to get to work.

The day flew by as Duke got regular updates and visited the maintenance hangers frequently. Writing the four letters to the downed men's families was the hardest thing he had ever done, but he knew it was a commander's duty. He prayed if he survived the morning attack, he wouldn't have to write anymore, but he had an uneasy feeling that might not be the case. Finally, as the sun was touching the horizon, Sergeant Murphy came rushing in with an urgent dispatch from General Allenby to meet him at headquarters in Cairo.

Corporal Shaw had the Rolls Royce command car warmed up and waiting for him outside. He rushed to the General's headquarters in downtown Cairo, carefully weaving through camels, goats, nomads, and troops of all the Commonwealth nations who battled the Germans and Turks under the British Union Jack. Within the hour, he stood at rigid attention in front of the tense General, who asked for a personal briefing of the events of the past twenty-four hours.

Duke efficiently provided a report and carefully left out his time with Max. Finally, as Duke detailed the plans for the morning attack, the General's rigid stare melted into a smile, and he ordered, "At ease, Captain. You have the fighting spirit of Lord Nelson and the wisdom of Wellington! I like your plan, but it is quite a gamble,

Captain. Are you sure this will succeed?" General Allenby had a frown of concern on his thick black eyebrows.

"No, sir, but we have the element of surprise on our side, and I doubt the Germans expect an aerial attack. They have no idea the range of our group and much less the fighting spirit of my squadron. They have only been in El Alamein for the past month. Intelligence reports indicate very little anti-aircraft or other defense against aerial assault, especially out of the sun at first light! We will give them hell, General! But I do expect some losses," said Duke.

He anxiously waited for the final OK from his General.

"I heard from Colonel Balfour, who made contact with the remains of the enemy concentration your group attacked. Tomorrow, he plans to finish the attack you started. He related many casualties and a complete loss of supplies and organization but feels he can easily finish the job if we have control of the air. Having air superiority is critical for his success, so I approve your plan and wish you Godspeed," said the General with a smile.

Duke stood at rigid attention and saluted his General, saying, "Yes sir!" and spun around to leave the office.

"One more thing before you leave, Captain," whispered the General while nodding to his adjuvant, who walked over with a silver case. "Effective immediately, I am giving you a field commission and advancing your rank. Congratulations, Major! I wish I had more officers with your fighting spirit! Go get 'em, tiger!" said the General.

Duke didn't know what to say or do but saluted briskly after the adjuvant placed the Major's oak leaves on his field jacket. He spun around before he passed out from shock.

"Yes sir, thank you, sir!"

He walked downstairs and across the street, telling Corporal Shaw to pick him up in five minutes in front of Shepheard's Hotel, where he was going to have one celebratory drink before heading to the airfield. When Duke entered the long bar packed with officers, there was a curious silence before a lanky English artillery Lieutenant barked, "Attention!"

Suddenly, Duke realized he was the ranking officer in the bar, now with Major's emblems on his shoulders. He said, "At ease." Then he pulled up to the bar for a neat glass of Lagavulin single malt scotch from the Isle of Islay, Scotland—his favorite!

He drank and tried to absorb the enormity of the last 48 hours. Death, war, discovery, and promotion; he had never dreamed any of this was possible just two days ago. It all seemed so unreal; he wondered if he was dreaming but was quickly brought back to earth as his friendly supply Colonel, Rob Scott of South Africa, walked in and sat beside him.

"Congratulations, Major Thomas. Your success has brought long-overdue recognition to this front! The General ordered me to open all supplies to you for anything the 77th LRG needs. I also wanted to let you know, we have just received the new, incendiary ammunition used on the Western front for balloon and ground attack missions."

Duke returned to the here and now and said, "Colonel, you are very kind. Thanks for your support. I used that ammunition during my time in France, and we desperately need it immediately! Is it possible to get it tonight?"

Rob responded with his African practicality, "Would I not shoot a bull elephant if I had the weapon and opportunity! Of course, I will have it delivered within the hour. Anything else you chaps need?"

Duke decided to go for broke with his supply request.

"I need more anti-personnel bombs, aircraft, two cases of your best scotch, and as much Guinness beer as you can round up for my overworked staff and crews," he said. "Also, three of your best trucks with fuel, aircraft spare parts, trenching and building supplies, including ammunition, weapons, water, and food for three months for my emergency airfield in the far western desert," Duke said.

He knew if he didn't use the supplies now, at least he would have them at the Oasis for his future full exploration of Alexander's tomb when this bloodbath ended.

Of course, that's assuming the desert bandits don't steal them, he thought.

"I can do everything except more aircraft within the next fortnight. I will have my staff en route to your airfield immediately. I do have one more Triplane still crated to deliver with the other supplies to the emergency airstrip. Tommy Sopwith sent it for your personal use with his congratulations on your success," responded Colonel Scott with a smile.

The Colonel continued, "Oh, by the way, there's a new chap at the bar who was also just promoted. Major Lawrence is better known as Lawrence of Arabia and just defeated the Turks at Akkaba! That's him at the end of the bar with his Arabian white robe on."

Duke looked at the deeply tanned officer with no signs of British military dress; he was wearing a white turban wrapped with a gold strap around his forehead and a flowing white Arabic robe with sandals. He looked Arabic except for the piercingly intelligent blue eyes that focused on Duke's congratulatory gaze.

He raised a glass to him as he likewise was aware of Duke's recent success and had a nose for military talent. Duke returned the silent toast as they both shared the smile of warriors about to return to combat. Duke to the Western Desert and Lawrence to Damascus, both critical players in General Allenby's upcoming strategic campaign to defeat the Ottomans in the Holy Land and take Jerusalem and victory on the Middle Eastern Front.

Duke then turned and said, "Thanks, Colonel! You may

have turned the tide for our mission and this front! I will have my crews awaiting your delivery, and this is all very hush, hush!" exclaimed Duke.

He swallowed the last of his scotch and headed to the door. He nodded to Major Lawrence, who smiled and winked as Duke slipped out of the long bar.

Corporal Shaw saw the shining new Major's insignia and jumped from his driver's seat to salute Duke. He jumped back into the Rolls Royce and immediately headed back to base, making excellent time as he dodged the camel caravans completing their autumn migration into town.

Duke had all hands on deck as Colonel Scott's supply trucks arrived full of incendiary ammunition, fragmentary bombs, and supplies for the officers' club.

He instructed the armorers to load every third round with the new, incendiary rounds and replace all bombs with the latest shipment, which were more suited to damaging enemy structures than personnel.

By the time all aircraft were repaired, rearmed, fueled, and ready for action, it was well after midnight. Duke finally laid his head down for a short nap before the briefing. It was his first rest in almost forty-eight hours.

He slept the sleep of the dead. His dreams were filled with strange figures of human-headed lions like the Sphinx, and then Vivian, Juliette, and smoking, flaming aircraft of strange colors and configurations. It was fitting for Halloween 1917. By the time Sergeant Murphy awakened him, he was drenched in sweat from aerial combat with an imaginary foe.

"Good morning, Major," whispered the Sergeant.

"Yes, good morning. Please bring me my Turkish coffee, black with heavy sugar, as usual," said Duke.

"Yes, sir, and your briefing is in 5 minutes," noted the Sergeant.

"Of course," cried Duke.

He gathered his thoughts while dressing in his flight gear for the upcoming battle.

After putting his leather jacket over his thick fleece-lined flight suit, Duke carefully strapped on his grandfather's Colt and saber. He pulled up his calf-high leather flying boots and stashed his cashmere-lined leather helmet and gloves loosely in his flight jacket. His flying goggles hung from his neck.

He ran his hand through his blond hair, grabbed his Turkish coffee from Murphy, and headed at a brisk pace to the packed briefing room.

The small room was full when Duke entered. Raj called the men to attention.

"At ease, men," said Duke, and the pilots quickly sat down as he went to the front and uncovered the map.

"Now, we depart in thirty minutes to bring this war to the German airfield where they least expect us!" Duke said.

He pointed to the map, and the men responded by yelling, "Huzzah, Huzzah, Huzzah!"

"Thanks to Sergeant Majors' team, we have every available aircraft back in service. I will lead the first flight of FE2s, and Captain Holmes will lead the second flight into the enemy's airfield. We will fly at five thousand feet en route, and as we approach the El Alamein German airfield, we will descend to the best bombing altitude of one hundred feet," Duke said.

"The Fokker DR1 Triplanes should be lined up because the pilots are awaiting their morning briefing. They will probably already be warming up their planes as we are now, so hit them hard

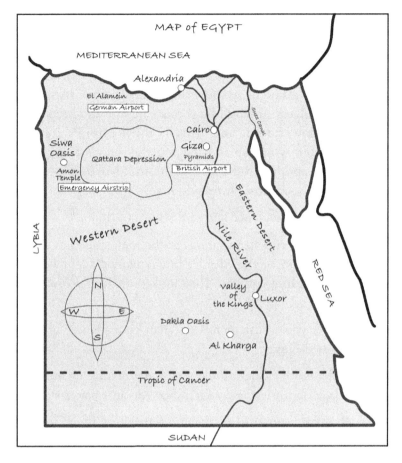

MAP of EGYPT

MEDITERRANEAN SEA

Alexandria

El Alamein
German Airport

Cairo

Siwa Oasis

Giza
Pyramids

Qattara Depression

British Airport

Amon Temple

Emergency Airstrip

LYBIA

Western Desert

Suez Canal

Eastern Desert

Nile River

RED SEA

N

W   E

S

Valley of the Kings

Luxor

Dakla Oasis

Al Kharga

Tropic of Cancer

SUDAN

on the first pass. Destroy all aircraft, anti-aircraft positions, hangers, fuel, supply, personnel, and structures on the airfield. I want to turn the place back into a desert wasteland!

"We will hit them out of the rising sun and make a second pass at treetop level as we return to our home base using our machine guns to finish off anything that wasn't destroyed on the first pass. I will be flying high top cover after the first pass with Captain Holmes in case any Fokker Triplanes slip away and try to cause trouble," he said.

"Here is our emergency strip close to Siwa Oasis, so if anyone can't make the return to base due to damage or low fuel, use this strip and its emergency supplies. Remember, we only have enough fuel for 15 minutes of combat power, so don't waste any time. Make every bomb and bullet count, especially the new rounds that were loaded last night, as those should easily ignite the aircraft, fuel, wooden hangers, and buildings. Also, be sure and keep a loose combat formation en route and focus on the fire from the exhaust stacks to line your wings up and stay together on your way home. The full moon is putting out a lot of light, so it will be easy to keep formation. Any questions?" finished Duke.

Raj broke the silence and said, "No, sir, Major!"

The room erupted in salutes as the men smiled at the unexpected promotion of their leader but remained silent with the tension of impending combat. They looked anxiously toward the door.

"Thank you, gentlemen. OK, man your planes, and good luck!" exclaimed Duke.

As the room cleared, Duke saw Raj was limping and had a heavy bandage on his left leg, which showed some blood staining.

"Raj, you know better than to ignore the flight surgeon's recommendation to not fly and to finish your recovery!" said Duke.

"Oh Major, it's just a scratch," smiled Raj with eyes as fierce as a snow leopard.

It was clear that no one would prevent him from paying back the Germans for the loss of four of his squadron. He even reached down and pulled out his almost two-foot-long Khukuri blade.

"If I get the chance, even more of those bastards will pay with their lives!" responded Raj with a quick smile as he limped out the door to his FE2.

Duke followed, and as he strapped on his vibrating Sopwith Triplane, he looked around at the squadron with deep satisfaction knowing the heart of these men and the weapons of war they flew would bring true red dawn to the Germans. They were all ready for take-off and focused on *Black Death*, which was straining against the chocks under her wheels and the two mechanics holding her tail from taking off too soon as her radial engine growled in anticipation of the upcoming strike.

Duke gave the thumbs up, and the crew pulled the chocks away and released the tail. He advanced the throttle, and the flames spewing from her exhaust stacks extended back to the cockpit. As the rest of the squadron followed, it gave an eerie glow to the airfield. All the watching staff wondered what this unworldly glow foretold; success or failure, and who, if any, would return from this high-stakes mission. As the planes departed, lifting into the light of the huge full moon, an eerie silence descended on the field, and the staff headed to the barracks for some much-needed rest, realizing that only time and fate could answer these life and death questions.

The take-off and flight to the target went well with no mechanical failures in the squadron. Duke fired his Vickers machine gun and watched as the third round glowed brightly and then saw the sky around him lighting up as other aircraft likewise checked their weapons.

It looked like fireflies twinkling all around him, and the smell of the salt marsh mixed with the scent of pines reminded him of the cool Georgia woods on a late fall evening.

He remembered the crackling bonfires that were a family weekend tradition during the evenings when the leaves were changing from yellow and orange to red. The whole family enjoyed the fruits of the hunting season with duck, quail, venison, and wild boar simmering on the open coals with steaming oysters wrapped in wet sacks lining the edge of the fire pit. He loved this time of year and especially loved holding Vivian close after their lovemaking in the old hunting cabin that sat on a tidal marsh teeming with oyster beds and migrating mallard ducks. They lay together and whispered plans for a large family they both wanted.

What a difference to November in the desert with no trees, water, or game to speak of—only dry heat, blowing sand, scorpions, and humans that he and his squadron were now going to hunt and be hunted themselves in the process.

Abruptly, he brought his mind back to the present and felt his senses vibrate with awareness and tension that only men at war feel as they risk their lives in combat. Every fiber of his being said not to take this chance with his life or his men's, but his traditional sense of honor, duty, and country pushed him forward, not as a hero, but instead to protect and serve the men who so faithfully followed him into battle.

Just as his forefathers had followed first General Washington and then General Forrest into battle, this was a modern-day cavalry, and he was leading a charge directly into an entrenched and well-manned enemy position. They could easily be waiting in ambush or mount a counter-attack on his depleted squadron, who were far from their home base and safety.

As these emotions flowed through him, he noticed the first brightening of the sky and checked the time. He realized the flight was behind schedule and was not going to begin the attack before sunrise. They must be encountering a strong headwind at this altitude, and he began a gradual descent to one thousand feet in hopes of picking up speed as the rest of the squadron followed him. He realized it was too late to change the arrival time and how the invisible hand of the winds could change the mission's fate and outcome. Should he turn back and regroup for another day?

His men were motivated, and his forces were at 100% with every surviving plane in service. He still had the element of surprise, which would be unlikely if he delayed this attack for another day. He thought of Alfred Lord Tennyson's poem, The Charge of the Light Brigade, "Half a league, half a league, half a league on-ward, All in the Valley of Death rode the six hundred. Forward the Light Brigade! Charge for the guns, he said; into the Valley of Death rode the six hundred."

Duke made up his mind, now was the time. Onward charged his squadron to tempt fate and death once more, just as the Light Brigade had done on October 25th, 1854, during the Crimean War with Russia. He hoped this time his forces would prevail since his decisions and leadership were at the tip of the spear, instead of behind the lines as the British commander had done, which would prevent miscommunication and defeat.

As the sun broke behind them and the reflection of the bright blue Mediterranean Sea became visible in the distance, Duke descended to an attack altitude of 100 feet and pushed his throttle to combat full power. He felt the surge of speed and performance as his Triplane jumped forward, ready to fire the first burst of machine-gun fire into the enemy aircraft.

He looked behind him and saw the FE2s of his flight spread beautifully into a Finger-Four attack formation to cover as much of the enemy airfield as possible on the first pass. He noticed Raj's FE2 lagging behind the others slightly and wondered if he might be having some engine problems.

There was no time to worry. He was surprised to see the German airfield's perimeter approaching fast and three lines of four Fokker DR1 Triplanes lined and warming up, awaiting their pilots. *Maybe we will all survive this,* thought Duke optimistically.

Could they possibly have caught the whole squadron on the ground? He lined up with the first line of DR1's and pressed down on his stick-mounted trigger while he carefully walked his tracer and incendiary fire up the line of Fokkers, hitting each fuel tank location and flaming three of the four planes in seconds. He kept the trigger down, feeling the Vickers .303 machine gun vibration sweep through his nimble mount while hearing the "AK-AK-

AK" of the deadly weapon.

He knew every pilot on the ground would see his black Triplane, which he had instructed Sergeant Majors to paint with a white *Grim Reaper* on each side of the overall black tail and the fuselage. He flamed two wooden maintenance hangers with Fokkers inside in various stages of repair as he released his bomb load before flashing past the far western perimeter of the airfield and climbing to cover the rest of the attacking squadron.

As he turned back while climbing steeply, he watched with satisfaction as each of his wonderful flights of FE2s made their bombs count, and more and more of the Fokkers exploded or caught fire. Then he saw Raj deviate from the last line of aircraft toward the far northern corner of the field where a large hanger with a huge Gotha twin-engine Bomber was hiding in the shadows!

Where did that come from? thought Duke. He watched Raj drop his bomb load squarely on the bomber and hangar, both erupting in flames. Then, to Duke's shock, he saw the second Gotha Bomber beside another hanger. He hoped the next flight would see it before using all their bomb loads on the fighters.

Before the next flight could release their bombs, Duke saw a sickening sight. Three German Fokker DR1s following a red and black Triplane with the skull and crossbones in black dove-like falcons out of the sky and began firing at the last FE2 approaching the airfield as the anti-aircraft guns began filling the sky with tracers.

Fight's on, thought Duke as he rolled on his back, pulled into a Split S, and came screaming down to defend his second flight. Simultaneously, Captain Tom Holmes began firing on the last undamaged Triplanes on the ground and released his bomb load, wiping out a hangar full of uncrated Fokkers, not yet assembled.

Before Duke could fire his Vickers, Max von Wagner had the last FE2 in flames, and it crashed into the only remaining undamaged structure on the airfield, which immediately caught fire.

As Max lined up on the second FE2, Tom and his wingman in their Sopwith Camels violently pulled around into a head-on pass on the Fokker Triplanes, which returned fire while breaking off the attack on the FE2s, who were then able to complete their bomb runs leaving total destruction on the ground. By this time, the low-level dogfight was in full display right over the German airfield, and the anti-aircraft gunners had to stop firing for fear of hitting their own aircraft.

Tom's Camel latched on to the tail of the last German Fokker Triplane, and under his accurate fire, it exploded and crashed into the middle of the airfield. Tom's wingman was under heavy fire from the other three German fighters, pulling and turning for all he was worth, but he could not shake the attackers who by now also had Tom in their sights.

Each British Camel fighter was so low that dust and sand were coming up from the airfield as they turned hard and fought for their lives. Finally, Max von Wagner had Tom in his sights and fired a long burst which destroyed his propeller. Tom skidded in for a crash landing at the German airfield's far southern corner and climbed out of his burning aircraft. He ran for cover to the remains of a destroyed hangar while firing his pistol at advancing German ground troops.

Duke's Sopwith Triplane was screaming well past the red line, its maximum structural speed, as he lined up with the last of the three German Fokker Triplanes and opened fire at point-blank range, sending his machine-gun fire directly into the fuel tank and engine of the enemy's aircraft. It immediately caught fire, forcing the German to crash land on the airstrip already filled with destroyed and burning aircraft.

As Duke lined up with Max's wingman, he was suddenly sighted by the Fokker's pilot, who took evasive action but couldn't shake the determined American. Duke fired short bursts into the wings and engine compartment, both of which caught fire and exploded mid-flight, sending fragments of wood and fabric all over the airfield.

Unfortunately, Max had shot down Tom's wingman in a fatal crash by this time, joining the death and apocalyptic conditions on the ground.

Now there were only two fighters in the sky and the last of the FE2s, including Lt. Raj. They made firing passes across the airfield and knocked out any remaining hangars and aircraft that were not already in flames. Raj and his wingman headed straight for the German Gotha bomber and were able to ignite multiple fires on the massive offensive bomber with the new, incendiary ammunition, which soon exploded into thousands of fragments.

However, Max's Fokker latched onto the tail of Raj's wingman, and his FE2 caught fire after a long burst of machine-gun fire, crashing in a huge fireball in the middle of the German airfield. Then, Max latched onto Raj's tail, which turned hard left and right but was unable to shake the faster, more maneuverable Fokker.

Max lined up for the death blow after sending multiple Spandau machine gun rounds into the frail aircraft and further slowing it down. But before he could finish off Duke's trusted flight commander, Duke fired at long range on Max, who immediately broke off the attack and attempted to aggressively turn into his worthy quarry and lure him into a head-on pass where the German's heavier armament with twin Spandau machine guns could once again win the day.

But Duke remembered his previous combat with Max. Instead of meeting him head-on, he pulled up—using his extra speed and superior climbing ability—into an Immelmann turn, a half-loop followed by a half roll resulting in a 180 change of direction.

At the same time, Max had bled off his energy and speed, attempting to lure him into a head-on pass. This gave Duke the momentary edge as he lined up behind the German Ace and Blue Max recipient. He fired a short burst directly into the tail's surface with multiple hits before the great ace quickly snap-rolled, and Duke flew right by him.

Max immediately fired on Duke's tail as he was briefly exposed, and he felt multiple hits along his fuselage, which began to vibrate at high speed and power setting.

Duke now was right above the enemy runway, and as he turned, he was so low that he left a trail of dust behind him, with Max hot on his tail.

Duke pulled into a hard left turn while the three wings of his Sopwith fighter, The *Grim Reaper*, dug into the thick morning desert air, and combined with the torque of the rotary engine, produced the tightest left turn he had ever experienced. But he also had to fight the positive G forces, which loaded his body and aircraft to over seven times their normal weight and began to drain the blood from Duke's brain and eyes.

He tensed his stomach muscles and lungs while yelling out, "Dixie!" to prevent G-loc, which would render him unconscious and lead to certain death.

Duke held on by the thinnest of edges while his vision narrowed into a small cone of forward visibility. But by a miracle of time and space, he was able to barely see the black skull and crossbones on each side of Max's red Fokker crossing right in front of him. He fired one last desperate burst that ran up the fuselage's length, through the black skull and crossbones, and then into the engine, which immediately caught fire.

His vision began to return, as did his hearing, as he reduced the G forces and followed the burning Fokker as it crash-landed on the airfield, throwing Max from the aircraft, which was fully engulfed in flames.

Duke couldn't believe it, but he prayed Max had survived,

so he made a last pass over the enemy field as the anti-aircraft fire resumed. As Duke flashed over the downed enemy at full combat power with his landing gear barely missing the dirt, he saluted his gallant adversary, Max, who returned the salute while limping away from his destroyed Fokker.

The German anti-aircraft fire resumed as Duke surveyed the total desolation of the airfield while he lined up and put one aggressive anti-aircraft position out of action. He had seen his friend and flight leader, Captain Tom Holmes, holding off the advancing ground troops at the corner of the airfield. Suddenly, he saw muzzle flashes as the ground troops were almost to Tom's position, and just in time, Duke fired a long burst into their midst, killing or scattering the now disheartened German troops.

Duke had an idea as he chopped the power and slipped into a rough landing, rolling to a stop beside his lightly wounded friend.

"Get in!" yelled Duke.

"No way, boss, we will never make it. There is another truckload of Huns heading our way," said Tom as he fired the last of his pistol's ammunition into the truck.

"That is an order, Captain!" yelled Major Thomas.

He had fire flaring in his blue eyes as small arms fire produced geysers of dirt all around the *Grim Reaper*, whose Clerget rotary engine rumbled angrily at the unexpected interlude from full combat power and action.

Tom ran over and grabbed onto the wing walk, wedging himself against the fuselage, throwing away his now empty Colt 45. Duke gunned the Clerget 9B 130hp rotary engine, which happily exploded to full power as he turned the Sopwith Triplane toward the open runway, only to see a truck full of screaming German infantry speeding toward them while firing in their direction. Suddenly, he was out of options.

Duke thought, *was this really how my life was going to end?* Time seemed to slow down. Then, mysteriously, the truck exploded and skidded off the runway, opening a small section of runway for the Sopwith's escape, and an FE2 Biplane screamed overhead with Raj, the true Nepalese Gurkha warrior swinging his lethal Khukuri blade overhead in a victory salute to his commander.

Duke gave the rotary engine the good news and roared away into the now bright rising sun while taking light small arms fire as he exited the perimeter of the airfield but did not sustain additional damage. Raj formed up on his commander, and they shared a smile of survival, both whipping away sweaty goggles and shaking their fists in triumph. They were alive and flying, but they had big problems.

Raj's engine was running poorly, and he was barely able to keep up with Duke's aircraft, which continued to vibrate more and more violently due to the tail damage from Max's attack and accurate Spandau machine gunfire.

Tom was holding on for dear life but had wounds that were quickly weakening him, and there was no place to land in the endless sea of sand dunes just below them. Duke pulled his belt off and looped it around Tom's shoulder, giving him some much-needed support as he tried to decide how to save these wonderful men and the aircraft. He was now on reserve fuel and badly vibrating due to battle damage.

Then, as if a guiding hand directed him, Duke saw a falcon in the distance and suddenly realized they had only one chance: the emergency airstrip at Siwa Oasis beside the Valley of Death from Earth and Sky. Duke prayed they had enough fuel and power to nurse the aircraft to a safe landing.

The two British planes limped slowly toward the safety of the Siwa Oasis emergency airstrip as the sun climbed higher in the morning sky. Duke watched his fuel gauge fall to the emergency level as Raj dropped farther and farther behind with his engine, now occasionally stopping before angrily resuming its unsteady revolutions.

Finally, the tiny supply cabin and old stream bed became visible, and Duke dropped like a falcon for a smooth landing on the tumbleweed-covered but usable sandy strip. He quickly pulled in beside the supply shack and switched the magnetos off while watching the spinning disk hiss to a stop as the now unhappy engine hotly crackled in response.

He leaned his head back on the black leather headrest of the Triplane and, after taking a few deep breaths, reached under his leather flight jacket to tightly rub the Alexander the Great coin that he always wore for luck. He said a silent prayer of thanks for surviving such a close brush with death.

134

Tom spoke quietly, asking where he was, and it was apparent he was now in a state of shock from his wounds and exposure to the desert elements.

By the time Raj had limped in for a landing, Duke had placed Tom on the small cot in the supply cabin under blankets and with drinking water, which seemed to revive his spirits.

Raj limped over and saluted his commander, who quickly embraced him and thanked him for saving their lives. Duke silently planned on recommending him for a Distinguished Service Order as he was also going to recommend Tom. But first, they had to survive until they repaired their aircraft or help arrived.

CHAPTER 16 •
Valley of Death From Earth and Sky

It was midday, and the heat was intense in the open desert of the remote strip. Tom was sleeping fitfully in the supply cabin while Duke and Raj were busily working on replacing two shot-up cylinders on the reliable Beardmore 160hp engine for Raj's FE2 Biplane.

They took a short break and searched for enough fuel to re-fill the long-range FE2 tank. Fingers crossed, they pulled the eight-foot prop through by hand prior to test running Raj's Beardmore engine. It was ready to go. Duke checked again on Tom. He had a high pulse rate, and his abdomen was tense and tender to the touch. Duke had dressed the gunshot wound to his arm, which was no longer bleeding. The bullet had gone clean through his bicep muscle.

Duke remembered his dad telling him how serious internal abdominal injuries could be due to trauma, especially a splenic fracture. He was worried this might be the case for Tom. He knew it was a matter of life and death to get him back to Cairo soon for expert medical care.

"Raj, how did the German airfield look after your last pass?" asked Duke.

His curiosity about the mission's success overcame him while they rested and drank the warm salty water from the cabin's emergency supply.

"Boss, we got them all! Even the two Gotha bombers that were being loaded for a surprise raid on either us or HQ! Not one aircraft was serviceable, and almost all the hangars were on fire. I didn't see any anti-aircraft emplacements firing, but von Wagner was standing by his smoking Fokker, firing away with his Luger as I followed you out. You took him and his best pilots out in flames, sir! I have never seen better flying," he said.

"If you count the four planes you destroyed on the ground and the three in the air, you now have fifteen aerial victories! Congratulations, sir. That makes you one of the highest living allied aces in the Middle Eastern war theatre," exclaimed Raj with a huge smile and fire filling his eyes.

"Well, I will drink to that! Your masterful destruction of the Gotha bombers was critical, Raj! Tom also took one out and several on the ground, as did the rest of the squadron. It was a team effort and the best I have ever seen!" exclaimed Duke.

He scavenged some tin cups and a bottle of Laphroaig scotch he found hidden away in the cabin. He filled the tin cups to the brim, and they enjoyed the soothing nectar that warmed their stomachs and eased their adrenaline-filled bodies. They both smiled with relief at escaping death one more time. They believed a true warrior never knew or worried when his time would come but savored the sweet breath of life when the danger passed.

"We lost some great men today," said Duke as they raised their drinks to the departed and whispered a silent prayer to the Almighty. He hoped the remains of his squadron would safely reach their Giza airstrip.

Raj bowed his head, put his hands together, and chanted a Buddhist prayer for his fallen comrades.

Duke took a moment to tell Raj he would recommend him and Tom for the Distinguished Service Order and rank advancement to Captain for Raj for his outstanding service and bravery.

Raj was overwhelmed with emotion as he embraced Duke, and they shared a moment of deep attachment and friendship, unlike either had felt before. Raj told Duke of his cousin, who also served the British Empire in the Middle East and his wife and twin sons who lived at the large family compound in Kathmandu where his father served as Minister of Education. He was very proud of his son, who continued the family tradition of military service. He expected he would return from service to a high position in the Nepali Flying Service.

Duke told Raj he would add his recommendation for this position.

"I think General Allenby can rest easy now after getting the news of our victory and will agree with my recommendation. It may be the end of this Senussi Campaign/Rebellion and Jihad if Colonel Balfour's Cavalry has similar success now that we have total air supremacy! Let's have another toast to you, my dearest friend, Captain Raj!" said Duke.

He smiled as he refilled their tin cups with the smokey dark nectar. They both enjoyed the burning scotch and once again embraced, enjoying the trust and companionship of friendship in wartime.

After a few minutes of quiet reflection, Raj said, "I do have some bad news."

"Fire away, Raj," replied Duke.

"Your plane's tail is done for, and honestly, I don't know how you got it here in one piece. That German, von Wagner, almost got you! We don't have any spares here," Raj said with downcast eyes.

"I know, my friend. All we can do is tie the Sopwith down securely behind this shack, and I will wait for relief. If you look to the west, there is more bad news," said Duke.

They walked outside, and Raj suddenly noticed the western

sky beginning to fill with the brown haze of the dreaded Ghibli wind, a hot, dry southeastern gale. It would soon fill the air with choking sand and prevent any flying for days.

"Not good!" exclaimed Raj as they downed their drinks and rushed to finish filling the FE2 fighter bomber's fuel tank.

Then, ever so gently, they loaded the unconscious Captain Holmes into the front of the FE2 after removing the Lewis .303 gun and all the extra ammunition boxes which were still almost half full.

Raj jumped in and switched on the dual magnetos yelling, "Contact!"

"Contact!" responded Duke as he swung the pusher-mounted prop into an angry blur while the engine coughed several times before it warmed.

"I will wait for relief here. There is plenty of ammo to make a stand if needed. Get Tom to medical help quickly. Fly safely, my friend," yelled Duke over the now sweetly humming engine.

Raj poked his thumb up and flashed a hopeful smile for both of them as he fired off a salute, which Duke returned with a smile, and then gave the Beardmore engine full power. The heavily loaded FE2 fled down the desert strip as the first waves of dirty brown sand began to fill the sky.

Duke saw Raj just clear the rocky area at the end of the short strip and then lost all sight of him in the Ghibli winds and blowing sand. He rushed to tie down his trusty Sopwith Triplane against the fury of the elements and just managed to crush the small cabin door closed and collapse inside the cabin. Then, the full fury of the winds engulfed the cabin, blowing through the cracks; it sounded like the howling wolves of Hades.

CHAPTER 17 • THE VALLEY OF DEATH; SUCCESS

Duke sat in the supply cabin and kept his mouth covered with his wet flying scarf to prevent inhaling too much dust. He reached for his briefcase, which he had brought in from the Triplane. For the first time since leaving the *Leviathan*, he had time to review the translated documents of Ptolemy.

As he pulled out the translations, Duke realized that he had neglected a second smaller document in Latin and written by Governor Marcus Tiberius. In the dark cabin, he settled down to read the rest of the tale by torchlight as the winds howled with hurricane-force outside.

In shaky, often smudged ink, Tiberius began:

After Caesar defeated the last of the Ptolemaic forces at the Battle of the Nile, he installed Cleopatra as Pharaoh and ruler of upper and lower Egypt. I reported my shocking discovery of the truth of Alexander's tomb and treasure to my General. He hesitated only a moment and, with a smile, instructed me to find this tomb whatever the cost but to do it in absolute secrecy. He then told me to report only success with no other details in writing.

Before he left the throne room, I showed him the helmet and Jewish tablet fragment from the Ark.

He said, "My loyal commander and friend, if you find this great treasure and unworldly power, I will make you the richest man in the Roman empire and governor of Crete, your new home! We have fought non-stop together for too many years, and now the time has come for us to reap the rewards of our labors. Now, I go to Rome to become Emperor and claim my long overdue prize and you, my friend, to find the greatest treasure and power on earth. You must return these sacred findings to the tomb when you do. Then, reseal the tomb undisturbed with all treasures inside, and keep the location known only to you! Do you accept this task, Commander?" exclaimed Caesar.

"With all my heart, my emperor!" I exclaimed and knelt before my General and uncontested Emperor of the Roman empire. He lifted me, and we embraced. Neither of us knew at the time, but we would never see each other again in this world.

For the next two and a half years, I searched the Oasis and Egyptian desert with my faithful, handpicked twelve elite Gallic warriors. We dressed as local Berber tribesmen but still fought repeated engagements with local bandits and wandering tribes as we reprovisioned or searched closer to the Oasis Siwa. Our numbers had been depleted by death in these engagements to half our original contingent, and I was losing hope.

Finally, about two years into the journey, far in the desert at an unnamed oasis, we heard one day from a passing caravan of a deadly pride of lions that prevented anyone from approaching a small spring and hidden valley near the

Oasis of Siwa. So, we made our way back to this area we had somehow missed, and then during the Blue Khonsu, we found it in that very valley! The lions were there and attacked and killed three of my remaining Gallic warriors while we searched and finally discovered the tomb.

The treasure was immense and incalculable; Alexander's solid gold sarcophagus with a huge male lion mounted on top, the gold Ark of the Covenant with fragments of Moses' Ten Commandments around it, chests overflowing with silver and gold, precious stones of all shapes, sizes, and colors, piles of ivory, golden statues, piles of silver and gold coins, bars, and so much more! It was overwhelming, and we stood in utter amazement.

I returned Alexander's helmet and Moses' broken tablet to sit beside the other tablet fragments at the side of Alexander's mummified body in his massive golden sarcophagus, as instructed by my General. I took a moment alone to look at the undefeated General/Pharaoh/God and King, who had conquered the known world by the time he was thirty years old. His perfectly mummified body was intact and wearing his golden armor, which showed many battle scars but glowed an unworldly color in the torchlight.

His face had a peaceful but sad expression. Perhaps he regretted missing his next battle, had foreknowledge of the impending breakup of his giant kingdom, or knew none of his true descendants would long survive or rule and that his mother would soon follow him in death.

Atop Alexander's gold and silver engraved chest armor rested a large gold coin with Alexander's head in profile wearing a lion's mane, a beautiful diamond fitted into his eye, and a heavy broken gold chain. I promised my Caesar that I would remove nothing, but this coin seemed to cast a spell on me as I realized Alexander personally wore this in battle and life and must have valued it greatly. I gently reached in and lifted the 300-year-old coin, which filled the palm of my hand and flashed in the torchlight, sending out beautiful rays around the chamber.

I did not disturb or dare touch the beautiful solid gold Jewish Ark of the Covenant. The two beautiful golden cherubim measured four by three feet. I instructed my warriors never to touch this powerful relic. I learned long ago from my Jewish friends the awesome power of the Ark.

We were almost finished resealing the tomb in complete secrecy and slept inside the last night for protection from the lions. In the morning, I awoke after what I thought were strange dreams of flashes and screams. I found instead my remaining Gallic warriors' burned and lifeless mummified bodies surrounding the Ark.

They had been unable to resist the temptation to discover the contents of this priceless Ark and attempted to open the vessel against my orders. The horrible death masks each of my warriors now wore for eternity showed their terrible pain, and all that remained of their clothing were the chain mail and blue circular tattoos on their bodies. I resealed the tomb alone and left my warriors as permanent guardians.

I immediately set off alone for Alexandria, arriving in February, almost three years since Caesar had dispatched me on this mission. I sent a single-word message to Caesar: "Success" and awaited his reply.

Within three weeks, my Emperor's reply arrived with a lifetime Roman consul's ring and a document confirming my Governorship of Crete.

"My loyal commander, I applaud your success and have immediately and irrevocably appointed you Governor of Crete for life with ownership of all Roman property and tax authority to you and your immediate descendants. I will meet you in a fortnight, at the Palace of Knossos in Heraklion, Crete, to hear of your success! Travel now in stately fashion with all honors, ceremony, and safety accorded your powerful position and wealth!" signed and sealed with Caesar's ring and dated March 14th.

After I arrived in Crete two weeks later, I heard the horrible news of my Emperor's murder during the Ides of March, only one day after he penned the letter of my rank and appointment. Mark Antony would soon convene the Senate and confirm all of Caesar's appointments, including mine. It seemed the legend that whoever controls Alexander's tomb and body could never be defeated in battle also extended to political appointments. I took a relieved breath.

I remained Governor of Crete and loyal Consul of Rome for the remainder of my life. My Roman forces have never been

defeated in battle as long as I led them, and so I confirm
this legend is true. I never returned to the Valley of Death
from Earth and Sky nor discussed Alexander's true tomb's
existence or location to anyone, including my sons and family,
as I promised and dedicated to Caesar, my Emperor and
friend, thirty-five years ago. This I confirm on my deathbed in
my own hand and seal; signed this May 4th."

Duke dropped the document in utter astonishment. He wondered if he was dreaming. He grabbed the remains of the Laphroaig Scotch and poured a large drink after carefully wiping the sand from the tin cup. He savored the burning sensation as he swallowed a large mouthful. It lubricated his mind and relaxed his nerves as he drifted into a deep, badly needed sleep with visions of Caesar and Alexander flashing through his dreams.

Duke awoke to strange calmness and quickly looked at his Rolex, which showed it was almost noon... or *was* it midnight? He found his torch and switched it on, showing sand filling the cabin's bottom edges to over a foot but without reaching the center area where he had slept. The window was covered. He tried to push open the door, but it wouldn't budge! Panic started to seep into his heart; was he buried alive, and would anyone ever find or help him? He grabbed a shovel, went to the leeward side of the cabin, and tried to pry open a plank, but it only let in more sand.

"Stop! Take a deep breath and relax. You can figure this out," he said aloud.

He pulled the cot over to the back of the cabin and used a metal bar to slowly lift the tin roof. A splash of bright light rewarded and accelerated his efforts. Within an hour, he was out in the bright midday sun, digging his way back into the door of the cabin, which was fully encased in sand and looked like a sand dune. He could not see any evidence of the emergency runway or his faithful Sopwith!

Sand filled the horizon. But he could almost make out the old creek bottom that was sheltered from the worst of the Ghibli. He felt like he was floating on an ocean of sand.

After a hard day of digging, Duke cleared the front door and window and the worst of the sand from inside the cabin, collapsing after a cold dinner of canned bully beef and biscuits. How would his squadron find him, even with an intense search or much less be able to land and pick him up? There were no landmarks, and the Giza airfield was probably covered in sand as well! *Oh well, tomorrow is another day*, he thought, and he fell into a trance-like sleep.

On the second day after the storm ended, Duke realized his water supply was almost exhausted. He heard no sign of life or aircraft. He had to try for the Valley of Death and the small spring that sustained it to replenish his water supplies.

Using timber from the cabin supplies, Duke made an awkward SOS with an arrow pointing in the direction of the valley. He finished the last of his water and bully beef, packed up his Colt, Bowie knife, spare canteens, briefcase, saber, compass, two torches, and any other supplies he could stuff in the knapsack, and began trudging up the old, dried creek bed toward the valley. He wondered if it would still be there. Had the stream dried up? How would he deal with the lions? Could he find the tomb and use it for shelter as Governor Marcus Tiberius had done two thousand years ago?

He trudged through the loose sand as the sun descended and his mouth grew drier and drier. Hope pushed him on, but he realized without water, his life would quickly pass. Finally, in the twilight, he found the small, partially obstructed entrance to the valley and eventually burst through into the little green oasis. He rushed to the stream, dropped his gear, and buried his face in the cool, clear water. He drank until his stomach bulged. He rolled over, seeing the first of a million stars in the crystal-clear desert air, and laughed at the joy of hydration and life.

He soon snared a gazelle that didn't see him in the dark and quickly began roasting his first fresh meat in days. With the fire built as large as possible and banked against the side of the rock cliff face, he stayed awake, Colt pistol at the ready in case the lions approached.

They came at 3 a.m., the quietest, most deadly time of night when only evil creatures were awake and thriving. Their roar split and shook his body like a lightning bolt, and he was quickly adrenaline-soaked and on his feet against the cliff wall, Colt pistol at ready as he watched the pride circle the camp closer and closer.

The bright evil yellow eyes flashed hungrily, obviously angry at the invasion by the hated human smell. The female burst into the firelight and grabbed the remains of the gazelle before disappearing into the darkness. Then the male exploded from the darkness as big as a warhorse and fearlessly rushed Duke. He was knocked to the ground by the impact before raising his Colt, which was thrown from his hand. The beast's breath smelled of fetid death as he released a roar of such power; it vibrated Duke's chest like artillery fire and left him motionless. He pinned Duke to the ground with his massive paw, which tore away his jacket and tunic, exposing the pale white skin of his chest and neck for imminent death.

Then, the fire flashed as sap from an old log sizzled to life, and the beast looked at the large gold coin with a diamond eye, which was flashing an array of spectacular colors in the glow of the fire onto Duke's chest, right into the beast's eyes, and this seemed to puzzle the man-killer. Suddenly, the lioness was there, nuzzling the great beast with low growls and pushing him aside as she also was mesmerized by the flashes of the large diamond in the gold coin.

This hesitation and movement allowed Duke to roll free and grab his Colt, which he leveled at the great beast, but to his astonishment, the pride was walking away and didn't even look back!

Duke looked down in shock and realized the large Alexander coin did indeed flash brilliantly in the firelight, reflecting off the clear multifaceted diamond eye.

Then it dawned on him; Alexander had also been spared, perhaps at this same spot and with this same coin! Could this have been the reason why, and not that he was a God, as the Oracle and his best friend Ptolemy had said?

As Duke stood up, he realized his back and chest were bruised from the encounter with the lion. The deep cold of the desert was worse than he expected. He threw another log on the fire and curled up with a thin army blanket, praying that the pride would not come back to finish him as he drifted into a fitful sleep.

CHAPTER 18 • DISCOVERY

Duke awoke too stiff and sore from his encounter with the lions to do much more than warm up in front of the fire in the cold, still morning. He looked up at the rock face to the hidden ledge where he had previously discovered the mark of Ptolemy and wondered if there truly was a tomb. If so, would the contents remain after over two thousand years? He was conflicted about his military duty and if he should refill his canteens and return to the shed to await rescue or continue his quest for the truth about Alexander?

Then he remembered the work of the Roman poet Horace in Odes from 23BC, which was also during Governor Marcus Tiberius's life, which read, "Carpe diem, quam minimum credula postero. *Seize the day, put very little trust in tomorrow!*"

He would embrace this day and opportunity wherever it led him since the truce with the lions was tenuous at best, and he needed to find the truth. He splashed into the clear pool and swam, floating long enough to ease his bruised body.

As the sun rose and warmed his wet body and the green hidden valley, the animals of the desert, foxes, addax, oryx, Barbary sheep, and even an ostrich family, quickly made their way to the clear, life-giving spring and drank their fill before disappearing into the morning mist. Even African silverbills, Nubian bustards, and a flight of Mallards arrived to thrive and chatter in the comfort of the spring pool. Above them, Duke saw the beauty of two Peregrine falcons awaiting their morning meal.

Stiffly, Duke made his way to the hidden ledge about ten cubits above the valley floor and began searching the sheer rock face for any evidence of the tomb or cave entrance.

With the morning sun throwing unusual shadows, the whole area around Ptolemy's seal looked different, and Duke noticed a hidden crevice in the depths of one of the shadows. As his eyes adjusted to the dark, Duke eased his way slowly to the dead end, watching for any unusual man-made markings on the stone but saw nothing.

He retraced his steps over and over, but it was a completely natural stone cliff face with no signs of man other than the seal. Then he remembered Ptolemy had buried further instructions below the capstone. Duke quickly grabbed a sharp stone and began prying the seal out of the soil. He saw nothing buried below it. He lifted the limestone engraved seal gently in his hand and turned it over.

There were markings on the back! After he washed the loose dirt away with water from his canteen and held it up to the sun, Duke saw the diagram to the entrance of Alexander's tomb! There was a recessed stairway chiseled in the rock at the corner of the ledge, but it began seven cubits above the base of the ledge. No wonder he couldn't find it! Even with his arm fully extended, it was out of reach.

The heat was building, and his stomach told him he needed to hunt again, but first, Duke knew he needed to stack some blocks of limestone on top of each other in the corner to reach these hidden stairs. He slowly slid several blocks to the far corner of the ledge. He stacked the progressively smaller blocks on top of each other until he was able to climb high enough to reach back in the depths of the crevice and feel an indentation in the rock wall, which was invisible to the eye. He felt higher and found another and realized these were the chiseled primitive steps in the rock wall leading up, completely hidden in the shadows.

He pulled himself up and climbed, by feel alone, along the hidden staircase, which seemed to twist around and widen until he could no longer see the valley floor. Finally, he pulled himself up onto a secondary ledge covered with loose stone, obviously man-made with multiple chisel marks.

He stood up on a ledge the size of a small balcony and saw the cut stone entrance marked on each side—with the sign of the Pharaoh! Could it be? He fell to his knees, trying to regain his breath, and he looked again to make sure he wasn't hallucinating. But how could he possibly access this site? It was completely blocked with cut stone as tall as he was and sealed so tightly that not even his Bowie knife could pass.

"Patience and fortitude," Duke whispered to himself as he took deep, calming breaths. He glanced around the corner and realized he was at least 100 feet above the valley floor and invisible from sight with an overhanging shelf and old smoke stains still visible. Duke knew from previous field excavations that this indicated a campsite had been here and used extensively in the distant past.

As Duke gathered himself, he looked more closely while the midday sun reflected off the adjacent rock face. He realized there was an area of smaller, re-cut stone along the edge of the ledge farthest from where he stood.

After several hours of work, Duke removed enough of these smaller stones to crawl into the entrance of the dark recesses of the tomb complex. He could see nothing in the total darkness until he pulled his torch from the knapsack. As the beam cut into the darkness, his first sight was of three otherworldly beings dressed in chainmail with faces fixed in screaming agony. They appeared to look directly at him. He dropped the torch and sprang for the light of the ledge. Once outside, he collapsed and breathed in the clean desert air.

Duke gathered his thoughts and laughed as he realized these must be Marcus's Gallic warriors, left as eternal guardians after touching the Ark. He then eased back into the tomb as his initial fear and shock gave way to curiosity and excitement.

Duke picked up the torch as the macabre scene changed with the beam of light flashing from the solid gold Ark to the huge gold sarcophagus with the giant golden lion on top, then to chests overflowing with precious stones, gold, silver, and more wealth than he thought existed in all the world.

He stood up shaking and leaned against the beautifully cut and engraved wall of the tomb. He walked slowly toward Alexander's partially open sarcophagus, careful to avoid the piles of ivory, gold, and silver bars as well as gold statues and closed chests of untold treasure. The gold reflected the torchlight, lighting the whole chamber in an unworldly glow which revealed intricate, colorful, gold-painted frescoes on the ceiling and walls, showing scenes of Alexander's battles and conquests.

Finally, he reached the partially open, solid gold sarcophagus and slowly shifted the light to the mummified figure inside. The bright gold battle-scarred armor and helmet sitting beside Alexander's head reflected in an intense golden glow. His expression was peaceful. Duke gingerly reached in, lifting the gold and silver-plated helmet. He gently turned it around and read: ALEXANDER OF MACEDON!

Duke's knees gave way. He collapsed to the floor, holding the priceless helmet. He almost knocked over the two largest tablet fragments written by Moses in Hebrew leaning against the sarcophagus, where Marcus had placed them two thousand years ago. The light revealed the well-known first inscription and commandment, which translated read: "You shall have no other Gods before me."

Duke's head was spinning, and he couldn't catch his breath as he stumbled to the narrow opening. After carefully placing the helmet outside the entrance, he switched off the torch and scrambled out to collect himself. He leaned against the solid cliff wall as he shook his head, and after he filled his lungs with the crisp desert air, he screamed at the top of his lungs the rebel yell, "Yeee Haw!!!!!"

His yell echoed again and again off the cliff walls of the bright green Valley of Death, flushing the ducks off the spring pool far below. A huge smile creased Duke's face as the reality of his discovery began to settle into his soul. Slowly, the complexity of properly handling the greatest archaeological find since British archaeologist Frank Calvert found Troy fifty years ago filled his mind.

Thankfully, Duke's archeology degree had trained him in art. He could draw all of his discoveries in the tomb in detail. He eased around the small balcony of stone until he could see the rapidly setting sun on the western horizon. He pulled out his sketchpad and pencil to draw the sunset on this momentous day one of discovery.

The orange glow of the setting sun reminded him of the gold reflection that filled the tomb from the light of his torch as he watched the horizon change slowly from orange to red and finally an eerie purplish glow. The moon and stars quickly took control of the sky from horizon to horizon.

Duke realized how thirsty he was and drank deeply from his canteen, now almost empty. He began to formulate a plan as he gazed at the southern cross. He had to change gears. Instead of a military officer and Major, he now needed to become Dr. Duke Thomas Ph.D., archaeologist, to correctly record and preserve everything he could of this earth-shattering historic site.

There was priceless treasure, artifacts, and mummified human remains of the most famous General of all time that would rewrite all of history and an Ark of unworldly power, which had been lost to mankind for millennia and could change the future of the planet. He now started to understand the legend that whoever possessed Alexander's armor and tomb could never be defeated in battle!

This was a monumental task and would take every ounce

of his strength and brainpower to protect and preserve. Perhaps Ptolemy, Caesar, and Governor Marcus Tiberius had been right to keep this hidden from humanity, but now, it was only a matter of time before the truth came out. Duke was acutely aware that Max von Wagner was alive and close enough to independently explore and discover this site, no matter how well Duke covered his tracks. He also knew in his heart that Max would not be able to resist this treasure, and the tomb would be plundered.

Dr. Duke Thomas now purposely and reverently reentered the Tomb of Alexander the Great. The thick, dark air of the chamber settled heavily into his lungs as he stirred the dusty floor with his careful footsteps and began to walk the perimeter of the tomb, taking detailed notes and measurements. As he reached the back of the tomb, he noticed a secondary chamber hidden behind the giant golden Sarcophagus of Alexander. He flashed the laser-like torch beam into the space and saw the mostly intact funeral cart of Alexander!

It was magnificent and measured about twelve feet wide and eighteen feet long with a vaulted barrel-like roof, covered in gold shingles with precious stones set between them! On each corner stood statues of Nike in gold, except two had fallen or broken off over the ages. On top of the roof was a huge olive wreath of solid gold, similar to what an Olympic athlete would win. It reached to the decorated ceiling of the carefully cut tomb.

The chamber's roof was supported by gold columns of the Greek style with golden ropes and climbing vines in between, all perfectly sculpted in gold. Atop this colonnade, four panels of Alexander's military might were reproduced in greater detail and volume throughout the tomb walls and ceilings. These panels showed ships in combat, cavalry awaiting a charge, elephants clad in war gear leading an infantry Greek phalanx, and finally, Alexander seated in a chariot holding a scepter, surrounded by attendants and honor guards.

154

Under this image at the rear of the cart was an open doorway. As Duke flashed the torch inside, he gasped as he saw two solid gold, full-size lions on either side of the entrance with heads turned and watching him! He entered and sat between them, seeing mesh-like golden netting which would have been hanging between the elite mourners and Alexander's mummified body. Many precious stones littered the floor, perhaps gifts from his commanders and satraps.

After drawing in his notepad the funeral hearse measurements and the horde of treasure in the cart, Duke reached down and picked up the largest emerald and diamond he had ever seen, almost filling the palm of each hand, and placed them in his knapsack. The gold and silver coins and bars were too numerous to count. Duke couldn't resist; he moved past the gold mesh and sat in Alexander's throne seat, admiring the immense treasure lining the floor as he allowed his torch to sweep inside the stunning hearse.

Then, as he flashed the torch up and down, the two thousand three-hundred-year-old throne seat on which Duke sat and that Alexander had last rested on his way to this burial site collapsed! Duke landed heavily on the hearse floor on a rectangular jeweled gold box hidden inside the seat of Alexander's throne, and as he admired it, he noticed it was sealed. It had elaborate scenes of seafaring life, with mermaids, sirens, and Poseidon with his trident all intricately carved and all the fish and giants of the deep carefully engraved and inlaid with precious stones.

On the back, carved in gold, was an elevated central large island surrounded by reef, and engraved in silver was what looked like an ancient Egyptian letter 'A' immediately outside the pillars of Hercules. Could it be Atlantis? No? It was stunningly beautiful, and why was it hidden in the secret royal throne seat? Duke decided to add this important find to his knapsack to open and study in more detail later.

He stepped out of the funeral hearse and shone the dimming torchlight on the iron-rimmed wheels with golden spokes, each hub a golden lion's head holding a spear between its teeth. Four great golden bells hung at each corner of the magnificent hearse and in front where the team of horses would have pulled the great cart. Finally, in the front of the cart were fragments of four poles surrounded by the skulls of eight great beasts that pulled the hearse, all with golden crowns, bells, and collars set with precious stones beside each of the war horses. Duke wondered if Alexander would have used any of these great animals in battle?

Duke was stunned! He meticulously recorded each detail with roughly a quarter-scale drawing in his notepad, which he had thankfully stuffed with extra pencils into his bag. He had always enjoyed drawing and the creativity that it allowed, and thankfully he was good at it since he didn't have a camera, nor could it possibly encompass this immense tomb! Finally, Duke completed his circuit of the tomb. He had lost touch with time as he was immersed in another world from two thousand years ago and felt strange energy and power as he worked through his discovery. Duke worked intensely as he continued his inventory and drawings. The dwindling torch was eventually reduced to the dimmest of illumination and finally died.

Duke's energy was fading fast as well. He fell asleep, and the notepad and pencil dropped from his hands.

CHAPTER 19 • SURVIVAL

Duke awoke from a dead sleep to a shaft of light pouring into the tomb from the small entrance. He was confused and dizzy, but he saw the light reflecting off the Ark and suddenly realized he was not dreaming; he had just made the greatest discovery in modern archaeological history! If he only lived long enough to claim his prize and place in history, he thought.

He removed his British Major's field jacket with his name emblazoned beside his rank and placed it on two golden ceremonial spears, which he placed at the entrance. He carefully climbed out onto the ledge.

He was parched and starving and consumed the last drops of water in his canteen as the desert's midday heat assaulted him while he meticulously resealed the tomb. By the time he finished in the late afternoon, it had looked exactly as he had found it. He placed Alexander's helmet gently in his bag as well as the giant precious stones and mysterious gold throne box, then carefully made his way down to the valley floor.

His skin was red from the heat and sun. He was risking heatstroke but pressed on. Near sunset, he located the spring and stumbled to it. Duke delicately dropped his knapsack and plunged into the cool life-giving spring pool, drinking and absorbing the badly needed water, which revived him, body, mind, and spirit.

Finally, Duke stepped out of the water and started a fire after spearing a large rainbow trout with his Bowie knife. He warmed himself by the glowing crackling fire as he cooked the giant trout on a spit while wondering if the lion pride would again attack him. He felt at peace with them for some reason, as if a truce based on his recent contact with Alexander's remains and spirit was flowing through the valley.

He was ravenous, and he consumed the delicious flaky white fish and survived the night, which passed so swiftly that it seemed time had accelerated. Perhaps he was in a whole new world that was at peace, he imagined, as he refilled his canteens in the morning and shot a large gazelle that hesitated a moment too long in the spring. But he knew that was only a dream as he headed back to the reality of his cabin and a world at war.

He carefully concealed the entrance to the valley and arrived exhausted in the twilight to his sand-covered cabin, unsure of how he could survive and return to his squadron and if he should reveal his find. He fired up the stove, quickly warming up as he cleaned the gazelle and roasted the tenderloins to a crispy golden brown. The aroma filled the shed, quickly raising his spirits.

Digging through the sand-covered supplies, he found an old bottle of French Bordeaux, and after popping the cork from the aged treasure, he savored the meal as if he was dining at Shepherd's Hotel in downtown Cairo. His spirits were much refreshed.

The remainder of the Gazelle he cut into strips and smoked over the fire that night, making it into a nice jerky before finally falling asleep for a few hours.

The next morning, Duke awoke with a light cough but felt fully refreshed. He looked at his watch and realized instead of two days, he had been gone for four days. How had he lost track of time, or had time slipped somehow while he was in the Valley? He walked outside and looked up, hearing the screech of a Peregrine falcon circling high above his camp. Suddenly, as if Alexander was guiding him, he realized the only way out of his isolation was in his falcon, the Sopwith Triplane.

He began slowly uncovering his mount. It was completely encased in sand, with only the tip of the rudder showing. He was disappointed no one had attempted to find him but realized perhaps the squadron was in worse shape than he suspected. He was on his own and embraced the challenge.

Three days later, the Tripe was fully uncovered, and he began pulling the cylinders one at a time—carefully inspecting, lubricating, and freeing them from all the sand which had seeped into every opening. The work was grueling and hot, and he soon had to take another two-day hiatus to make a resupply trek to the spring and replenish his water and meat.

He savored his time in the valley and felt a deep peace and tranquility, which revived him and fired up his resolve as if Alexander himself was infusing his being. Suddenly, two days turned into two weeks as if he had stepped into a time warp. His body felt stronger and even younger, or was that his imagination? The animal residents and visitors to the spring seemed to accept him as part of the family. Even the lion cubs, who began wandering into his camp and tumbling in play with each other, were seemingly fearless of his presence until their mother growled in the brush, causing them to scamper back to the pride.

Duke left every cleaned gazelle carcass near the lion's lair at the valley's far edge beside the stream. This seemed to enhance the Truce of Alexander, as Duke called it, between himself and the magnificent lion pride, and he was able to sleep deeply under the uncountable stars every night with no fear of attack. He slept, and his dreams were filled with thundering war elephants, charging chariots, and victory celebrations with Greek warriors who embraced Duke as if he were their leader. Duke lost touch with time as the rhythm of peace, life, and death in the valley infused his being.

It was a balanced flow of nature with nothing lost in the rhythm of time. Eventually, his dreams became more current, showing him in aerial combat in *The Reaper*, firing his Vickers machine gun and achieving victory after victory, no matter the odds he faced. He saw a red Triplane and a sleek schooner under full sail with flashes of cannon fire in the mist, and finally, Juliette reached out to him, yearning for him to return to her during what would turn out to be his last night at the valley.

Juliette and duty finally pulled Duke back to his work at the airstrip. His body felt years younger, and he no longer had the terrible nightmares he had experienced since his last crash in France. He returned fully revived and stocked, ready to complete his work on *The Reaper* as he now called his Sopwith Triplane.

Duke worked steadily and finally reached the Triplane's tail. It was a mess. The rudder was hanging on by one ruined hinge with little fabric left, and there were multiple holes in the elevator, which also had heavy fabric and rib damage. How would he repair this with his limited material? Then he remembered the gazelle hides he had cured in the sun. He would use them in place of the fabric, and the desert ironwood trees he had seen in the Valley of Death could be shaped into ribs to repair or replace the damaged ribs and tailplane. He would use the door hinges from the cabin, baling wire, and dope that survived the storm to finish the tail repair!

His pace increased as the materials and vision of success became apparent, and finally, almost three weeks later, it was finished. The center of gravity would be off due to the heavier repaired tail, causing the Triplane to be dangerous to control unless Duke compensated for the heavy tail by adding extra weight upfront in the empty ammunition boxes.

However, his instincts told him to keep one full of ammunition just in case, so he gathered all his spare rounds and filled one box with .303 shells. But what could balance the changed center of gravity in the aircraft that had the most weight per volume, he wondered? Then it came to him: gold! And Duke knew where to get it.

He made his final trip to the valley the next morning with a heavy heart as he had grown accustomed to the serenity of the desert valley with its daily rhythm of life. But today was different. He sensed and heard loud breaking brush and palms as he entered the valley with dust filling the air. *What was going on?*

Then, out of the brush thundered a huge North African Bull Elephant with tusks as large as a man. The elephant shook his head in full glory as he plunged into the spring pool and buried his trunk deeply in the cooling water to drink to his heart's content. He rolled and bathed for hours, enjoying the date nuts which covered the ground around the pool after his messy entrance.

Duke was downwind from the largest land-based mammal on earth. He watched transfixed as the wild desert elephant thrashed in the pool, making it muddy brown, relishing the soothing waters before lazily leaving the pool and wandering to the far eastern edge of the valley oasis to feed and rest.

Duke quickly and quietly made his way up to the tomb, and after reopening the almost invisible entrance, filled his knapsack with gold bars, dated coins, and a small fragment of the ten commandments. THOU SHALT NOT KI-was all that was written in Hebrew on the fragment he collected. He once again meticulously sealed the sacred tomb while whispering a prayer of thanks to Alexander and God.

Duke carefully left a note in his military jacket pocket detailing the location and quantity of gold, precious stones, coins, and the fragment of the ten commandments he had removed and for what purpose. He also noted that he had Alexander's gold helmet to prove and claim the find. He had made such a tiny dent in the volume of treasure that it was unnoticeable. Still, he was committed to returning every item or placing them on public display in the British Museum or Smithsonian.

After dark, he finally returned to the cabin with his last torch dim and quickly grabbed a few hours of sleep. Juliette came to him that night in his dreams as real as the bull elephant in the valley. She was radiant in her white silk gown as she embraced him and covered his mouth with hers. He inhaled her erotic smell as she buried her tongue in his mouth and then stripped him to reveal his manhood in full glory.

In his dream, Duke tore away her thin silk gown and found her wetness. With eager fingers, he gently stroked her, slipping into her deep warm flower.

She moaned with pleasure and arched her back as he pulled out his fingers and slipped them into his mouth, savoring her sweetness as she straddled his manhood with a smile. She rode him madly and wildly, like the bull elephant tearing into the green foliage of the valley. Throwing her head back and thrusting her hips up and down, she firmly pushed on his chest while moving faster and faster.

He could hold back no longer. Juliette pounded him into full submission and yelled like a female panther in the Georgia swamps until they climaxed together. Then she screamed madly again and again in erotic ecstasy, and Duke opened his eyes to enjoy her pleasure and realized it was a dream, and he heard the hunting lion pride in the distance. They must be pursuing game flushed out of the valley by the bull elephant's bathing and feeding frenzies.

As the dawn broke of his eighth week at the emergency cabin, Duke loaded Alexander's gold in the ammunition boxes well forward of the Triplane's center of gravity. Duke kept one full ammunition box left over from the raid, primed and loaded in *The Reaper*. He also had two nearly full ammunition boxes, which Raj had left when he evacuated with Tom in his FE2 Biplane and attached them in readiness to the extra Lewis .303 machine gun, which Raj had also left out of necessity.

It was now January 1918, and Duke wondered if his squadron was deployed to a new theatre of combat in the Middle East since he felt sure the German's squadron was firmly defeated here in the Western deserts. He had to get back to his duties and brothers at arms but first had to overcome the difficulty of finding the emergency aviation fuel, so he had enough to get back to Giza and Cairo. Duke found several buried barrels of aviation fuel, and miraculously, one was full, so after exhaustedly manhandling the barrel over to the side of *The Reaper*, Duke topped off the fuel tank with a siphon.

The airstrip had been swept flat again by the strong southern winds, so after walking the strip's length and removing some large stones, Duke felt it was safe for use.

The back-breaking ordeal of fueling and clearing the strip took all day. Finally, Duke did a test run of the reliable rotary engine as the sun settled in for a spectacular sunset. The engine ran rough until Duke reset the magnetos timing and cleaned the plugs again carefully in the dying purple glow of what he hoped would be his last night away from his comrades.

As he settled in, Duke noticed some glowing cooking fires along the caravan route to the Oasis and hoped they hadn't heard the final smooth sunset test run of the 130hp Clerget 9B rotary. He felt uneasiness in his gut and decided to set Raj's Lewis .303 machine gun up in a depression behind the cabin, which would place the morning sun behind him and allow a clear field of fire up and down the runway, just in case. The Berbers were notorious for predawn attacks on their fast mounts and would focus on the cabin when they saw it. They had no love for the British, especially after the punishment Duke's squadron had rained down on them this past year.

The cold night passed slowly. Duke drifted into a light sleep after checking his Colt and saber. He hoped his gut was wrong. He had been lucky so far and didn't want to end up as lion bait after surviving so much!

As the first yellowish red hue of dawn crept up behind him, Duke was wide awake and thought the dawn seemed unusually quiet. Even the normal desert sounds were absent.

Then he saw them. They approached on horseback from both sides of the runway at a silent canter behind a single man on foot who was pointing toward the cabin and Triplane. There were at least three dozen horsemen and many more on foot, all carrying modern rifles at the ready, and the leader of the horsemen wore a German uniform. He had a Luger pistol and a familiar-looking saber at the ready!

Duke wondered if it was Captain, no, Major von Manstein whom Duke had spared in France. Duke said a silent prayer and took a deep breath as he primed the Lewis gun and checked that his ammunition belt and boxes were clear. He was thankful he had carefully taken apart and cleaned the Lewis gun the previous evening.

Then, like the horsemen of the apocalypse, the Arabs broke into a gallop with yells of excitement at the prospect of easy killing and booty. Duke waited until the line of cavalry was almost to the cabin and lowered the machine gun sight to belly level and pressed the trigger, unleashing hell into the left flank of the galloping hoard and swept in a continuous burst across to the far right. Like a stroke of his grandfather's civil war saber, he cut the horsemen down one after another, watching the tracer rounds light up the predawn gloom and continued firing into the foot soldiers until his first aluminum case of .303 ammunition was empty.

He quickly pulled his second case over, and by the time he loaded and began firing, the survivors were almost on top of him, led by the gallant German officer Major von Manstein. Duke once again lit the morning gloom with tracer rounds and flying lead as he cut down many of the remaining attackers until the Lewis machine gun jammed from the heat of the barrel and sand, which was surrounding the muzzle, and he was almost to the end of his second box of ammunition.

By this time, the surviving Arabs and German were on the

run to the horizon, but Duke knew they would regroup and return.

Duke spiked the Lewis gun and ran to the Triplane. He set the magnetos to hot, cracked the throttle, and pulled the prop to life as the Clerget engine coughed and the prop disappeared into a blur.

Out of the gloom, two attackers jumped from the ground where they had been faking death and flew at him with unsheathed swords and a Luger pistol. Duke pulled his Colt and fired at the white-robed screaming Berber at the same time the enemy fired at him with his Luger. Duke felt a burning sensation in his left thigh while the enemy collapsed after Duke emptied his pistol into him and then dropped it. He then turned his attention to the second screaming attacker.

Duke unsheathed his grandfather's wristbreaker saber just as the Arab lunged high at him with his short, curved sword. Duke ducked just in time under the blade which whistled over his head like the Ghibli wind, and then with a clean, pure stroke, cleaved the enemy in half with his razor-sharp blade and watched the dying attacker's blood soak the sand to a deep red.

He was wearing a gold and red turban with more ornate jewels. Duke thought he must be one of the rabble leaders, and he reached down and pulled the bejeweled Arabic sword from his lifeless fingers.

Duke took a deep breath as he felt the blood fever coursing through his heart, enhancing his mind and vision with death approaching from all quadrants. He saw Major von Manstein approaching alone on horseback.

He bowed deeply and then raised his sword to his forehead, indicating a duel. He must still want payback for the last engagement that Duke won in France in what seemed like another life. Duke brought his now bloody wristbreaker cavalry saber to his forehead to accept the challenge.

While this chivalrous battle began, the remains of the horseman were reorganized for another assault. Duke knew the Major was trying to delay him and allow his surviving force to reorganize, and he realized he must prevail quickly.

Duke's wounded left thigh made his left side vulnerable, so he moved to place the now smoothly idling Triplane behind his wounded thigh to prevent the German from exploiting that weakness. The Major's hackles were up, and he madly dashed straight at Duke. He missed seeing the deep depression just before reaching him.

As he tried to jump his charger over the depression at the last moment, the poor animal misjudged and tumbled into it, throwing the Major flat-faced and empty-handed at Duke's feet.

Duke brought his sword to the Major's neck and said, "Sir, do you yield and live to fight another day with honor?"

The Major hoarsely said, "Yes, Major, I yield," and then removed his sword and Blue Max medal and surrendered these to Duke, who sheathed his sword and spared the Major's life in return. Duke reached over and also removed his Luger.

"I hope we meet again in better circumstances and can enjoy some schnapps together, Major," said Duke.

"I will look forward to that Major, but I must warn you, my 100 Arabs follow no civilized rules of warfare, and now they will have a blood feud with you since you have killed the son of their leader ingloriously, which they see as angering Allah," said von Manstein.

He looked disdainfully at the cleaved torso of the Arab at his feet. "So, the chance of our reunion is remote. I see no hope for your survival," sneered the Major.

"Your kind concern is touching, but you are wrong, of course. There are no longer 100 Arabs at your command," smiled Duke. Then, Duke released the German Major who bowed and jumped on his horse, who was just standing up from his fall, and kicked him to full gallop toward the surviving advancing tribesmen still half-hidden on the far undisturbed edge of the airfield.

Duke then looked around, absorbing the macabre scene. It was a bloodbath around the shed and Triplane and was especially brutal on the runway adjacent to the cabin with blood and bodies strewn in death and wounded agony. Horses bedecked in bright tassels and ornate saddles ran randomly around the airfield. Then, miraculously, his mind cleared from the adrenaline-soaked struggle for life, and his heart rate slowed as if a guiding force was infusing him.

He turned toward the Sopwith Triplane and struggled toward his only escape from this hell, but his left leg collapsed. He fell beside the head of one of the attackers he had dispatched with the lethal Lewis machine gun. Blood poured from Duke's wounded left thigh. He grabbed the white turban from the sightless head of the enemy and tightly wrapped his thigh, and stood up again, limping to the Triplane.

Suddenly, two Arabs rose from rocks behind the Triplane and ran straight for Duke with curved swords raised. The first ran into the spinning prop and exploded into a fine mist of blood with only his outstretched right sword arm falling intact at Duke's feet. The other avoided his comrade's fate and came straight for Duke, who raised the Luger pistol to defend himself and heard a click after click as the weapon misfired or was empty. He now had no chance and saw his life flash before his eyes.

Time compressed into slow motion, and Duke felt a great sadness, knowing he would never see his unborn child. But he held his head high as he watched the sword draw back for the impending death blow, and the eyes of his attacker squinted into an evil smile.

But then, a yellow flash and roar exploded from the dried creek bed behind him! The wild female lioness flew over Duke's head and grabbed the white turban attacker by his neck, which she shook once with an audible snap and dropped the inert body at his feet. After a moment's hesitation, while she looked at Duke with an unworldly glow in her piercing yellow eyes, she disappeared into the rocks.

She save my life!

What force and power had she possessed to intervene moments before Duke's certain death? But Duke had no time to ponder this connection and his salvation as he shook his head, trying to focus.

Duke was in a trance and near shock-like state, but he heard the roar of the surviving Arab horsemen once again galloping toward him, firing wildly at top speed. He dragged himself into his only hope of escape: his black Sopwith Triplane, *The Reaper*, and gave her full-throttle without even putting on his safety belt.

He just cleared the rocks at the short end of the airstrip where there were fewer dead Arab bodies to avoid on his takeoff run as the attackers raged, yelled, and fired away below him.

He stayed low to prevent any lucky rifle shots and soon flashed over the Valley of Death, where he saw clearly from above the secret ledge of Alexander's tomb. What a difference an aerial view provided, and Duke committed that if he survived this endless war, he would explore similar desert plateaus and desolation in the American southwest or the trackless South American jungles for future archaeological discoveries.

Duke decided to use the last of the ammunition to destroy the remains of the cavalry unit and protect this valley and the pride of lions that had protected him. He dropped back to horse height, turned around the hidden valley, and unexpectedly appeared at the rear of the survivors who were galloping toward the valley.

They saw him at the last moment and turned to fire, but he pressed the Vickers machine gun trigger and held it as he walked the explosive rounds through the remains of the Arab henchmen on two passes, leaving no horse or man standing.

Dead men tell no tales, Duke thought as he prayed Alexander's tomb and lion pride would remain safe until he could return after enough men had died to end this war.

He then began a slow, steady climb to the thin cold air three miles above the desert floor to maximize his range while leaning out his fuel mixture.

Only one set of enemy eyes remained open, hidden in the edge of the valley: Major von Manstein, and he quickly galloped away toward Siwa Oasis to telegraph news of this terrible defeat to headquarters.

Duke saw a grey mass throwing up dust as it quickly moved to his left, away from the Valley of Death, about a thousand feet below his climbing Sopwith Triplane. It was the North African bull elephant striding swiftly away from the chaos of the valley. He raised his head at the unexpected heavenly noise and threw back his trunk and tusks in rage at the unnatural human presence.

The bull elephant continued on his lonely quest to the next secret desert oasis that only he and the small female herds knew existed. The bull would never return to the Valley of Death now that it was contaminated with human sounds and scents. He embraced the endless freedom and safety from man as he rushed away, as did Duke, who hoped conversely to return here and establish his name in history.

CHAPTER 20 • The Cross

Duke flew like a falcon as he streaked toward the Giza strip and salvation. He felt steady vibration from his makeshift tail repair, and it required constant attention to keep the Sopwith Triplane level. His wound was throbbing, and the white turban was red around his thigh, but he was able to stop most of the bleeding by pulling it as tight as possible. His father had often shown him this technique to control bleeding from the extremities by using a belt or cloth as a tourniquet, and he would not be alive now without this knowledge.

As he descended back into the hot, bumpy desert air while preparing to land at his squadron base, he saw the wreckage of Raj's plane on the perimeter of the field but didn't see any other aircraft or personnel. Many of the hangers were gone, and by now, Duke was light-headed from blood loss. He landed poorly, bouncing until he slowed to a steady roll. His engine was running rough, but he taxied into the open and intact old hanger close to his office and shut down the Clerget engine, which crackled and hissed as it cooled in the eerie quiet of the empty field.

He slowly and painfully pulled himself and the precious cargo carefully out of the Sopwith and stored it in his old traveling chest, which still sat in the hanger's corner, and locked the ancient and beat-up family heirloom. Then he heard cocking weapons and turned around to face the two Gurkhas he recognized as base security.

They looked like they were seeing the Buddha himself as

they dropped their weapons and smartly saluted, saying, "Sorry, Major! Didn't recognize you with your heavy beard and sunburn. We thought you were dead, sir!"

Duke was now white as a sheet from blood loss and exposure. He collapsed as the Gurkhas rushed forward and caught him before he hit the ground.

Duke woke again briefly, now for the second time due to combat wounds in the Cairo military hospital, wondering what the fuss was about as he saw blood and plasma pouring into his volume-depleted veins before drifting off again to a troubled sleep. He thought he heard Juliette weeping, but nothing was clear until two days later when he awoke to the bright morning sun filling his corner room.

It was Juliette! She was exhausted after serving non-stop as his nurse for the past two nights and tightly embraced him, sobbing, "Oh mon amour, we thought you weren't going to make it! I love you!" And with that, she planted the deepest, longest kiss of his short life on his now moist smiling lips.

"Oh, my darling, I thought I was dreaming, but it is you, and now I feel completed and once again alive," croaked Duke through his quivering vocal cords as he broke down for the first time during the war in tears of shock, loss, and happiness. They held each other while tears flowed endlessly from both of their eyes, and they kissed again and again.

Finally, the questions started to flow. Duke learned that Juliette, soon after hearing Duke was missing and presumed dead, had been posted here at her request, and with help from her famous French uncle, a Foreign Ministry official. But she had known in her heart that he was alive.

She explained that Raj had crashed as his FE2 Biplane approached the Giza strip in one of the worst Ghibli sandstorms of the century and was still in a coma here, in the next ward. After an emergency splenectomy, Tom survived and was released fully recovered after a week in the hospital.

He now commanded the 77th squadron, which had moved to Palestine and participated in the Battle of Jerusalem. The victory on December 30th,1917, with General Allenby was possible because the squadron had cleared his western flank of the enemy. The General now had the Ottomans on the run and would eventually capture Damascus with the help of Major Lawrence of Arabia.

Tom had related his rescue and the events of the German El Alamein airfield attack, including Duke's heroic actions and additional victories confirmed by the rest of the squadron survivors. Still, he had complete amnesia regarding anything after leaving the German airstrip with Duke. With Raj in a coma, Duke now understood why no rescue had been attempted. No one knew he was at the emergency strip, and he had become an MIA and presumed dead in this horrific conflict.

Then, Juliette smiled, "My darling, I have wonderful news! You have been awarded the Victory Cross for gallantry, fifteen aerial victories, clearing the Western desert front of the enemy, and other heroic actions in battle, including saving Tom. General Allenby is now coming here in person to congratulate you!"

She kissed him again and quickly left the room. Chaos ensued outside as the General walked in, surrounded by his staff in full dress uniform.

Duke sat fully upright in bed while briskly saluting the most successful General of the First World War.

General Allenby walked to his bedside and said, "Enough of that, my friend. It is I who should be saluting such a gallant officer," which he did, followed by every member of his general staff.

"You have done more to help win this war than my whole army could have done in a year, and I want to congratulate you on your bravery and achievement of the Victoria Cross. As you know, it is the highest medal in the British empire for bravery and is the equivalent of your US Medal of Honor. Well done, Major! Now, tell me what happened and why you took a vacation for these many weeks when I needed you most and came back with this fresh wound!"

Duke carefully related the military events of his time at the emergency strip, but with some guilt, leaving out his experiences in the Valley of Death and Alexander's tomb. He felt that secrecy was critical, and it wouldn't have any military bearing on the ongoing war. He related the attack of three mornings ago and handed the General the bejeweled short sword from his bedside. He described the horrific encounter in detail, including the tremendous number of enemy casualties he had inflicted and the German Major von

Manstein's involvement, as well as his narrow escape.

The room was dead silent as the General officers looked at each other in amazement. Allenby broke the trance saying, "Major, once again, I salute you as one of the finest and bravest officers I have the honor of commanding! I had heard from Colonel Balfour's Cavalry command that a German Major was reorganizing resistance near the Oasis, and now I see you have single-handedly destroyed it. I will send them in to mop up any survivors," said the General as one of the officers bolted from the room to send the message.

"I also, as is my privilege as your commanding officer, once again give you a raise in rank and field commission to full Colonel and issue you a Distinguished Service Order to add to your Victoria Cross," he said.

"You are hereby ordered, once you have sufficiently recovered from your wounds, to report to Buckingham Palace to receive these honors from King George V himself. I hope your family will join you there for the ceremony, followed by eight weeks of leave, the same amount of time you spent in the desert fighting this heathen enemy for the empire! Well done, Colonel, and don't forget, I need you back to help finish our conquest of the Holy Land and defeat the Ottomans!"

General Allenby then stood up, saluted his protege as did the rest of the staff, and before Duke had time to salute, he was gone.

Duke was shocked. He had hardly enough strength to digest the tremendous honor that had just been bestowed on him, but his friend was in the next ward.

He weakly sat up to make his way to Raj's bedside. But before he could stand, Juliette was back at his bedside, reading his intentions and saying, "Darling, you must slow down. I will get you a wheelchair, and then we can go see Raj."

As Duke rolled into Raj's room, he bowed his head and folded his hands, saying, "Namaste," the traditional Nepalese greeting of peace to his friend who had saved Tom's life and his. He could feel the heavy sadness that pervaded the staff as Raj sat motionless and silent with a heavy bandage around his head. He had withered since Duke last saw his animated face at the Oasis airfield, and now he was clearly on death's very doorstep.

Duke held his hand, lowered his pale face in earnest prayer for his friend, and wept while thanking him again for saving his life. Juliette rolled him away and quietly placed him back in his fresh, clean white hospital sheets as he drifted off to much-needed rest and recovery.

A week later, Duke climbed aboard the HMS Dragon and headed for London with a stateroom of his own, befitting his rank as full Colonel with his private nurse Juliette at his side, attending to his every need as well as a batman to help with his military needs and attire. At least, that was the official version for his nurse's presence, but with their insatiable love affair and given the glorious state of his current affairs, it was completely acceptable. It would have been impossible to keep them apart anyway.

They had been together at Raj's funeral, where Duke had spoken of his friend's heroic actions and courage and how much he would be missed. He sent a letter of condolences to Raj's family and recommended him for a Distinguished Service Order (DSO) as he had likewise done for Captain Tom Holmes, who had become squadron commander of the 77th LRG, or 77th Destroyer Squadron as it was now called, in Palestine.

This name change was due to the high victory count and air to ground tactical success it had achieved both in the Western desert campaign and now in Palestine.

Raj's cousin, who was a Ghurka Sergeant on the Palestine front, was in attendance and presented Duke with one of Raj's Khukuri blades, saying, "Raj loved you like a brother, Colonel, and would have wanted you to carry on the fight for him with this."

Duke bowed his head, accepting the ancient, two-foot razor-sharp reverse curved lethal blade with pride.

He said, "I will use it in his memory with honor. I also
want you to know that I recommended an elevation in rank to
Captain for Raj, which has been approved. His family will receive
his back pay and pension. One day, I plan to visit them in Kathmandu and personally thank them for his service. He saved my
life and was one of the bravest men I have known, in addition to
being my friend." Duke bowed deeply as he walked away with tears
streaming from his eyes.

On arrival in London a week later, Duke was much refreshed and beginning to regain much of the weight and color
he had lost with his near-death wound. He had brought his sea
chest from the Giza airstrip. It remained sealed with all the historic
wealth inside. He had decided it must go to the United States,
safely and securely with his parents and brother Robby, who were
en route to attend the glorious ceremony, as was his wife, Vivian.

He wasn't sure what he would do when he saw her. Duke
had not discussed it with Juliette either, but she seemed to know
his heart and smiled with love at all he did.

London was chilly and wet in late January 1918, but Duke
loved the civilized culture and security that seemed to permeate the
city. The Zeppelin airship raids still occurred occasionally, but the
risk of injury or damage was slim, and Duke relished the damp,
cool air after so many months in the desiccating desert.

Duke had caught up on the news from home by reading all
the letters he had not had the time or access to while en route from
Alexandria. His parents and Vivian were scheduled to arrive in two
days, and the ceremony at Buckingham Palace with King George
V was the day after, on Friday.

Duke had taken rooms in the Savoy Hotel and had been

invited to the St. James Club now that he was a full Colonel. Here he was able to relax with other General officers of the Royal Flying Corps and catch up on events on the Western Front.

The bloody Red Baron, who flew a blood-red Fokker DR1 Triplane, as did his cousin Max von Wagner, was much on the minds of these flying officers. His Flying Circus, as it was called due to the multicolored array of aircraft, was inflicting heavy losses on the Allies.

Duke's fellow Americans were now landing every day, and the Allies knew a major spring offensive by the Germans to try and defeat them before America was fully engaged was inevitable. The Germans were negotiating the Treaty of Brest-Litousk with Russia after the Communist rebellion had led to Russia's military collapse on the Eastern Front. This would free up a whole army of Germans to reinforce the Western Front.

Duke savored a glass of scotch as he discussed aerial tactics at the St. James Club with a fellow Colonel, Rich Ramsell. He was just back from front line service where he commanded an SE5A Biplane fighter squadron.

"The Huns are like butterflies compared to our new 200hp Hispano-Suiza powered SE5A Biplanes. Albert Ball and Jim Mc-Cudden, both aces in my squadron, have scored many victories in these birds against the best Fokker has to fly against us. The Camel is more maneuverable, but with the power and strength of these SE5s, you can just soar away from a bad fight or outrun any of the buggers! I have bagged four of the bastards and can't wait to get back for more. What do you fly, Colonel Thomas, and have you had any success?" asked the inebriated Colonel.

"Well, sir, I'm flying the Sopwith Triplane and do love its maneuverability. I've been lucky enough to bag 15 Germans, most of them on the Middle Eastern Front outside Cairo. I'm looking forward to getting a little R&R, then I'm going back to help General Allenby whip the Ottomans out of Damascus and beyond," said Duke.

"Well, God Save the King, you're the American chap that's been in the papers who is about to get the Victoria Cross from old King George himself! Well done, mate! Next round's on me!" shouted Colonel Ramsell. "And if you want to get into the real war, I could sure use a man like you in my No. 56 squadron! Although I hear the American Expeditionary Air Force needs good leadership, so they may try and kidnap you," added the Colonel with a loud Scottish laugh.

The evening wound down, and Duke stumbled back to the Savoy Hotel. He was starting to realize what a high honor he was about to receive! Juliette was waiting for him in her beautiful see-through white silk gown with the silver heels that made her almost as tall as Duke. He was in awe of her beauty as love filled his mind and body.

Passion overwhelmed the couple. Duke embraced her while she expertly stripped off his dress uniform. He quickly pulled her gown over her head as she rolled over on her knees with only her heels on.

Their ecstasy was so loud that a phone call from the front desk due to complaints from the adjoining rooms was met by Duke yelling, "To hell with those buggers!" After their passion had been exhausted and Duke's breathing and heart rate began to return to near normal, Juliette squeezed in tightly between his arms under the crisp Egyptian cotton sheets and whispered, "I love you, Duke."

"I love you, baby."

"I have a surprise for you," Juliette whispered in his ear as she stroked his manhood, gently urging him on.

"Oh, I know you do, you devil!" cried Duke with a mischievous smile.

He pulled her close, feeling her breasts rub against his chest while he grabbed her high heels and lifted her up for more love-making.

"Darling, I'm pregnant," whispered Juliette.

"What, my love?" Duke asked in a slurred voice.

"I'm going to have our child in about four months," cried Juliette, looking as happy as Duke had ever seen her.

Then, suddenly, despite the multiple rounds of single malt scotch, it registered! He was going to be a father! Duke grabbed his beautiful love, kissed her all over, and then noticed the slight bulge in her belly and carefully placed his hand there, hoping to feel a kick.

Then, ever so gently, he laid her back in bed and made mad love until the first light of morning broke into their love den, and they both fell into the deep sleep of true lovers.

When Duke woke with a start, he realized not only was it afternoon, but he was ravenously hungry and couldn't stop smiling with the excitement of fatherhood.

Juliette was already up and dressed to the nines. She seemed even more beautiful now with the hormones of motherhood coursing through her supple body.

They couldn't keep their hands off each other as they ran across the busy street in the rain to The Wellington Pub for bangers and mash with pints for all the soldiers and families in the place on Duke's tab to celebrate the news of his impending fatherhood.

The pub soon was awash with fellow soldiers and Londoners, hugging the ecstatic couple and wishing them well. An officer mentioned his impending Victoria Cross presentation from the King, and the pub exploded in song, "God Save the King!" Every officer and soldier proposed round after round of Guinness stout to the couple until he and Juliette escaped, laughing and kissing into the cold, gentle London rain.

When they left, it was already dark, and they rushed to the suite and began where they had left off earlier that day, making mad passionate love. The exhausted sleep of lovers soon followed as the next momentous morning dawned bright, clear, and cold.

Duke knew his parents and Vivian were arriving today, and it was time to face the truth. He had already told Juliette he was married, and she accepted it blandly with Parisian understanding as if it was merely a temporary inconvenience.

Duke, on the other hand, was horrified. Viv's letters were so full of love and excitement at his accomplishments, and she was so looking forward to seeing him. She had been a faithful wife and even helped raise money for war bonds, and she had strictly followed the wartime rationing while helping Duke's dad at the hospital and clinic.

She did frequently mention their mutual family friend and classmate, Phillip Huguenot, who had inherited his family's cotton and timber plantation, which was closer to St. Simons Island and was twice as large as his father's. He had lost his wife to the Spanish flu, and Viv explained she had been kindly helping with his young 2-year-old daughter over the past several months.

Duke's mom was from one of the oldest and most tradition-al families in Georgia, so Duke knew she would be very disappoint-ed in his infidelity, and Duke's dad's lineage was legendary in the South. His great-great-grandfather, Johnathan Thomas, had been the Captain of General Oglethorpe's ship, who founded Georgia in 1733 and established Savannah as the 13th and last American Colonial capital.

King George himself had granted him thousands of acres of prime plantation land just south of Savannah that had grown many times over until the tragedy of the War of Northern Aggres-sion when most of it had been lost to Yankee carpetbaggers and back taxes due to the loss of so many family members in the war.

Thankfully, due to his grandfather's engineering degree from the University of Georgia, the family was able to hold onto Peru, their original family plantation, and establish a small shipping company. This had prospered and now was one of the largest on the Eastern seaboard, allowing them to maintain houses in Savannah, Charleston, and other smaller plantations.

He would be shocked when he learned of Duke's infidelity, and his mother would probably disown him, but this was love in a time of war, and he had a baby on the way!

Duke wondered how he should handle this. Should he follow his head and Southern tradition and renounce his true love, Juliette, and their future child, or follow his heart and embrace the love of his life? He looked at Juliette as she excitedly and fearlessly dressed in her fabulous style with tight khaki pants, black calf leather knee-high buffed riding boots, and a white blouse showing off her cleavage under her tight black leather riding jacket.

She topped it off with beautiful diamond studded earrings, a pearl necklace, and an Aussie expedition hat that made his breathing almost stop at her eye-popping beauty. She showed no signs of pregnancy while her skin glowed with health and radiance as if the gods favored her. But Duke especially loved her contagious smile and spirited Parisian voice, which lightened his war-weary heart.

Duke knew immediately, in his gut and his heart, how he would handle this. Juliette was his soulmate, and he would do anything to protect and love her and their unborn child for the rest of his life, even if his family and friends disowned him. He would approach this with honor and do the right thing for Viv with a generous divorce settlement, and he knew Juliette would understand as he looked at her and smiled. She smiled back knowingly and ran over to plant a long, wet kiss on his lips, which seemed to fire his heart with resolve.

She said, "Mon amour, it will be OK! Your family will be so excited to see you, and I can't wait to meet Viv! I know we will love each other."

Duke smiled with relief, she was truly amazing and had already saved his life physically with her nursing, and now she was saving his heart with her unconditional love.

He had not yet told her or anyone else about the contents of the battered but secure family chest that sat in the corner of his hotel room. It was the size of a quarter cord of wood and weighed even more. Duke suspected Juliette knew because his eyes sparkled each time he mentioned the contents as extra souvenirs that he was going to send home with his family.

Duke looked at his trusty Rolex watch as they rushed down to the lobby of the Savoy Hotel to meet his family. He was already fifteen minutes late.

He straightened his dress uniform and medals while the bellman opened the lift at the lobby. He heard them chatting with that beautiful, slow southern accent and rushed to embrace his mother.

She must have felt his presence since she turned and opened her arms to her firstborn son with a loving touch and kiss. Duke buried his face on her shoulder as the tears of happiness flowed, and they held each other as he regained his composure. No words were necessary. His mother looked at Juliette and immediately opened her arms and heart to her.

Viv was surprised, but in her elegant way, embraced Duke as they shared an awkward hug.

"Hello, Duke. You look like you need some good Southern cooking, but mighty glad to see you, son!" said Dr. Johnathan Thomas with a huge grin on his face as he admired his son's medal-bedecked Colonel's uniform and embraced him strongly.

"This must be the nurse who brought you back to life. Twice, I understand. We are all so indebted to you, my dear! It's a real pleasure to meet you, Juliette! I'm a huge fan of your great grandfather Marshall Ney who was also an idol to my grandfather, whose sword Duke is carrying. Duke mentioned how talented you are, but he should have told us how beautiful you are as well!"

Duke's blushing father likewise hugged the smiling Juliette, who responded with her Parisian accent, "I'm so glad to meet you all too!"

Then, out of the corner of his eye, Duke saw a young man rush in. He suddenly threw a crushing bear hug on Duke, at nearly eye level. Duke was shocked to see Robby had grown so tall for a fourteen-year-old.

Robby flashed a salute to his older brother, saying, "Honored to meet you, Colonel!" The whole family started laughing as the brothers caught up on some long overdue horsing around.

Duke broke away as the brothers struggled to catch their breath and dropped onto a couch with an affectionate but impressed smile on his face at his brother's strength. He felt the effects of a year at war and two serious wounds more than he realized, and Robby smiled at his brother with the knowledge that he was different, but he was not sure why.

Viv walked over and elegantly sat on the lobby couch beside him.

She said, "Duke, I'm so glad to see you. I have been worried about you after hearing of your wounds, but now we can celebrate your new medal together! Darling, you are so skinny and pale, but with your nurse, it seems you are healing quickly?"

"Thanks, darling," said Duke with a half-smile on his face as he awaited the emotional attack.

"Well, when should we discuss our future?" said Viv.

"I'm in love with Juliette," said Duke with a determination that surprised him, and the lobby seemed to hush with the tension of the moment.

Duke would face the impending battle head-on, just like he did in aerial combat.

Viv hardly moved as she absorbed the news and flashed her beautiful smile. Duke squirmed on the elegant leather couch while his tailored uniform seemed to have shrunk two sizes and was suddenly way too tight. He felt sweat forming on his brow but held Viv's eyes with a caring but determined smile.

Viv looked deeply and knowingly into his eyes and said, "I think we both have news of the heart, and I thank you for being honest. I have become involved with Phillip, and he has asked for my hand. I told him that I would have to wait until you returned safely, but now I see we both are well-loved and can follow our hearts. I hope we can always be friends."

Duke released a deep sigh of relief while they embraced. He too hoped they would always be friends. Juliette and the rest of the family surrounded them with love and support as the lobby seemed to fill with fresh air again.

Duke fell into Juliette's arms, and tears of relief welled in his eyes as they all walked to the hotel bar for some much-needed refreshment.

The next morning, Duke was escorted into the presentation room at Buckingham Palace, surrounded by his wide-eyed family as they were ushered into King George's presence. After a deep low bow, he moved forward for the award presentation.

The King was elegant and dressed in his formal military attire, complete with more medals and ribbons than Duke could count. "Congratulations, Colonel, it is a small medal, but it is our highest for bravery, and I thank you for your service to our country," said the King as he hung the red-ribboned Victoria Cross with the coveted Distinguished Service Order bars around Duke's neck.

"General Allenby tells me you are among his best officers and has also sent a telegram for you. Now that America is fully engaged in this conflict, we all hope the bloodshed will end soon! Can you introduce me to your family?" said the grey-haired monarch who showed deep lines of fatigue across his sharply cut aristocratic facial bones.

"Yes, sir!" said Duke as he proudly introduced his blushing family. When Juliette bowed, the King said with a twinkle in his eye, "Madame, what a pleasure. My father spoke very highly of your grandfather Marshal Ney."

"Merci, my Lord," said Juliette as she bowed as he kissed her hand.

"Perhaps you and the Colonel can join us for dinner before you leave my island?" said the King knowingly.

"It would be an honor, my Lord," blushed Juliette as the King made his way to greet the rest of the family.

The King greeted Duke's father and said, "Dr. Thomas, my great grandfather often spoke of the talented Captain Thomas, who was General Oglethorpe's Captain when he founded our last and favorite American colony. I'm glad to see you have kept your family's military tradition of service to the motherland intact. I thank you, sir."

Dr. Thomas bowed awkwardly but smiled proudly and said, "Thank you for remembering our family, Your Majesty. It's an honor to fight side by side with our English brothers."

The King patted Robby on the head, who blushed while attempting a bow.

"Oh, by the way, Colonel, the US Ambassador has asked you to drop by his residence, and my military attache has General Allenby's letter and package for you," pronounced King George V.

He smiled and winked at Juliette as he left the room to attend another awards ceremony.

"Yes, sir!" responded Duke with a deep bow as the ushers

led the family out through the elegant wood-paneled grand hall. It was filled with suits of armor and paintings of monarchs and heroes from William the Conqueror to Queen Victoria.

The family was exhilarated by the royal experience and began chattering like a flock of seagulls as they exited the Palace grounds. Robby stared in wonder at the bear hats on the motionless, red-suited palace guards and then ran over to Duke, asking to touch his new medals. His eyes shone brightly as he said, "Duke, I want to be a pilot and join the air service just like you!"

Duke's mother knowingly wrapped her youngest in a bear hug and said, "Hold on Tiger. First, you get your college degree, just like Duke. Then we can talk about sending you to Americus, Georgia, to fly those Curtiss Jennies and earn your wings just like your big brother did. Until then, no more talk of service!" said his mother, Anne, as she winked at Duke.

Duke smiled and joined his mother.

He said, "Robby, you will love Americus, especially the cornbread, fried chicken, grits, and fried okra! And don't forget the best peaches in the world, especially on your ice cream," added Duke as his stomach started to growl.

CHAPTER 21 • London

After settling the family and Juliette back at the Savoy Hotel, Duke opened and read the sealed message from General Allenby in the carriage on his way to the ambassador's residence. The General's package also contained his Colt pistol, which he dropped after emptying it during combat with the Berber's while at the desert emergency airstrip.

My dear Colonel, I am pleased to return your empty pistol, which Colonel Balfour found personally and returns to you with his compliments. We have also analyzed the sword from your engagement at the Oasis. After Colonel Balfour's cavalry tracked down the sole survivor and captured Major von Manstein, we discovered one of the men you killed in single combat was the favorite son of the Sheik, Abdul Muhamed. He started the uprising, which is now defeated. Unfortunately, he has placed a bounty of 12,000 gold pieces on your head as revenge for killing his son and the other 119 Arab soldiers that died in combat against you. I advise against returning to this theatre of conflict, although I will sorely miss your skills.

In the East, these blood feuds can be dangerous with assassins of all nationalities, relatives, or tribesmen hunting for an easy payday, but you will be far from these devils on the Western Front. I have sent word to my friend, US

American Expeditionary Air Service General "JJ" Grant, of your great service and have no doubt he will be calling on you soon.

Good luck and Godspeed.

General Allenby.

Well, thought Duke as he climbed out of the carriage at the elegant ambassador's residence after tucking the Colt into his dress jacket pocket. *It looks like I'm in for a new assignment.*

"Welcome, Colonel Thomas!" said the doorman as he took the heavy dress coat from Duke, and wide-eyed, he admired the shining Victoria Cross.

"The ambassador and General Grant are expecting you in the gun room, sir."

He led Duke into the dark wood-paneled room with a roaring fire in an oversized fireplace surrounded by many general officers. "Ambassador Page, may I introduce Colonel Thomas," said the doorman as he presented Duke.

The Honorable Walter Hines Page from New York had been the US British ambassador since 1913. The stress of a world at war with the US now fully engaged showed in his eyes as he walked over and personally welcomed Duke. "So nice to meet you, Colonel Thomas, and let me be the first to congratulate you on receiving the Victoria Cross.

"Did you know, the bronze used to make The Cross Pattee with the Crown and Lion superimposed with the motto, 'For Valour,' comes from melted Russian cannons captured at the Siege of Sevastopol? "

"No, sir, I had no idea," said Duke with curiosity.

"I see you also have a red ribbon bar with a second Distinguished Service Order award bar for further gallantry in action in the deserts of Egypt and Libya. Well done, my boy! You are the first American in this conflict to be so highly honored!" said the ambassador.

"Thank you, sir," said Duke.

One of the tuxedo-dressed staff brought him a large Lagavulin Scotch, neat.

Duke wondered how they knew his tastes. He swirled the dark, smokey nectar in his crystal glass and took a full sip, letting it slip down his palate while it quickly warmed his stomach. They moved together toward the roaring fire to meet another General.

"Allow me to introduce you to General "JJ" Grant, our American Expeditionary Air Service Commander," said Ambassador Page. The General was much sterner and more intense than General Allenby.

He said with a smile through his bushy black eyebrows, "Congratulations, Colonel, on your achievements and honors while serving in the Lafayette Escadrille and with my friend, General Allenby. He is very disappointed you will be unable to help him with his next campaign, but I'm very pleased to offer you command of the 94th Aero Squadron, also known as the 'Hat in The Ring' squadron," he said.

"It is composed of our best American aviators, and you will retain your rank of full Colonel in the US Air Service. Just as you did in the Egyptian desert, allowing General Allenby to defeat the Germans and end the Senussi Jihad last year, we need to gain command of the air. This war needs to end, and I intend to put our boys out front as soon as possible to accomplish this feat. I need you to help clear the air of the Huns! What do you say, Colonel?"

Duke was amazed as he slowly inhaled another large mouthful of scotch while reflecting on the circumstances of his last year at war. He eased closer to the crackling fire. The heat infused his body as the scotch relaxed his mind. He admired the ambassador's collection of English Purdey double-barrel shotguns, neatly standing upright in the dark rosewood gun case, which covered the whole side wall of the high ceiling, wood-paneled room.

Not only had Duke risen to this offer of command, but he had also discovered one of the greatest treasures of all time. He had received the Victoria Cross with two bars of The Distinguished Service Order, the Medal of Merit, the Legion of Honor, and Croix de Guerre from France.

He had also achieved a score of fifteen aerial victories but paid an enormous price physically and mentally. He watched his hand tremble as he gazed into the fire. His shoulder and thigh still ached in the damp English cold. Duke considered this assignment's responsibility, but he was a loyal Southerner and American, and he knew his country needed him. If he could help gain air superiority over the Germans, he could significantly reduce the American and Allied casualties, which was worth the price.

After one more deep swallow of the smoky scotch, Duke said, "General Grant, it would be my honor, sir!"

"Wonderful, Colonel, I hope you can take command after you finish recovering from your wound and the well-deserved leave, but no later than the beginning of April. As we all already know, a major spring offensive is in the works," said General Grant.

"Yes, sir!" responded Duke as he was ushered over to meet General Grant's staff, with whom he discussed logistics and the details of the assignment, including staff and aircraft requirements.

"You will be facing the best of the German air service, including Manfred von Richthofen, his brother Luther, and cousin Max von Wagner, whom we understand you know quite well. The General has asked us to provide everything we can for the squadron and make it the best on the Western Front. We have requested the new SPAD French fighters to replace our aging Nieuports, and you will have Eddie Richenbacker, the famous racecar driver, in your squadron. What else do you need, Colonel?" asked Major Keith Carpenter.

"I will need a modified Sopwith triplane and my mechanic Sargent Fred Jones, who is on the front lines, and I hope still alive. He was assigned there by Major David Vann several months ago as a vendetta against me when he assigned me to the Egyptian theater of conflict. I want him assigned to my command and Lieutenants Frank Wilson, John Patton, and Jimmy Franklin. We will need the new, incendiary ammunition and the newest SPADs available," said Duke firmly.

"Yes, sir! I have also been assigned to your staff as Executive Officer and look forward to serving with you," said Major Carpenter as he stretched his thin frame to his full height of 5 feet 11 inches.

"Glad to have you, Major. Where are you from, and what flying experience do you have?" asked Duke.

"I'm from Dothan, Alabama, sir, and have over thirty hours of flight time in a Curtis Jenny, but no combat time yet. I graduated from West Point three years ago at the top of my class and requested the Aviation Branch, which allowed me to train in Americus, Georgia, just like you did, sir!" said Major Carpenter.

"You're right about that. What a wonderful town. The meals at the famous and elegant Windsor Hotel still make me miss the place, not to mention the beautiful Southern ladies! Pleased to have you on board. I will be out of touch until I return from leave on April 1st to take command of the 94th. If any emergencies arise, please post to me through the London war office. Work our pilots hard and get the boys in the air with gunnery, bombing, and local training as much as possible. It will save their lives when we start full-time combat patrols in all conditions.

"I want the squadron at full strength and ready for action when I arrive. Push as hard as you can to get those new SPAD XIII fighters ASAP since the Fokkers, especially the Triplanes, outclass the Nieuports we now have. The first offensive will follow as soon as the spring weather allows, and I want us leading the fight from above," said Duke.

"Yes, sir. Proud to be serving under you," said Major Keith Carpenter as he saluted.

Duke quickly made his exit after saying his goodbyes to the General, Ambassador, and staff.

As Duke walked out of the toasty ambassador's home, he took a deep breath of the cold, damp London air while climbing into the waiting carriage. His hands were shaking, and the cold dug through his heavy military dress jacket as he realized how badly he needed leave. His body ached and felt frail, but his mind was sharp.

His family, including Viv, were leaving in the morning, and he and Juliette would be able to spend the next weeks of leave relaxing, allowing him to finish healing and put on weight. He would send the chest filled with gold, precious stones, and Alexander's helmet to his Georgia home. Its secret would be safe with his father, deep in the family vault on Peru Plantation. He would address the treasure and discovery of a lifetime when and if he returned home from this conflict. *It needed to remain a secret*, Duke thought, perhaps permanently, but he had to recover both physically and mentally right now.

When Duke arrived at the hotel, Viv met him in the lobby and coldly embraced him as she saw the stress of the meeting with the ambassador in his eyes.

She said, "Duke, I know we leave tomorrow, and I wanted to give you these marriage annulment papers in hopes you will agree, and we can both move on with our lives. I don't want anything other than all the funds in our bank account and your home on River Street in Savannah, darling. I'm so glad you have found happiness, and I am excited to begin my life with Phillip. I spent time with Juliette this evening, and she is wonderful and loves you so much."

Duke scanned the document and then quickly signed and said, "I wish you and Phillip all the happiness in the world."

After looking at the signature, Viv sardonically smiled and said cruelly with a dark look Duke had never seen before, "If you survive the war, beware, as one day I will repay your betrayal twice over when you least expect it! As the good Book says, 'an eye for an eye,'" said Viv as she escaped to the lift.

Duke collapsed into the lobby couch, closing his eyes and taking a deep breath. He felt he had just taken a body blow from a heavyweight fighter, but now he was finally free to fully commit his life to Juliette.

CHAPTER 22 • RECOVERY

After seeing his family off with more tears than any of them could remember, Duke and Juliette headed to the harbor. They chartered a fast, private schooner recommended by the King's attaché whom Duke met at the London war office. It was the only way to get quickly and relatively safely across the channel and into the North Atlantic during wartime. Duke could afford it.

The couple quietly boarded *The Wolf*, an 87-foot twin-masted masterpiece crafted in Portsmouth, England, by the best shipbuilders in the last century. Even then, every scrap of sail counted for speed in battle or blockade running, both of which this schooner was rumored to have participated in. Their stateroom featured beautiful dark teak. It had an old whale oil lamp which swung tightly in the corner of the room as the ship slipped quietly under London Bridge and out of the harbor on that cold, wet afternoon of February 1918.

Juliette was beaming with excitement as she thought of the voyage ahead and over a month of alone time with the love of her life. She had spent many summers in Brittany with her family and loved the sea and sailing.

Duke did too, ever since his childhood spent on the waters of the Georgia and Florida coast, where he often sailed the family's fifty-foot schooner, *Freedom*.

Every Christmas holiday, the Thomas family sailed to the Florida Keys, staying with his grandparents who had a large winter vacation house beside the Key West Lighthouse on Whitehead

Street. Duke loved diving in the clear, aqua blue waters on the third largest reef in the world, only six miles offshore.

My escape on the W.f.

He shot giant grouper while spearfishing and enjoyed the tender white meat that could be cooked in so many ways—especially fried, his favorite. But he savored the large Florida spiny lobster and giant stone crab claws the most. The family cook, Isabelle, loved to spoil him, often adding the sweet, delicate white lobster to his scrambled eggs and cheese in the morning. But the giant stone crab claws Duke would only eat with melted butter. His stomach growled as he remembered the delicate flavors.

He had always dreamed of sailing to the Caribbean, and after stowing his bag in their small private stateroom, Duke grabbed Juliette. They ran up on deck, hand-in-hand, to watch the crew hoist sail and grab a fast beam reach as they headed off into the salt-soaked air of the English Channel.

Captain Jones said, "Good afternoon, where are we off to, Colonel? I have loaded the provisions you requested for a six-week voyage."

Duke and Juliette smiled as they both exclaimed, "Somewhere warm and as far away from this war as possible!"

"Well, we can make a run for the Virgin Islands, but it may take a week or so to get there," noted Captain Jones as the crew tightened and trimmed sail.

They soon cleared the last lighthouse and coastal patrols with the Union Jack and American flag both flying freely in the late afternoon breeze.

The couple exchanged excited looks and agreed. "Let's do it, Captain! My father has told me of the spectacular scenery of the Grenadines. I remember he told me about an island there that still had a whaling station and palm plantations with water so clear, it looked like gin! Any idea which island it could be?" said Juliette.

"Yes, ma'am!" said Captain Jones with a twinkle in his eye. "That is Bequia!" And it flowed off his lips like honey.

"The island of the clouds, as the war-loving race of ancient Arawak Indians called it. They are all dead now, but the locals are as friendly as Tahitians and are excellent boat builders and fishermen. But I think the whaling days are over."

Juliette jumped into Duke's arms with excitement. "Yes,

darling, that is it!" And after Duke nodded to the Captain, they rushed to their stateroom, not to be seen again until late the next morning at the Captain's table for coffee and biscuits.

"Good morning, sir and ma'am," said the Captain with a knowing smile. He always addressed Duke as sir, even though he was over twice his age.

"Darling, I'm famished," whispered Juliette as she surveyed the biscuits while inhaling her coffee.

"George, get your ass in here!" yelled the Captain. The cook and first mate popped his head through the gangway.

"Yes, sir!" said the coal-black giant of a man who had to duck his head to get through the door. He had a large bald head shaped like a billiard ball with eyes and teeth that shone as white as pearls. His nickname was Black George.

"Cook these fine folks a decent breakfast," said the Captain.

"Yes, sir, but we have a ship crossing our bow ahead, and it looks like we may be hailed," noted the mate.

"Captain, please show me the kitchen, and I will take care of it," said Juliette in her silky French accent. "I think I can handle myself in your kitchen," she added with a knowing smile.

"Well, ma'am, it's called a galley, and we would love to let you run the show," said the Captain without hesitation as he lifted his six-foot frame and followed the mate out on deck.

And with that simple statement, Juliette took over the galley for the outbound journey and used the simple provisions on board to produce some of the best meals the crew had ever experienced. They all fell under her spell and jumped to her assistance at the slightest misstep or slip as if they were caring for a small child. Each meal was a heavenly experience, and the men jostled for the first seats at the table while filling their plates to capacity and then bowing deeply in thanks as they rushed off to their duties.

Soon Duke began to fill out, and his black buffalo leather belt approached the old worn spot where it had been before the war. The couple were never more than an arms-length apart and seemed to glow in each other's company as *The Wolf* raced toward the warmth and peace of the Grenadines.

Their time on deck was glorious as the North Atlantic faded behind the stern. Soon, dolphins and even the occasional whale appeared in the deep crystal blue waters of the Caribbean. Duke helped with navigation and steering while the Captain took sextant sightings every noon, and they excitedly charted their progress. The winter trade winds held true day after day as they made excellent time in *The Wolf*, which seemed to fly on the water.

Even Juliette learned how to navigate by the sun and stars as she absorbed life onboard. The sun and salt spray only enhanced her beauty, and Duke found himself wondering how he was so lucky to have fallen in love with her.

Then on the morning of the eighth day since leaving London, they heard a cry from the crow's nest, "Land ho!"

By lunch, *The Wolf* was dropping anchor in Port Elizabeth, Bequia. The smiling British harbor master and magistrate, Eric McCambell, soon boarded and proudly shook hands with the only aviator and war hero he had ever met. He invited the couple to dine with his family for lunch and offered his palm plantation beachfront home as accommodation. Duke happily accepted, but only if they agreed to accept full payment for their plantation paradise in the palms.

The white wooden plantation-style home featured large open windows, shutters, and slow whirling fans. It had a wraparound porch and high ceilings. It was spectacular and reminded Duke of his family home in Georgia. It was fully staffed and positioned within a stone's throw of the white sandy beach with crystal blue water gently lapping against the shore, sending the couple into a trance of peace and endless love.

Their lovemaking was a mix of passion and pleasure as they seemed to learn new ways of satisfying each other with deeper feelings of ecstasy each passing day. Juliette would often send the staff away after breakfast and wear nothing but her high heels all day. She would parade around the house finding mysterious things to bend over and pick up as Duke tried to concentrate on reading the latest newspapers, which were already two weeks old but usually ended up on the floor. He would take her from behind while grabbing her hair as she screamed in pleasure.

Later, they would lay on the beach blanket sipping excellent French Chardonnay from the Bourgogne region, which Juliette carefully selected from the well-stocked shelves of the General store in Port Elizabeth. It was only a five-minute carriage ride away from their isolated paradise. She wore nothing as they sipped wine and fresh coconut milk while downing fresh broiled lobster and other local delicacies until they could no longer resist the pleasure of each other's bodies. They made passionate love in the shade of the palm trees, rolling in the deep lush grass as the warm salt-infused trade winds rushed over their tanned bodies day after glorious day.

Finally, the realization came that it was almost time for departure and a return to reality. A large pouch of forwarded mail from Georgia finally arrived toward the middle of March, two weeks before Duke was to report to his new command. It included the official declaration of annulment from his marriage to Vivian.

He grabbed Juliette in excitement and exclaimed, "Let's get married, darling," while he showed her the official document.

She collapsed in his arms in tears crying, "Oui, Oui, baby!"

The whole island seemed to come together for the biggest wedding the small Episcopal church had ever seen. The ladies surrounded Juliette in her bright white flowing gown that had been carefully fitted to her growing but still barely visible belly. At the same time, flowers of all shapes, colors, and aromas flew on the island breeze as the couple left the ceremony to the cheers of the whole town of Port Elizabeth.

The local Governor and Duke's best local drinking partner and friend, The Honorable Tom Stone, had been the best man and offered his local mountain top home as their honeymoon retreat.

They jumped into the waiting carriage and found all the horses had bells and flowers draped carefully about them. They were dragging a line of tin cans that announced their passage to more smiling locals. They hurried off to the governor's cottage hidden on the peak of the lush Mount Pleasant. It had a view of the harbor and the tranquil blue Caribbean sea. Their lovemaking was nonstop and epic as the fresh mountain top breeze seemed to send them to new levels of pleasure. The sounds of the tropical birds of the rainforest around them was music to their ears.

The Honorable Tom Stone made a special trip back in his capacity as British Governor to see them off a few days later with the personal greetings, congratulations, and the well wishes of his Majesty, King George V.

He presented the couple with ceremonial flower wreaths of freedom and a special honor bestowed by order of his Majesty, granting them British citizenship with a lifetime exemption from taxes should they decide to make the islands or any other British possession their home.

Duke embraced his friend, humbled by the majestic gift. The governor blushed and said, "Be safe, Duke. You two will find that once you have been in paradise and tasted the peace, freedom, and beauty here, you will forever long to return. And when you do, we will greet you as friends and citizens, and we will celebrate your return with a party fit for a conquering hero!"

The couple was speechless, and Duke couldn't help but

think of his connection with Alexander the Great, wondering if Tom knew something. Then he realized that was impossible and broke out in his infectious laugh of pure happiness as they were rowed out to *The Wolf* by the star-struck crew who joined in the laughter and pulled strongly while singing, " Yo ho ho and a bottle of rum!"

Once aboard, Captain Jones pulled anchor, and *The Wolf* was suddenly under full sail, racing away from their sanctuary. The couple needed to rush from their cozy teak-lined cabin to watch their wonderful island paradise of Bequia dissolve into the distant horizon and evaporate into the Caribbean blue.

Once underway, Captain Jones performed a special on-board marriage celebration of his own. The crew laid palm fronds freshly cut from Bequia on deck for the couple to dance on. Black George played a series of nostalgic wedding dances on his fiddle as the crew cheered and clapped, all happy after a triple portion of dark Mt. Gay Barbados rum.

"We wanted to congratulate you in our own way, Colonel and Mrs. Thomas," said Captain Jones with a beaming smile as if his own son had just been married.

"Merci Captain, it is the best onboard symphony I have ever heard!" said a beaming Juliette. Duke winked and nodded his head in gratitude to the capable Captain who had become more than a friend on the journey.

Duke considered naming his unborn child after this gallant man who had achieved the rank of Captain in the Royal Navy before retiring due to injuries he received leading a party of Marines during the Boxer Rebellion in China.

The journey across the North Atlantic back to a world at war was rough and stormy. Juliette suffered from bouts of morning sickness that left her confined to the cabin for much of the day. Her previous cooking duties were taken over by Black George, who did his best in the pitching galley but couldn't match Juliette's wonderful French meals.

Duke and Captain Jones spent hours on deck discussing the merits of *The Wolf* and her previous sixty-plus years as a blockade runner and smuggler during the Civil War and other conflicts. He now enjoyed her as a private charter vessel but confided in Duke that he felt something was missing without the danger.

She was the fastest schooner Duke had ever sailed, and her raked sharp lines contributed to her name and reputation. The captain even had two ten-pound deck guns lashed to the closed gunports in the unlikely event of an enemy or pirate encounter.

He described his years of sailing in Royal and private vessels, and they shared their mutual love of the sea and nature.

The Captain even told Duke about the loss of his only son during the Battle of the Somme in 1916 while serving as a Lieutenant in Kitchener's Army. He had received a Distinguished Service Order (DSO) for leading his men in the first and most successful part of the battle. But when a German counter-attack threatened the new gains, he led a desperate attack and was cut down by artillery fire, and none of his remains were recovered. He said Duke looked and acted like his son.

Duke embraced the Captain, who unsuccessfully fought to hold back tears, and they drank to his son's memory.

Duke began taking watches while steering *The Wolf*, and when the weather cleared, he also took sextant readings. He realized that when the war ended, this would be the therapy and life he and Juliette would need to recover from his daily fight for survival on the front. A slow trip around the world with this fabulous vessel and captain, whom he considered now as a second father, as well as the crew and new child would cure anything, or so Duke dreamed, but only time would tell.

Then, on the morning of March 29th, two days ahead

of schedule, *The Wolf* dropped anchor in the shadow of London Bridge.

Duke embraced Captain Jones and said, "Sir, if you would allow me to reserve *The Wolf* for a year or more charter when the war ends, I would be in your debt."

Captain Jones smiled and said, "We will await your arrival with great anticipation and excitement. Consider *The Wolf* your ship at any time, Colonel! Keep yourself safe."

Duke had left prepayment in his stateroom, unknown to the Captain, and he smiled and returned Captain Jones and the crew's salute as he quietly went ashore and settled Juliette back at the Savoy Hotel. He had seen tears in the Captain's eyes as he left the ship.

Duke then reported to the war office where he received urgent dispatches from the war office and his squadron in France.

The first ordered him to report to the Sopwith Aviation Company in Ham, England, as soon as possible to pick up his new triplane, *The Reaper,* with better performance and armament than what he had used in Egypt. The first dispatches from his Executive Officer, Major Carpenter in France, were good, with reports of a fully-equipped squadron including his head of maintenance, Sargent Fred Jones, who had been recalled from the trenches and elevated in rank to Master Sergeant at Duke's request.

Both Lieutenants Jimmy Franklin and John Patton had been reassigned to the squadron as flight leaders from the 95th squadron along with Eddie Rickenbacker. LT. Frank Lewis was killed in aerial combat just a few weeks before, which greatly saddened and burdened Duke.

The dastardly Major David Vann was now demoted and had been sent to the front as a lowly Lieutenant platoon commander, verifying the tradition of "what goes around, comes around"!

The last dispatch from March 27th revealed the squadron

was being rushed to the front due to the beginning of the Luden-dorff Offensive on March 21st, which had already pushed the Allies to the brink of collapse. The squadron had been called to the front in a desperate attempt to stop the Huns with their last reported position close to St. Quentin, France. Major Carpenter asked for Duke's assistance immediately!

Duke suddenly realized that without his leadership, the whole squadron could be destroyed before he even arrived at the front. He rushed to the Savoy Hotel to spend one last evening with Juliette, who felt much better and looked like an angel as he swept into the room, his face flushed with the excitement of war mixed with the deep tan of the Caribbean.

"Darling, I have to leave first thing in the morning," exclaimed Duke as he embraced Juliette in a passionate but tender hug.

"But, mon amour, we have three more days," lamented Juliette with tears in her eyes.

"My love, I would do anything not to go, but the last great offensive of the war started a few days ago, and my squadron desperately needs me!" exploded Duke.

Juliette saw the pain in his eyes at the impending separation and knew his honor and duty would never let him stay beyond this last night. She relented as she smiled and kissed him, saying, "Then we will make it the best night ever!"

With a smile on his face the next morning, Duke made his way to the Sopwith factory in Ham, England. A brief but astonishing and exhilarating test flight confirmed the new 160hp rotary Gnome engine, with two Vickers .303 guns instead of one, indeed made the Sopwith triplane the best fighter he had ever flown. Not only would it climb like a homesick angel, but it was even more maneuverable and rolled, looped, and turned on a dime.

The ground crew, including Tommy Sopwith, were ecstatic

at the low-level rolls and loops Duke performed and were cheering as he came in for a final pass upside down only feet off the runway!

Duke landed and asked the crew to arm the aircraft fully. He spoke with Tommy Sopwith, saying, "Yes, sir, it is the best yet! The rate of climb and turn has doubled even with the extra weight of the additional gun and heavier 160 horsepower Gnome engine. But after losing before to more firepower, now the Huns will never have a chance."

Sopwith responded, "I wish the Flying Service would agree with you, but this is the only one they have approved."

"Yes, sir, I agree. Please make a backup triplane for me, and I will prove through my actions the value of your design. If they won't pay for it and more that I may request, I will!" said Duke as he strapped on the triplane.

He yelled, "Contact!" after switching the magnetos to the hot position.

Tommy Sopwith himself grabbed the long wooden prop and yelled, "Contact! Good luck and Godspeed!" And after flinging up his leg as if beginning the Charleston two-step dance, he pulled the prop through. It immediately disappeared into a blurred disk of motion as the engine happily coughed back to life, belching white smoke as it was eager to return to exploring the endless uncharted realms of the sky.

With a quick thumbs up to Tommy and the ground crew, Duke thundered off to the front one more time after making a low high-speed pass followed by a victory roll to the cheers of the factory staff. It was time to return to the inescapable reality and the cruelty of "the war to end all wars."

The only question was would he return to the love of his life and unborn child to travel the world in the therapeutic schooner *The Wolf* and reveal the truth of Alexander the Great, or would he join the millions in Valhalla's halls of death.

CHAPTER 23 • FRANCE

As Duke raced the setting sun across the English channel, he felt like Mercury flying on rays of purple light as the sun sank lower in the horizon behind him. Flying always seemed to be the tonic that freed his mind from the tyranny of earthly concerns. It expanded his thoughts and dreams as he flew faster than a streaking falcon to his new command in France. He smiled in anticipation of the challenge as he entered French airspace and the combat zone.

The cumulus clouds took on a life of their own as he recognized the old bull elephant and lions in the shapes and shadows they formed in the dying twilight. It brought his mind back to the Oasis of Siwa and his brush with death against the raging Arabic enemy cavalry at odds of 100:1 or more. He wondered aloud how he could have been so lucky. How had the lioness been there at the exact time of his imminent death to save him?

Suddenly, the hair of his neck prickled, and his sixth sense awoke as he saw a flash reflected from the dying sun high over his right shoulder. He knew he was being hunted. The four specs fell from out of the dying sun like arrows of death as Duke awaited the last second before turning hard into the unsuspecting flight leader trailing bright red streamers from the struts of his overall white Fokker Triplane.

He saw the flashes from the enemy's twin Spandau machine guns, but his unexpected turn caused them to overshoot his overall black Sopwith Triplane, *The Reaper*. Duke pulled back hard on his joystick, and his vision began to fade as the positive G forces pulled the blood from his brain, draining the vision from his eyes until only his central cone of sight remained, and then his ears began to ring from lack of life-giving blood.

He was out of flying condition and needed airtime to acclimate and regain his G tolerance and learn the nuances of this fantastic, modified triplane. But this was war; he found courage, and as the lead Fokker DR1 triplane flashed by, Duke fired a short, accurate burst to flame the leader's aircraft and scatter the remains of the flight who now changed from hunters to the hunted. At least his marksmanship and aim were still good, and the twin Vickers now created a wide swath of death and destruction.

Duke's heart rate slowed as his killer instinct took over, and an eerily calm confidence filled his head. Time seemed to compress, and he felt like the aerial combat was in slow motion. He dove hard after the remaining flight, which tried to evade the Sopwith as he lined up with an overall yellow Fokker that had black stripes on the tail. The German Triplane turned hard left and right as the pilot looked over his shoulder in utter fear with his mouth open in panic and his white scarf streaming behind him. Duke could feel his fear and tried to fire at his engine, but the line of streamers from his pounding twin Vickers .303 guns flashed through the cockpit after destroying the engine, and he saw the pilot collapse and then lifelessly fall from the Triplane as it rolled into a death spiral.

Then, suddenly, he realized by some innate warning that he was in danger and looked over his shoulder in time to see the two remaining Fokkers lined up behind him. He pulled hard on his joystick as the line of enemy bullets and tracers from the enemy Triplanes briefly surrounded him. He felt hits on his tail and fuselage, and his windscreen exploded in front of him before *The Reaper* briefly escaped the deadly fire by rocketing vertically due to the powerful new 160hp Gnome engine.

Normally, he would have felt panic, but it was as if he was being guided and protected. He was calm and clear thinking as he kicked hard right rudder while pulling the joystick into his belly, producing a violent snap roll that threw off the aim and timing of the trailing Fokkers while slowing him to a crawl. The two Huns flashed by each side of him, allowing him to quickly dive on their tails.

The pair of German pilots were good and provided mutual protection with hard turns and violent pulls in the three-dimensional sky, quickly consuming the altitude until they were just above the ground. Duke now finished off the wingman in his blue and white checkerboard painted Triplane, who plowed into a tall windmill after a burst of fire from Duke's twin Vickers machine guns.

Now, just the talented co-leader remained, whose Triplane was candy red with white stripes on the wing and LO painted in white on the fuselage.

He flew like a demon as he rocked his wings left and right, sometimes seeming to scrape the very ground while throwing dust up from the freshly plowed fields. Finally, he dove under a bridge with German soldiers lining the railings and bank. Still, Duke followed him under it while matching his every move and slowly firing short three-second bursts of machine-gun fire, which tore fabric and wood from the wings and fuselage.

Then, a lucky shot from the German ground troops hit Duke's engine just as he fired the last burst of his ammunition into the Fokker's engine, which began smoking as the prop stopped, and the German crashed into a plowed field beside the Marne river. Duke flashed over the helpless German who waved in admiration as the Sopwith raced in the gathering dusk toward the front lines and his Allied airfield; his trusty Gnome engine continued to growl while occasionally missing from the damage. Little did Duke know, this was Lt. Ernst Udet, also a Blue Max recipient who would survive the war as the highest living German ace with sixty-two confirmed victories, and that LO was his girlfriend at the time.

What a great pilot, *[illegible handwritten caption]*

Duke knew he was close to the last reported position of his squadron at St. Quentin but was disoriented from the long dog-fight. As he approached the trenches, he was shocked to see them empty as he realized the Germans had made great forward progress in the ongoing spring offensive.

He saw grey-colored troops on the move toward Paris, and he received steady but inaccurate small arms ground fire as he crossed the fluid front-lines and finally began seeing the blue colors of the retreating French soldiers as he took a deep breath of relief.

Now, if he could find the field before his engine and the final twilight faded, his luck would be complete. He felt as if an inner force of power was directing him as he banked hard right, and several minutes later, he saw the outline of an airfield covered with Nieuport 28s with roundels of central white surrounded by blue with red in the outer ring lined up beside a row of hangers. These were American Aircraft on Chateau Albert airfield as the Germans had overrun St. Quentin. In the last dusky light of his first day back in France, Duke lined up for a landing, just as his Gnome rotary engine growled away the last of its power, and the prop froze from battle damage.

The men came pouring out from the Officers' Club and mess as they heard the rough running rotary engine followed by silence as the Sopwith Triplane performed a perfect dead-stick landing right in front of them.

Duke rolled to a stop beside the hangers, removed his belts and goggles, then pulled himself shakily from the cockpit. The men gathered around the heavily damaged Triplane in shocked silence while the mechanics led by Master Sergeant John Majors scratched their heads in awe.

Then they saw *The Reaper* painted in white on the Sopwith's black fuselage, and Lt. John Patton called out, "Attention men, this is your commander, Colonel Thomas!"

"At ease, gentlemen!" whispered Duke as he jumped from the cockpit and pulled off his fur-lined leather helmet and gloves while returning the men's salute. The old and new faces gathered eagerly around him.

Duke said, "John, they damaged my new girl pretty bad, but I sent four of the enemy to the scrap yard!"

The whole group broke out in laughter and began cheering, "Huzzah! Huzzah! Huzzah!" and surrounded Duke with back slaps and handshakes as they headed for the Officers' Club.

"The first round's on me, boys!" Duke said to another series of cheers as he eased into a table while the barman poured a large neat Lagavulin scotch as if he already had been briefed on the needs of his commander.

The Officers' Club was in an old barn covered inside with trophies of air battles and downed enemy aircraft. It included enemy Spandau machine guns, props that were being used as fans, and rotary enemy engines converted into light fixtures. Many German imperial black crosses cut from downed aircraft lined the walls, as well as serial numbers cut from the cotton fabric which covered the aircraft.

The squadron mascot, a nearly full-grown lion, named Junior, paced the floor, occasionally rubbing the legs of his favorite pilots. He seemed to be drawn to Duke as he settled in behind his stool and quickly dozed off with Duke gently rubbing his thick yellow mane. Duke poured the dark brown smokey scotch into his dry mouth, and as it filled his palate with peaty flavor, it also burned his adrenaline-soaked body into a temporary state of relaxation while he got to know the talented members of the 94th squadron.

He had assembled the most talented squadron of American pilots in France, including Lt. Eddie Rickenbacker, whose reputation as a race driver matched his skill in the sky.

He excitedly told Duke, "Yes, sir. One day, I will have as many victories as you, Colonel Thomas!" in his heavy American-Swiss-German accent.

Duke laughed and said, "I sure hope so, Ed, but until you do, I want you to fly as my wingman, keep my tail free from trouble, and watch what I do! The Nieuport 28s of our 'Hat in the Ring' squadron are no match for the Fokker DR1 Triplanes, but with good skills, we can win!"

Lieutenants John Patton and Jimmy Franklin broke into the conversation excitedly, congratulating Duke on his last four kills that had just been confirmed by Allied observers on the front. "Congratulations, Colonel!" both men shouted as they slammed their pints on the oak planking of the Duke's table and shouted to the exuberant pilots, "Add four more kills for the 'Hat in the Ring' 94th squadron on the board and the Colonel's tally! Now he has 19!!"

The pilots began shouting and cheering even louder as they embraced the accomplishments of their leader as validation of their hard work over the past month. It was as if the invincible Hercules or perhaps Alexander the Great had just landed in their midst.

After the pilots calmed down, Duke pulled the two men aside and asked them to be flight leaders of A and B flights and to choose their members. He explained to his old friends that they had urgent orders to provide air cover to the retreating Allied forces as they moved closer to Villers where they hoped to stop the German onslaught. The two men excitedly spread out among the pilots and formed their flights with take-off scheduled for first light after a 0500 briefing.

Master Sergeant and chief mechanic for the 94th, Fred Jones, slipped into the celebration and whispered into the Colonel's ear that he could have three flights of Nieuport 28s ready for the morning flight but that Duke's Sopwith was going to need more time.

Duke smiled and said, "Fred, I'm so glad you are running the show, and I'm sorry for what you went through on the front lines."

With tears forming in his eyes, Fred said, "I'm honored to be in your squadron, Colonel, since I know we are going to take the fight to the Huns! The bastards gassed and gunned down wounded men in no man's land, and now after that hell, I know how to handle anything! I'm just happy to be alive, and thank you for remembering me!"

"I know how to take care of my talented, loyal crew, and as long as I'm the Commanding Officer, I won't forget what you and the other men have done! But I need you to get *The Reaper* flyable for our first squadron mission together to keep the morale and esprit de corps strong. We need to also add more ammunition since the factory added a second Vickers gun to her but didn't add extra ammo capacity," said Duke.

His piercing blue eyes were confident and seemed to penetrate Fred's reluctance, inspiring him to a greater effort.

"Yes, sir, I will personally take care of her, even if it takes ALL night!" replied Fred as he hustled back to the busy maintenance hangar with renewed motivation.

"And Fred, add anti-personnel bombs to all aircraft and full loads of ammo to each flight. We will need it. I saw more grey uniforms than ever moving toward us. They looked like ants, and we have to slow their progress," said Duke.

"Yes, sir!" replied Fred as he rushed to the hangers, ready for a long night.

CHAPTER 24 • FIRST BLOOD

As the first streaks of orange and red filled the eastern sky, one flight after another from the "Hat in the Ring" American 94th squadron lifted off from the grassy Chateau Albert airfield and sprang toward the front, following Duke in *The Reaper*.

They sounded like a swarm of angry hornets as the combined roar of the rotary engines echoed off the ancient oaks surrounding the rectangular airfield and slowly faded into the distance.

Fred and his exhausted crews had worked nonstop all night. They completely replaced two cylinders of the Gnome engine while patching fabric and splicing broken wooden wing ribs, replacing the destroyed windshield, and finally adding another ammo container. The engine was successfully test run less than an hour before the scheduled take-off in *The Reaper*. The crews filed into the enlisted barracks and dropped into an exhausted sleep, even skipping breakfast. They knew the loud noise of rotary engines would wake them in less than two hours for more work as the fighters returned from the front.

Duke watched proudly as the three flights formed tightly around their flight leaders, who spread them into line abreast as they approached the area Duke had crossed along the fluid frontlines last evening. They flashed over blue-colored French troops who crowded the choked roads, pushing toward the rear lines in exhausted slow motion as enemy shells landed randomly around and among the men. Duke realized he needed to silence those guns. They were being directed by several enemy balloons he saw floating in the distance. But first, they needed to slow the rapidly approaching German troops.

The squadron was spread out like the fingers of a hand to cover the rear of the French withdrawal and immediately began firing as groups of German soldiers began firing into the fast-moving Nieuports. It was like watching wheat being harvested as grey forms fell while muzzle flashes winked from all enemy quadrants.

Duke saw one of the Nieuports of A flight peel away, trailing smoke as he lined up with his wingman Ed on two large field guns, rapidly firing at the defenseless French troop withdrawal. Duke dropped one of his bombs on the first pass, taking out the larger of the two field guns. As they pulled hard to line up on the second pass, Ed dropped his last bomb on the anti-aircraft battery, which took it out of action and allowed Duke to drop his last bomb directly on the second gun, ending its death-dealing.

Duke now raced toward the first of the three balloons and, despite picking up hits from the heavy anti-aircraft fire, exploded the gas bag with his burning tracer rounds on his first pass as the observer jumped safely away under his parachute. The next two followed quickly as the observers bailed out before Duke arrived, and he sent both down in flames then climbed for safety.

Duke smiled as he saw Ed glued to his wing and the other members of his flight following closely, and then it happened again. A sixth sense warned Duke to check the rising sun as the hair on his neck suddenly stood on end. He saw many dark specs diving toward his flight, and he wagged his wings, pointing skyward to warn his flight.

He immediately turned into the enemy, which caught them by surprise as his flight fired first, sending one Triplane crashing into the muddy dark earth as one of his Nieuports from B flight began trailing smoke with a bright red and white Triplane glued to its tail.

Duke turned hard as his vision briefly greyed under the G forces, but the Sopwith Triplane turned on a dime. He fired a long-range burst of machine-gun fire into a yellow Fokker that exploded as the incendiary rounds found the fuel tank.

Two more Fokker Triplanes flashed by, firing on John Patton's Nieuport 28, which was trapped at treetop level and already shedding fabric despite his hard turns left and right. Round after round, bullets crashed into his wings. Duke pulled hard on his control stick, going up into the tightest Immelman loop and half roll of his life, and he briefly lost sight of the dogfight as he fired a burst on top of the loop at a black checkered Fokker Triplane which filled his gun sight momentarily.

He saw its engine ignite in flames as he rolled out in the Immelman maneuver, diving at combat power after the two enemy aircraft on John's tail. He knew John was done for if he didn't clear his tail quickly, and he once again fired at long-range and watched his bright yellow tracer rounds rake both Fokker's, sending one down in flames and causing the other to break off its attack.

John looked back, rocking his wings in thanks as Duke locked onto the surviving plane whose pilot looked desperately over his shoulder. At the same time, Duke fired a burst of twin Vickers machine-gun fire into the bright black and white Fokker as they streaked back toward the front lines and the relative safety of the Chateau Albert airfield. The German tried to turn right, then left back toward the German side of the lines, but each time, Duke fired tracer rounds across his nose and pointed toward the Allied lines.

They were now at treetop level as they raced over the heads of the cheering French army, now no longer under artillery fire.

They reached the airfield, and the Fokker made one more desperate turn for his lines. Duke fired into his rotary Oberursel 110hp engine, putting it out of commission, and the Fokker crash-landed on the field and was quickly surrounded by American troops as the dejected but uninjured pilot was captured and escorted off the field.

Duke saw the rest of the squadron was back on the airfield, and his spirits were high on adrenaline and survival. He pulled up into a loop and then streaked across the airfield, making six victory rolls for his three balloons and three Fokker Triplane kills this morning.

He landed and could hear the men cheering as his fierce Gnome 9-cylinder 160hp radial coughed angrily to silence. He pushed himself up and out of the cockpit while shedding his bearskin flying suit, revealing his flying jacket with an American flag sewn into the right sleeve and DT monogrammed on his silk scarf.

His Victoria Cross shone brightly around his neck as he unzipped the warm leather calfskin flying jacket. His smile of success was contagious as the men surrounded him and lifted Duke to their shoulders, carrying him to the Officers' Club.

The 94th squadron had scored a mighty victory.

Duke heard from Jimmy Franklin that he had destroyed one enemy aircraft without any losses but had two damaged planes in his flight. John Patton had recovered from his close call and was deep into his drink but excitedly said his was the only damaged aircraft. His flight had sent two Triplanes down and were awaiting confirmation. Duke's flight had suffered no damage other than his aircraft, which Fred rushed in to tell him would take the rest of the day to repair but should be ready for combat again in the morning. Duke grabbed his maintenance officer and thanked him while calling to the barman to bring over a pint of well-earned Guinness for his friend.

Major Carpenter, who was Executive Officer (XO), rushed over to tell Duke that five of his six victories were confirmed as well as two of the three other victories from A and B flight, giving the squadron a total of seven victories today and four from Duke's flight yesterday. When the eleven total victories were posted on the squadron Victory Board, the pilots began singing "God Bless America!"

The German pilot Duke brought down over the field sat silently in the corner with two Gurkha guards posted at the Officers' Club entrance. Duke walked over to speak with him as the German Lieutenant jumped to attention, saluting him, and in broken English, thanked him for not shooting him down in flames.

Duke smiled and said, "Relax, Lieutenant, and have a seat. Tell me how my friend Captain Max von Wagner is doing?"

Duke then turned to the barman Sergeant Murphy and said, "Sarge, bring our guest a pint of your best ale, and I need a large Lagavulin Scotch up neat!"

"Yes, sir!" responded Sergeant Murphy with a smile, quickly bringing the much-needed drinks over.

As both men began to relax at the battered table with large sips of their respective beverages, the German Fokker pilot, Lt. Goethe, said, "Colonel, your reputation precedes you, and it is an honor to meet you. Although, I wish I could be buying your drink at our squadron bar."

They both laughed and took another sip as Lt. Goethe cautiously watched Junior walk over and sit beside Duke. The lion groaned in contentment as Duke rubbed his mane.

"Captain Wagner has his own squadron close to Flanders, although you may see him in this sector soon due to our recent success as Captain Richthofen has asked for reinforcements. I am a flight leader in his squadron, but he wasn't involved in the recent engagement. He is just now returning from leave and will not be happy with our results today," said the German Lieutenant.

"I'm sure he won't, and I look forward to meeting him over the front as soon as possible!" said Duke with a smile.

He enjoyed another deep swallow of the dark peaty scotch while Lt. Goethe tipped his beer up and finished with a deep satisfying swallow.

"I hope your visit with us has been relaxing, and I wish your future confinement to be short and comfortable. Unfortunately, I must return to my duties," said Duke as he stood up.

The German pilot sprang to his feet and saluted him, and he headed to his office, following Major Carpenter, who told him he had an urgent phone call from HQ.

General "JJ" Grant was on the phone and said excitedly, "Well done, Colonel! The French Army commanders said the 94th knocked out several balloons and guns which were harassing their withdrawal and that now the enemy has stopped advancing in your sector. I also understand you personally led the squadron and shot down all the balloons and three of the hated Fokker Triplanes of the Red Baron's group! Did you get the red devil himself yet?"

"No, sir, but we really damaged their Flying Circus! After speaking with Lt. Goethe, the pilot I brought down over our airfield, I understand Captain Richthofen is returning from leave, and Captain Wagner will also be moving his group here from Flanders. We should have good hunting and will bring the Baron down soon!" said Duke with the fire of combat still pumping through his veins.

"Well, I hope you kill the bastard," said General JJ Grant. "I'm recommending the 94th for a unit citation with recognition from both the French and American forces. You will be honored for meritorious and gallant service during the Ludendorff Offensive and helping save the French during their withdrawal and contributing to stopping the offensive in your sector!"

"Thank you, sir, I will inform the men!" responded Duke.

"One last thing, Colonel Thomas, I'm recommending you for the American Distinguished Service Cross, and the French

General, Ferdinand Foch, would personally like to award you a second bar to the Legion of Honor and Croix de Guerre. You are to report to HQ in Paris in three weeks to receive these honors, followed by a fortnight frontal tour of the other American squadrons to help train them to your standards. Is there anything I can do to help the best American squadron on the front?" said JJ Grant in a fatherly tone.

"Thank you, sir, for these great honors, although I would prefer to give them to my whole squadron. Yes, sir, we could desperately use the latest SPAD XIII fighters since our Nieuport 28s are outclassed and worn out," said Duke humbly.

"I will get them to your squadron before any other Americans receive them, but I understand there is a 2-month production backlog, so can you hold out until then?" said the General.

"Of course, sir. I know Tommy Sopwith can produce his specially-modified triplane for us immediately, and it is my personal favorite. If we could get a dozen of those to add to our current inventory, I know we will make the Germans pay dearly!" pleaded Duke.

After a short pause, General JJ Grant replied, "Consider it done. By the time you leave for Paris in three weeks, a dozen Sopwith triplanes will be on their way! Keep up the good work, Colonel." And with those final words, the line went dead.

Major Keith Carpenter had heard most of the conversation and stood with his mouth open as Duke eased himself into a leather office chair. He leaned back and put his spit-polished but muddy boots up on the heavy oak table and gazed around the cluttered squadron office. It was lined with dark wood paneling, and it was covered in old hunting paintings and mounted stag trophies from the days when the Chateau was one of Louis XIII's favorites.

Duke reached over to the dark wooden cabinet behind him, opening several doors until he found two heavy crystal tumblers and a decanter, which he filled from his bottle of Lagavulin he had stashed yesterday on arrival.

He poured a generous neat glass for each man and stood up.

"Here's to the 94th!" bellowed Duke.

"Here's to you, Colonel!" responded Major Carpenter as they both downed a large swallow of the precious dark nectar.

"Assemble the men after lunch for the announcement of our first unit awards," Duke said. "My Triplane is out of commission, so Major, I want you leading the squadron this afternoon on another sweep of the same area. Put Jimmy Franklin's flight as high top cover and give those Huns hell! Unfortunately, I have to deal with this mountain of paperwork and supervise the repair of my bird," said Duke as he realized his victory total now stood at 24.

"Yes, sir! And thank you, sir!" shouted Keith as he rushed bright-faced to the door to begin making preparations.

CHAPTER 25 • *The Reaper*

Three weeks flew by as Duke worked non-stop, running the squadron, flying patrols, and handling media requests for interviews as his score of aerial victories continued to mount. He relished the mail each day as Juliette wrote frequently, updating him on her maternity and arrival back in Paris, despite his pleas for her to remain in London in case the German offensive on other parts of the front was successful. He also had to write several sad letters home to the United States, informing families of the loss of loved ones who had been killed in combat while serving in his squadron.

Late April 1918 was warming up, and as it did, the trees and flowers began to show their spring rebirth, and Duke began to hear the birds singing again, despite the roar of field guns in the distance each morning. He had time for a final mission before heading to Paris for his award presentation the following day and, most importantly, to see his beloved Juliette.

"Fred, let's get *The Reaper* ready for one last patrol over the front before I leave early tomorrow," said Duke as he rushed from the mess hall to his office on April 21st, 1918.

"Yes, sir!" replied the crack mechanic.

Duke erupted into his office, scattering his orderly and secretary to collect various documents he needed to sign authorizing leave, promotions, and awards to his talented squadron pilots before he left for a fortnight.

"Major Carpenter, you will be in command until I return.

You are becoming a crack pilot, and now with four victories, you will be an ace before I return, so keep up the good work! And don't forget, I want to know when the Sopwith Triplanes arrive so I can inform General Grant," said Duke.

He rushed to finish up last-minute details before joining the morning patrol, which was already warming up with a cascade of sound in the cool morning mist of the airfield.

"Yes, sir. I will let you know as soon as they arrive," snapped the Major. He had already answered this same question repeatedly for the past several days as his commander prepared to leave his beloved squadron and turn things over to his proud Executive Officer.

Duke left the stuffy, bustling office, and with the help of his batman, donned his bearskin flight suit and leather flight jacket. He added the monogrammed silk scarf that his mother had hand-stitched for him. He always wore his Victoria Cross with bars on its red ribbon tightly around his neck with pride and, of course, Alexander the Great's oversized gold coin for luck.

Even though it felt brisk on the ground this bright misty early spring morning, it would be brutally cold at patrol altitude. In preparation, Duke took a last long gulp of his steaming Turkish coffee, handed the mug to his orderly, and walked out to his warming plane.

The group of patrol pilots gathered around him expectantly for a last word. He assigned close cover for this mission to John Patton, who was B flight leader. Duke's flight would provide top cover for the three reconnaissance RE8 two-seaters that the 94th squadron had been assigned to protect on this critical photo mission of the front line. The massive German offensive was stalling, and HQ needed to know where to try and hold the new allied frontal position as US forces finally began arriving in large numbers.

Duke said, "Gentlemen, this is the time for us to show

them what we are made of. The Germans are desperate and will throw everything they have at us. I just got word from intelligence that the Red Baron's Flying Circus is now up to full strength in this sector, so today, we may get to bag the rascal and some of his men. Flight leaders, keep your formations tight. And wingmen, don't lose your leaders. Now let's give them hell!"

With that word of encouragement, the smiling men dispersed like a covey of quail and climbed into their waiting Nieuport 28s as the chorus of Gnome 160hp, 9-cylinder rotary engines throbbed off the thick ancient forest surrounding the large green rectangular airfield. It sounded like a chorus of angry buffalo waiting to stampede into the sky.

Duke strapped on his pulsating Sopwith Triplane, and as his orderly handed his shoulder straps to him, he inhaled the warm smell of burning aviation fuel while the prop wash stretched his white silk scarf toward *The Reaper's* dancing rudder. He pulled his fur-lined glass flying goggles over his ice-blue eyes to keep the castor oil, which lubricated not only the engine but the pilot as well, at bay. After a brisk salute to Major Carpenter, who stood with the other non-flying pilots watching and waving their hats in support, Duke gave *The Reaper* the good news and felt her jump down the runway for a fast takeoff.

There was a festive mood in the air as the pilots watched Duke lead the squadron in a trail of mist off the airfield like a herd of wild horses charging toward the front.

The men all seemed to sense something momentous was in the air, but would it mean good results for the 94th, or would some men fail to return?

The experienced flights spread out as they climbed while holding loose formation to give the anti-aircraft gunners more spread-out targets. Despite their efforts, the flak burst close, bouncing the squadron around like kites on a string until they cleared the confusing front line where the offensive remained in flux.

The observation RE8s were large clumsy two-seat Biplanes in which the observer and aircraft commander sat up front taking photos and navigating and the pilot sat in the back. The flight was spread out like a trident taking photos of the front lines and beyond. Duke, John, and the rest of the squadron looked around for the expected Fokkers of the Flying Circus.

It was cold and hypoxic at eighteen thousand feet, which was top cover altitude for Duke in his Sopwith Triplane, but the rest of his flight couldn't quite reach the full altitude in their worn-out Nieuport 28 Biplanes.

The steady hum of the Gnome radial engine running full throttle to hold altitude, combined with the insidious hypobaric hypoxia that created a lack of oxygen, ate away at Duke's alertness, and he felt himself slipping toward sleep. He slapped his red cheeks with his thick fur-lined gloves while singing Dixie at the top of his lungs to try and remain alert as the squadron penetrated deeper and deeper into enemy territory.

It was time to turn back as they reached the limit of their fuel supply and the point of no return. Duke felt relieved as the photo recon planes took the last of their critical photos, and the squadron finally turned for home.

This was their most vulnerable point, and the headwind they faced would make the long trip back even longer. And then, as had occurred each time before since Duke returned from Egypt, he felt an impending sense of danger send tingling pulses through his spine. He looked vigorously around, expecting to see the enemy, but due to the building cumulus clouds below between the two flights, his field of view was restricted.

He instinctively dove with his flight through the puffy white turbulent clouds and burst out just in time to see a large gaggle of multicolored Fokker Triplanes, led by a blood-red DR1 Triplane with commander's streamers trailing off each wing, dive toward the critical reconnaissance RE8 Biplanes.

Duke fell like a stooping falcon as he pushed *The Reaper* to the limit. He flew above the dangerous red line speed as he streaked toward the trailing black and white checkerboard colored Fokker Triplane at the rear of the flight. He calmly lined up and pulled the trigger of his twin .303 Vickers machine guns and watched the tracers disappear into the engine and root, which collapsed.

The Triplane's left wing tumbled away like a butterfly wing as the remainder of the Triplane spiraled straight toward earth, fourteen thousand feet below. Duke made brief eye contact with the pilot, who had just turned wide-eyed looking at his killer; his desperate eyes would soon close permanently. Humans didn't have the fierce fearlessness of the raptor's eyes which, even with severe injuries or on the brink of death, looked proud and free to the end.

The rest of the Fokkers exploded like a covey of quail. It seemed that all the squadron had locked onto enemy aircraft (EA), and Duke saw several Fokkers trailing smoke as he lined up one whose pilot displayed remarkable skill. He turned into Duke's Sopwith Triplane, causing him to overshoot and miss his target.

Duke was in a vulnerable position as the two pilots pulled hard on their elevators and turned into each other while staring into each other's eyes at less than 50 feet, hoping the other would make a mistake. The positive G forces pulled Duke hard into his wooden cockpit seat, and his vision began to tunnel in the telltale signs of impending G lock. He tensed his belly and screamed Dixie at the top of his lungs, trying to keep the blood from draining entirely from his head, which would cause him to blackout and end up like his last victim: a smoking hole in the French countryside.

Duke knew his aircraft could perform better due to the larger engine the Sopwith factory had installed but also realized the extra weight caused him to be unable to turn as tightly as his talented adversary. So, right before he reached the limit of his G tolerance and just as he saw a burst of tracers pass his left wing, he reversed his turn and pulled hard up into a vertical climb as he began a hammerhead maneuver.

The confused German pilot, who couldn't hope to stay with him in this vertical plane, turned and dove away. Duke kicked hard left rudder as his plane decelerated, bringing the nose down in a vertical dive, quickly catching the Fokker, which continued its plunge straight down. Duke pulled again on the machine gun trigger attached to the control stick while watching the tracers through his large circular metal gunsight walk up the fuselage into the engine and fuel tank, which exploded into a fireball.

No time for celebration as he found himself once again surrounded by tracer rounds while his Triplane was now approaching five thousand feet. He chopped the throttle while looking over his shoulder at the two Triplanes who had come too close in their eagerness to dispatch the nimble Sopwith.

They both flashed by in astonishment as Duke's Triplane seemed to stand on her tail, decelerating until Duke pushed her over, adding combat power. Now *The Reaper* locked onto the closer of the two Fokker Triplanes, which quickly exploded in flames under the hammering of Duke's twin Vickers machine guns.

As Duke turned to close on the other enemy aircraft, he saw that none of his squadron was around, and now he was alone and flying low at treetop level over enemy territory. He still had ammunition, and his plane was flying well despite a few holes in the wings, so he pressed his attack.

The Fokker was quick to turn as it maneuvered around tall trees and flew under a bridge lined with grey-clad enemy soldiers. They opened fire on Duke as he edged closer to his adversary while watching the water of the Somme River erupt in geysers of small arms and machine-gun fire all around his Sopwith.

But still, he pressed on until he realized this Fokker Triplane was red with squadron leader streamers flying from both struts. Could it possibly be the Red Baron? Known to be the highest-scoring and most talented pilot of the war with 80 confirmed allied kills to his credit? No time to think of that now! He tried to turn with this very talented enemy who suddenly pulled into a loop, trying to reach Duke's tail and sending a burst of machine-gun fire right past Duke's ear, exploding his windscreen.

Duke was thankful for his flight goggles and helmet as the glass fragments splashed across his face. Duke realized they were approaching the front lines when he saw an Australian flag in the distance. He knew at this altitude, neither pilot could escape, and this would be a fight to the death.

The Red Baron was now on his tail, sending burst after burst of fire with tracers seeming to shimmer off *The Reaper's* wings, despite Duke's constant turning and maneuvering. Duke's mind went blank as he realized he was under the guns of the most successful and lethal enemy fighter pilot of the first World War. Then he realized that he would never see Juliette or his unborn son if he panicked, and they needed him.

In that moment, as if a guiding hand reached out, he remembered the snap roll maneuver, which was unique to the Sopwith Triplane. Duke pulled hard on the stick while kicking full left rudder, and the world turned into a blur of motion as the Triplane twisted into two violent snap rolls at treetop level, which caused the Red Baron to overshoot and fly right past Duke as he leveled out.

As Duke's vision cleared, he realized he was now on the Baron's tail, who was shockingly momentarily level. He pressed down on the machine gun's trigger and watched the tracers and .303 Vickers machine gun rounds go right into the cockpit as both aircraft streaked over the Aussie trenches.

The Fokker seemed to shudder and fell into a sudden descent into a plowed field, where it landed intact but on its nose behind the Australian front line trenches. Then, as Duke flew over, he saw the Red Baron pull off his goggles and slowly lay his head back on the black leather headrest of his plane as if accepting his fate. Their eyes met momentarily, and sadly Duke realized that death would quickly take the world's greatest aerial fighter to Valhalla as the Aussie troops ran toward the downed aircraft.

The Baron was the first of Duke's victims to show no fear in his eyes as death was about to close them; it seemed only relief and disappointment at a life cut short filled them.

Duke was low on fuel and almost out of ammunition, so he headed at treetop level toward his airfield as his mind tried to digest the enormity of the last, most difficult, and longest aerial dogfight he had ever experienced.

He had engaged and downed four Fokker Triplanes, which

were all flown by the best pilots he had ever encountered since his combat with von Wagner in Egypt.

This must have been the renowned Red Baron's Flying Circus, and therefore, that had to be the Baron himself. He looked around at the wings through the fragments of his remaining windshield and was amazed at the damage to *The Reaper,* but still, she flew strong and true, or was there another power holding her together?

He felt again as if his life was being guided and protected by an unknown force. He had dodged death again and again while emerging victorious despite the tremendous odds against him. Had he just been victorious over the very aerial combat master himself?

There had been over a hundred enemy fighters in Egypt that he had somehow defeated on the ground and escaped from in his Sopwith Triplane. He had been outnumbered and cornered when he encountered Fokkers coming to France and repeatedly during the past month at the front and sent almost all twelve of his recent victories, including today's, to their graves, and yet, he had emerged unscathed. He now had thirty-six confirmed victories and was among the highest living Allied aces.

Now, as much as he doubted legends, Duke firmly believed that by discovering and now being the only living human to touch and possess the knowledge of the existence and location of Alexander's grave, armor, and body, he was being guided and protected. Was he the recipient of the protection and power prophesied: "Whoever possesses Alexander's body, tomb, and armor will never be defeated in battle."?

But was this a blessing or a curse? What about von Wagner, who also knew the location of the tomb? Was he likewise immune to death in combat? But he had never actually seen or touched the body, and he wasn't there when Duke found the entrance.

Should he announce his discovery to the world? His gut told him he should keep this ancient tomb and body a secret. This would prevent others from knowing about it and attempting to use this unworldly power for dark or evil purposes.

Duke's mind was racing with these thoughts as he streaked over the airfield. He decided to throw caution to the wind and answer those questions another day. Then, despite the heavy damage to *The Reaper*, he performed four flawless rolls to the cheers of his squadron before landing on the last fumes of his aviation fuel.

Major Carpenter rushed to the cockpit as the Gnome rotary coughed its last breath, and the air-cooled 9-cylinder engine began its agonizing cracking and tinking as it morosely began to cool down like a racehorse that, even though covered in sweat, was eager for more. Duke relished the sound and smell of his powerful radial as it reluctantly rested.

"Colonel, the Red Baron is dead!" shouted Major Carpenter.

Duke looked coolly into his eyes like a leopard and said sadly, "I know," and quickly added before the Major could put two and two together, "Did I lose any men today?"

"No sir, all pilots accounted for. You are the last to arrive, but we have a lot of aircraft damage, and four of our Nieuports had to crash land on our side of the line. I have sent two lorries with maintenance crews to recover them, but only mild injuries to our pilots are reported."

"John claimed two Triplanes and Jimmy one, as did one of our other new pilots, Summer Sewall. He also said that you had brought down two other Triplanes before they lost contact with you. Looks like you have a lot of damage to the Sopwith as well, sir," said Major Carpenter.

He put his finger in the bullet holes in the lower wing and looked at the destroyed windshield.

"Well, in case you can't count my rolls, add four more from me. Of course, they all have to be confirmed. That gives the squadron quite a day with eight more victories against four of our planes downed with no fatalities!"

"The first round is on me, boys!" laughed Duke as the squadron ran into the Officers' Club enthusiastically while singing *Dixie* in honor of Duke's and the 94th's high victory count.

Duke pulled up a stool at the bar while Junior ambled over and began nuzzling his leather flying boots. Duke rubbed Junior's mane while he rumbled his contentment and closed his hazel eyes, slowly licking his large paws that were already larger than a man's hand.

Sergeant Murphy, the barman, pushed a large neat Lagavulin Scotch into Duke's hands with a wink. Duke smiled at him and took a deep, burning drink that filled his palate with peaty flavor as the smoky aroma filled his nasopharynx, and the soothing burn flowed down to fill his belly and began to decompress his adrenaline-soaked mind.

Duke took a deep breath as he listened to the men who were laughing too loudly, drinking too deeply, smoking too heavily, and gesturing wildly with their hands. They showed the enemy plane with one hand and their plane with the other while demonstrating to their squadron mates the details of the morning combat and enjoying living through another mission.

All the odds were against their surviving more than a few weeks of aerial combat on the Western Front, so why not enjoy these precious moments of life to the fullest. These were his men, and he loved each and every one. He especially respected their courage, skill, and dedication to freedom while fighting tyranny in another country far from their homes and loved ones.

As the soothing dark scotch eased the morning's adrenaline rush from Duke's mind and body, John Patton came smiling as he walked over after just getting off the phone with HQ.

"Congratulations, Colonel, they have confirmed all but one of our victories this morning, and the 94th is now the highest-scoring American squadron on the front! The reconnaissance aircraft all returned with excellent photos, and we have been recommended for another unit citation," he said.

"Oh, and by the way, they have also credited you in your jet black Sopwith, *The Reaper*, with shooting down and killing Manfred von Richthofen—The Red Baron—at Vaux-sur-Somme. The Aussies gave a detailed description of the combat and have named you and your aircraft 'The Grim Reaper'!" exclaimed Lt. Patton with tears of joy and honor in his eyes.

"Colonel, you may have turned the tide in the air by destroying the greatest and most famous German Imperial aviator of the war!" shouted Jimmy Franklin from down the bar.

The men raised their glasses to honor their commander. The next thing Duke knew, his men had picked him up on their shoulders and were carrying him around the bar while singing, "For He's A Jolly Good Fellow!"

Finally, Duke was released from this circus, and after quieting the men, said, "Thank you, gentlemen. I only wish I could have brought him down alive. It was the longest, most difficult dogfight I ever experienced. He fought like the chivalrous warrior that he was and almost made me his 81st victory. I propose one final toast. To the Red Baron, may he rest in peace."

"May he rest in peace," echoed the squadron.

The Officers' Club settled into a temporary quiet as each pilot pondered his mortality and reflected on the loss of this feared but respected enemy.

Then out of the back of the Officers' Club came another toast, "And to *The Reaper*, may he continue to lead us to victory!"

The whole club erupted in, "Cheers to *The Reaper* and victory!" and the celebration continued.

Fred would paint Baron Killer in white on Duke's cowl to commemorate this epic aerial victory.

CHAPTER 26 • PARIS

The following morning Duke delayed his departure for Paris as Master Sergeant Fred Jones and his capable crew worked overtime to repair *The Reaper*. He was overwhelmed with telegrams and messages from all over the Allied world, including President Wilson who insisted he return to America to receive personally at his hand the Medal of Honor. King George V also wanted him to add another cluster to his Victoria Cross in London.

The most impressive was a message that Major Carpenter brought him. He said it had been dropped that morning by a single Red German Fokker Triplane at the 94th's squadron Chateau Albert airfield from the Baron's brother, Lt. Lothar von Richthofen. He was also a Pour le Merite (Blue Max) medal recipient and an future 40-victory ace, asking that full military honor be accorded his brother at his funeral. It also said that Manfred had admired Duke since meeting him over the front while saving his cousin's life and if he had to be shot down, then he would have been grateful to be lost to such a skilled and famous Allied pilot. It was also signed by Captain Max von Wagner who added that he had seen the final combat and was still in shock at the intensity and beauty of his cousin's final fight. He also agreed that Manfred died a hero's death after a magnificent air fight from the best Allied fighter pilot any had yet seen.

Duke collapsed in his chair in the small CO's office as tears filled his eyes at the loss of such a great fighter pilot and man by his own hand. He and all the other enemy pilots Duke had killed began filling his mind. He was responsible for countless deaths and injuries, no matter how hard he had tried to spare them. Would he forever be haunted by their loss as well as his squadron pilots during this meaningless war?

He had to do something to stop this endless bloodshed and loss of a whole generation of men, but what could he do?

Duke realized now was the time to honor the dead. He would delay yet again his departure for Paris so he could participate in this German hero's funeral and would insist on full military honors for his fallen foe.

He called his orderly and immediately dispatched a message to HQ explaining his delay, with the knowledge that they would bend over backward to accommodate him with his current notoriety. He then called Major Carpenter back into his office and said, "Major, I want to form an honor flight to overfly the burial ceremony at Captain Richthofen's funeral. It is taking place at Bertangles near Amiens. Get Jimmy, John, and yourself geared up. We leave in an hour and be sure the aircraft are fully fueled and armed."

"Yes, sir!" responded Duke's Executive Officer with a brisk salute as he realized the intensity in his Commander's voice.

Thankfully, as he had done before, Fred and his crew had worked overtime that night to repair Duke's Sopwith Triplane.

Duke walked to the flight line as the honor flight of four aircraft warmed up. He loved the sound of the large bore rotary engines barking and coughing in a muted roar as the smell of burning aviation fuel and oil filled his nostrils. A large grim reaper with a sickle was now painted in white on the black rudder of his newly repaired, overall black Sopwith Triplane with *The Reaper* painted in white on each side of the fuselage and Baron Killer on the engine cowl. Of course, Duke's Sopwith Triplane mount was sitting in the lead of the other four Nieuport 28 Biplanes, all idling and warming in the morning mist.

Duke had a word with his men and said, "Gentlemen, we go to pay honor to our gallant adversary as he is laid to rest in Bertangles. I want a tight, low-level fly-by, and we will drop a wreath as we fly over. Jimmy, you are in charge of that. I will fly lead, and as we approach the grave, I will pull up and away, creating a new formation to recognize our departed adversary—the missing man formation. You won't see me again until we return to our Chateau Albert airfield, but you are all to return here after the fly-by. Any questions?"

 honoring our gallant fallen foe

"No, sir!" they all responded and quickly ran to their warming mounts.

The morning was calm but overcast as the flight made its way to the ceremony. They arrived right after the pallbearers laid the coffin in place and the honor guard had fired three rounds. As the squadron of warbirds flew over at combat power and the wreath was dropped safely, Duke pulled up into the clouds and disappeared from the scene, performing the first missing man formation ever recorded. The officers and soldiers on the ground looked up in awe as the flight thundered away and returned to the Chateau, but Duke was not with them.

Duke climbed through the low clouds and broke out into the bright sun-splashed sky, bounding over the cloud tops shaped like sculptures of stone and otherworldly creatures. Duke mingled with the clouds and felt the rush of his amazing 120 mph speed as he flew through the misty cloud structures, which sometimes rose like hills or fell like canyons. Duke reached out and grabbed the clouds with his outstretched hand, watching the moisture roll off his glove as he rolled or looped into the fog of the clouds.

Then, he was tumbling madly out into the bright sunlight while climbing or spinning wildly back into the mist, enjoying the dangerous freedom of living in this three-dimensional space.

He closed his eyes, listening to the roar of his faithful Gnome rotary engine as he then began to climb and head east. He prayed for his fallen foe, Juliette, his unborn son, and all the men he had lost or killed during his almost year and a half of combat.

When he finally opened his eyes, his resolve had returned. He squinted into the reflected light of the morning sun that produced purple, orange, and pink hues off the misty cloud tops that now lay thousands of feet below *The Reaper*. Duke leveled into fast cruising flight and tested his guns. The familiar *"ak, ak, ak"* of the twin Vickers .303 was enough to fire his spirit and heart.

He knew what he had to do: kill the instruments of war which allowed this horrible conflict to continue and consumed his wonderful squadron mates and talented adversaries like chaff.

He felt at one with his Sopwith Triplane as the cold, thin, hypoxic air of his maximum service altitude of three and a half miles above the ground numbed his body and mind. He felt like General Nathanal Bedford Forrest, who had fought against unbeatable odds while Duke's grandfather rode with him and yet was never killed, although he was repeatedly wounded and had many horses killed beneath him.

"Get there first, with the most, and always surprise them," had said the famous General.

This rang through Duke's head as he gazed earthward from his high perch, knowing no one could be higher in the sky than he was this April morning.

The peace of the morning was an illusion. Duke knew this. He was now penetrating enemy territory at 120 mph, following an urge to fight solo against all odds.

For the first time, he felt a rage against this war, the machines of war, and against the Germans who had started it, and especially the politicians, monarchs, and generals that sustained it. All he could do for now was fight the enemy that was in front of him. This was his job and mission this morning, and he knew he was good at it.

He was reaching the point of no return when he saw far below him the specs of multiple enemy aircraft climbing toward the front. Duke began a fast steep descent, keeping the sun behind him as he fell like a black Arctic gyrfalcon on a flight of geese, but instead, it was the unsuspecting multicolored German Fokker Triplanes of The Red Baron's Flying Circus.

He was screaming toward the unsuspecting enemy, which began to form a tight battle formation. As they filled his windscreen and gun sight, Duke waited until the last moment and then pulled the machine gun trigger and watched as the flaming tracer rounds plowed into the last of the Triplanes.

It exploded into a mist of debris as the explosive tracer shells hit the fuel tank. Duke then pulled back on the stick and watched his tracers rake the length of the second and third unsuspecting Fokkers, which both fell away trailing fire and smoke, spinning madly to a terrible death. In Duke's anger and frenzy of fire, he felt he was killing the instruments of war, not the men that flew them.

The other Triplanes broke in all directions like a gaggle of geese when they saw the destruction of their brothers.

Duke latched onto the tail of the closest Triplane, painted a gaudy green and black. *Lena* was painted on the tail. He fired point-blank into the fuel tank and engine, which ignited into flames. It caught the castor oil-soaked cotton fabric, which blazed like a torch as the pilot flung himself from the flaming inferno to fall, spinning like a windmill to his death.

The killing was a blood fury that now filled Duke's brain. He fired again and again as planes flashed through his gunsight and field of view. He watched aircraft parts explode from his targets. He recalled countless mornings spent wing shooting at his family plantation on the coast of Georgia. He was a crack shot, often dropping two and sometimes even three swift flying teal or wood ducks with a single shot. Now he felt the same, as if he was on a bird hunt. He lost count of his victims and success in the blood lust of destroying the enemy, killing the war against his country and friends by destroying the machines of war that propagated it.

He felt like his innate shooting skills and flying was being guided by an unseen power, which caused him to lose touch with space and time and to become Shiva the Destroyer of these deadly tools of war.

When lined up for another shot, the now-familiar Alexander the Great warning instincts went off in his brain. Instead of firing at the Fokker in front of him, Duke pulled hard on his aircraft's joystick, sending waves of darkness through his eyes as the positive G forces drained the blood from his brain.

He heard the *"ak, ak, ak"* of machine guns firing behind him. As his vision returned, he saw the tracers just miss him. Two planes in tight formation flashed under his fuselage as he pulled into a vertical climb, then after kicking hard right rudder, he dove after them, turning the hunters into prey.

Duke latched onto the tail of the wingman, who turned and looked at him with cold shock in his eyes. He instinctually pulled the trigger and watched the black and blue checkered plane disintegrate as the .303 tracer rounds hit the fuel tank.

The leader, who trailed red and white flight commander streamers from each strut, flew a red and white Fokker DR1 Tri-plane with a black skull and crossbones on each side of his fuselage. He turned hard left and right, performing perfectly executed rolls trying to shake *The Reaper*, which stalked him and closed in to killing range.

Then, in desperation, the Fokker pulled hard into a blur of a snap roll and a half followed by a pull into a split S maneuver, which almost threw Duke as the Fokker raced toward the ground.

He had never seen another enemy pilot perform this ma-neuver, which had saved him before. But he seemed to be able to sense the moves of his opponent beforehand. He tenaciously stayed on his tail after pulling into a half roll followed by a hard pull into a split S toward the ground, right behind his enemy.

Now, as the dogfight reached treetop level, the enemy played his last desperate trick and pulled up into a perfectly executed Im-melman maneuver, a half loop and half roll. As Duke admired his skill, the twin Spandau machine-gun fire of the Fokker, which now was headed directly toward him, raked Duke's Sopwith Triplane.

Duke watched the flashes of the enemy's machine guns while holes appeared in his fuselage and wings. It shocked Duke back into the reality of life and death. They raced toward each other head-to-head at over 240mph in a nerve-testing, head-on firing pass.

Duke held his fire until the last second as he knew he was low on ammunition. He let out a rebel yell, "Yee-haw!" and held his course, determined not to flinch or pull up; he knew this would expose his Triplane to deadly enemy fire. Finally, he pressed down on the trigger, listening to the belching machine-gun fire as he spewed hit after hit into the Fokker, which pulled hard right at the last second to avoid a midair impact.

Duke pulled hard over the top into a half loop followed by a half roll and followed his quarry, which amazingly was still flying straight and level. Unfortunately, Duke's trusty Triplane was beginning to vibrate as he surveyed the damage from the German's head-on onslaught. The right wing was heavily damaged, but Duke knew he had to finish the kill while he had the chance and once again lined up for the coup de grâce.

Then, the fog of war began to lift from Duke's blood-fever-soaked brain. He realized this was Captain Max von Wagner, now a forty-five-victory ace who had once spared him in Egypt, and he also knew the man as a talented Ph.D. ancient linguist.

He was also the only other living man on the planet who knew the location of Alexander's tomb. Perhaps Duke was being given this opportunity to destroy him for a reason? But that went against his deeply ingrained Southern sense of honor and chivalry. This, he knew, was the moment of truth.

He filled the gunsight. His finger shook on the trigger with his friend (and enemy at the moment) directly under his guns. Hadn't Max just shot up his Sopwith in an attempt to kill him? But in the fog of war, he had also tried to kill Max, who would already be dead with his fellow Flying Circus pilots if he weren't one of the best pilots Duke had ever fought against.

As he hesitated, Max looked back, and to Duke's astonishment, raised his right hand and tried to raise his left in the air in the universal sign of surrender.

Duke took a deep breath and slowly removed his trembling finger from the trigger as he pulled up alongside him. He then pulled the trigger to fire off a burst of fire in recognition of his surrender but heard nothing as his guns were empty, and he was out of ammunition.

He removed his goggles and pointed with his hand to the Allied side of the line, and Max nodded his head in agreement and saluted as did Duke, and then bowed his head. *So, this was the way it was meant to end,* thought Duke as once again fate or some greater power had decided his immediate future.

The men flew in close formation across the battered, muddy brown front lines as Duke struggled to keep *The Reaper* in the air. Max seemed to fly unsteadily as well. The small arms and anti-aircraft fire were strangely silent since neither side wanted to risk shooting down their own.

It was a relief to leave the dank smell of death, which filled the sky above the front. Many bodies and body parts lay unrecovered and unburied in no man's land in the valley of death below them.

Duke was dangerously low on fuel and out of ammunition but insisted, using hand signals to Max, that he should land first as he appeared pale and perhaps wounded and was flying unevenly.

Max's landing was awful. He wiped out the undercarriage and landing gear and came to a stop on his nose. Duke circled, hoping his fuel would hold out a little longer. Finally, after he saw the medics remove Max from his heavily damaged Fokker, Duke threw caution to the wind and flew two passes, completing a total of nine rolls, one for each of his estimated victories this morning.

Then he landed the battered but still growling and proud Sopwith.

He slowly rolled to the hanger, the Gnome 160hp engine hissing and popping after Duke switched the magnetos off. He leaned his head back on the black leather headrest and closed his eyes in relief. He said a silent prayer of thanks for his survival and for those souls *The Reaper* had sent to an early grave.

When he opened his eyes, he found himself surrounded by his men, who silently saluted and then broke out in cheers as they carried him on their shoulders to the Officers' Club for a thorough debriefing.

Duke removed his gloves, reached under his silk scarf and below his Victoria cross, and grasped the gold oversized Alexander the Great coin, which he always wore. He gently rubbed it and felt an incredible peace and power.

His men were now cheering and singing: "For he's a jolly good fellow, for he's a jolly good fellow!" The men placed him at his favorite battered table beside a foggy window that faced the airfield. Junior quickly joined him, softly growling under Duke's firm petting as he reached up and licked Duke's hand in affection.

Duke took in the moment and the ambiance of the club. He looked at the German Imperial crosses hanging from the ceiling along with the enemy Spandau machine guns, props, and other trophies of aerial combat that the squadron had accumulated as their victories quickly mounted. And now, sitting beside his Sopwith at the edge of the Chateau's airfield was a shot up Fokker DR1 Triplane belonging to one of the most successful enemy aces of the war!

This only added to the mystique of Duke's squadron and leadership. He felt Junior nuzzle up against his calf. He reached down to rub the lion's thick yellow mane. Junior let out a deep but contented growl, sending shivers through the other pilots and causing Sergeant Murphy to hesitate mid-stride with Duke's scotch.

Junior and Duke had developed a bond only found in a wild lion pride, and he hoped to keep him after the war.

Duke laughed, "Don't worry, Murph. He won't hurt you! But I might if you don't get that drink over here!" The whole club exploded in laughter.

Duke took a deep mouthful of scotch. It flowed along his palate and tongue while the peaty flavor burned its way down into his stomach, allowing him to take a deep breath as the blood fever slowly slipped from his brain.

A smile crossed his lips for the first time in far too long as the nectar entered his bloodstream, and he absorbed the reality of one more day of survival and life. He remembered the engraving on the tomb in Crete, which contained the Alexander medal now hanging under his silk shirt. The same medal that Alexander himself had worn. It was also the clue that led Duke to discover Alexander's tomb and power. Duke knew he had to live every day to its fullest since it might be his last.

Let the boys enjoy this moment of victory with me, Duke thought, *as it brings glory to our squadron and eliminates more dangerous enemy aircraft to deal with on our next mission.* Duke looked at his men with a smile of contentment.

Duke shouted, "The next round's on me boys!"

The club shook with cheers as Lieutenants Jimmy Franklin and John Patton pulled up beside him with full pints of Guinness beer foaming and overflowing onto the table. They kept a watchful eye on Junior as they pushed Duke to spill his combat patrol.

The whole club was silent as Duke stood up and described his last fantastic enemy engagement. He left out the sixth sense he now possessed and attributed to his discovery of Alexander's tomb and the associated prophecy.

He hoped the story of his recent victories would help his squadron learn to watch their six and not fall prey to attacks out of

248

the sun as he had proven over and over can be lethal.

As he finished describing his aerial combat with the surrender of Max, Major Carpenter came in.

He shouted, "Colonel, the French front-line observers called in to say a black American Triplane had destroyed 11 German aircraft in single combat and escorted a damaged Fokker across the lines!"

The whole room exploded in cheers. The Major then whispered in Duke's ear that Captain Wagner's condition was critical, and he had asked to speak with him. Duke shouted to Sergeant Murphy to bring Junior a ham bone, then he downed his scotch and rushed to the medical tent.

Duke found Max pale with a chest wound, heavily bandaged. He spoke with the airfield medic since the French doctor had recently died of the flu after attending to patients at the Spanish flu-infested field hospital outside Paris. The medic explained that his left lung had collapsed, and the German Captain was dying.

Duke lunged at the medic, pinning him to the center post of the medical tent, and screamed, "Why haven't you put in a chest tube and called for evacuation to Paris where he can get proper care?"

"Sir!" gasped the medic. "He's a Hun, and we don't have chest tubes here or evacuation available due to the offensive! All the roads are full of our troops. I don't know how to put a chest tube in, anyway."

Duke took a deep breath, released the medic, and said to him, "Staff Sergeant Tucker, we do have blood here, so start a drip in both arms."

Duke saw Major Keith Carpenter had just arrived and was frozen in place at the sight of so much blood around the German Captain's bed.

"Get me Master Sergeant Jones, ASAP!" Duke shouted at him.

"Yes, sir," croaked Keith as he ran for the mechanic.

Duke leaned over and whispered, "Max, hold on, I can help you through this," as he squeezed his hand and got a feeble response.

No wonder he surrendered, thought Duke. He realized he had inflicted this wound in their last head-on firing pass.

Jonesy ran in, and Duke said, "I need a trochar with a clear tube attached to it now! Soak it in grain alcohol and get me a bucket full of water. Also, bring me alcohol!"

Sergeant Jones didn't hesitate. "Yes, sir!" He knew his commander well enough to know when to question and when to jump, and now he jumped and was back in less than five minutes with the supplies.

Duke had once watched his physician father save a farmer's life who had a collapsed lung after being kicked in the chest by an ornery field mule. He tried to follow the same process.

First, he exposed the left chest below the through and through gunshot wound close to the clavicle and wiped it down with grain alcohol until he found the second rib interspace right below the left armpit. Then, after washing his hands in the alcohol as the field medic, Allen Tucker, silently winced at the waste of good booze on a Hun, he cut the skin over the top of the second rib with a scalpel from the field kit.

Then, when Duke saw the white periosteum of the rib shining through, he grabbed the sharp trocar which Sargent Jones had delivered and forced it in just above the rib. Suddenly, a loud pop was heard, and as Duke told the medic to place the other end of the tube into the bucket of water, air began bubbling out of the line, and then dark blood followed until the water was black with the old blood.

Max opened his eyes fully and smiled at Duke as he secured the improvised chest tube with tape and bandages while the blood flowed into both arms. He was weak but alive, and now he could breathe again with both lungs since Duke had released the tension pneumothorax in his collapsed lung.

Duke stared at the staff sergeant who smirked at his commander and said, "What a waste of good alcohol."

Duke looked at the medic and turned to Major Carpenter, "I want him out of here today and transferred to front line service! Maybe there he will learn to respect our enemy as fellow men and treat all wounded soldiers equally!"

Major Carpenter cleared his throat and said, "Sir, that may be a problem."

"Why!" responded Duke as he struggled to control his anger at the medic who was violating the basic rule of his Hippocratic oath: 'First, do no harm.'

"Sir, this is General Grant's nephew who was assigned here at his specific request with instructions for us to assist him in all necessary ways. Evidently, he was kicked out of West Point due to problems with other assignments and alcohol," whispered Keith as the Sergeant scowled at Duke.

"I don't care if he is President Wilson's son, Major! I want him out of my squadron! And get Captain Wagner medically evacuated to Paris for proper care!" said Duke as he stormed from the tent.

Duke didn't bother to look at the medic as he walked quickly to his office to deal with squadron affairs, reports, and finish packing for Paris. It had been a surreal couple of days, and he longed for rest and peace from the raging conflict that engulfed his life and world.

Duke burst into his office, running out his secretary as he worked ruthlessly at his battered desk, filling out his combat report and claims for another twelve aerial victories as well as the other critical paperwork stacked on his desk. He now had forty-eight confirmed victories, including one captured Fokker Triplane and was still alive to talk about it. *How can I continue at this pace,* thought Duke as the visions of fiery aircraft and dead enemy pilots began to overflow his mind.

Duke leaned back, took a deep long relaxing breath, and gazed out the window at the runway, longing to hold Juliette and feel his growing son swimming in her womb. He wanted to make the world a better place for him and finish the job here, as his squadron fought like tigers to win air superiority over the aggressive Imperial German Air Force in this contested section of the front.

Today, he felt like he had made a dent in taking better control of the skies over the front. Perhaps even saving more of his pilots and Allied ground forces by having less of the enemy aircraft and their talented pilots to deal with.

He closed his eyes and tried to visualize Juliette, her bountiful breasts, and glowing, healthy skin. His musings were interrupted when suddenly the hair raised on the back of his neck, and he felt the now so familiar warning of impending danger.

He opened his eyes and reached for his closest weapon. It was his grandfather's wrist breaker Confederate cavalry sword emblazoned with CSA on the hilt, that he always kept close. It had never felt defeat, and he pulled the shining razor-sharp blade from the tight scabbard with a smooth, well-oiled scraping sound. The bright steel blade slipped smoothly from the sheath as he stood to his full six feet four inches, and he took a step toward the door, clearing his sword arm from obstructions just as the door burst open.

The muzzle flashes seemed inches away as two shots screamed toward Duke, whose sword arm flew like a cobra toward the attacker.

Duke's fight-or-flight reflex kicked in and pumped adrenaline into his body.

He felt a blow to his chest and burning pain in his left flank. Before the third, and likely fatal, round in the automatic pistol could be discharged, the flash of the razor-sharp steel cut through the attacker, his body cleaved in half by the cavalry sword. His Colt dropped loudly to the floor, followed by his body.

Duke looked into the wide-open, shocked eyes of the incompetent medic, Sergeant Tucker, who mouthed, "How?" Five liters of bright aortic blood pulsated quickly from his body, covering the rough wooden floor until the dull, now all too familiar, glaze of death reflected in the unseeing dilated pupils.

Duke dropped his saber on the desk and reached to his now painful left flank. On withdrawing his hand from his wet uniform, which was covered in blood, Duke collapsed into his chair with a sigh. *Did this American Sergeant accomplish what so many German pilots couldn't do*, thought Duke as Major Carpenter and Lt. Patton rushed into the room.

"Colonel, what happened? We heard shots!" shouted the Major as they stepped over the inert torso of the Sergeant while taking in the bloody scene.

"Looks like one of my men tried to finish what the Germans have been trying to do for a year and a half," whispered Duke.

He leaned his head back on his wooden chair in pain. He lifted his bloody right hand from the gunshot wound, which was now bleeding profusely from his left abdomen.

"Oh my God!" shouted Lt. Patton as both men rushed to his side, carefully lifting him between them as Duke hobbled to the medical tent, leaving a blood trail.

The other pilots came rushing from the Officers' Club and maintenance hangers, in shock at seeing the pale face of their wounded commander, and lifted him as a group while rushing him into the medical tent. A trauma nurse, Kimberly Nightingale, quickly placed him on a gurney, cutting away the tattered uniform shirt and binding the wound after bathing it in alcohol and starting an IV.

"Out!" she shouted to the gathered men. They scattered from the small medical tent until only Major Carpenter and Lieutenants Patton and Franklin remained.

"He is critical, and his blood pressure is way too low," whispered the nurse to the officers.

"He is bleeding internally, and I can't stop it here. All I can do is start whole unmatched blood and transfer him to the field hospital, which is hours away, but with these terrible roads blocked with our troops moving in all directions at the ongoing German offensive..." said nurse Kim with tears in her eyes. "He won't last an hour... two at the most."

The men looked at each other in confusion at the thought of the impending death of their invincible commander.

John Patton said, "But why can't we fly him there in the FE2 observation aircraft? It has two seats!"

"There's no airfield there," said Keith.

"So? I can land that crate on a dime! It would take less than 15 minutes to get there by air!" yelled John.

"I will fly as a fighter escort in my Nieuport 28!" shouted Jimmy as they looked at the Major for guidance.

"Let's do it! I will join you as top cover in mine!" said Keith after a moment's hesitation.

Then, the men shouted to nurse Kim to run as much blood as possible, but she had heard the plan and was already doing just that. The lieutenants ran to prepare for an immediate departure.

Keith leaned over and whispered in the Colonel's ear, "Sir,

we are going to get you the help you need!"

Duke said, "Keith, I heard the plan, but get me to Paris! It has better medical staff and facilities, and Juliette is there. It's only a bit farther."

Keith looked up at the nurse, and she shook her head no as she opened the IV wide open and prepared the other arm for another.

"Sir, it's another thirty minutes, and we don't know if you can last an hour!" said Keith.

Duke reached up and grabbed the Major by his shirt collar, opening his eyes fully, and pulled him close, saying, "That's an order!"

"Yes, sir!" responded the Major as Duke's arm dropped back to the gurney. His eyes closed in pain, but he felt a glimmer of hope as he heard the first rotary engine bark to life on the airfield.

When Duke opened his eyes again two days later, he was in Paris at the famous Val-de-Grace Hospital founded in 1645 by Louis XIV.

Juliette planted a wet joyful kiss on his weak lips as she excitedly yelled to the staff nurse, "He's awake!"

CHAPTER 27 • *The Wolf*

Juliette spilled the story to Duke of the life and death struggle his body had been through over the past few days, beginning with the arrival of the FE2 liaison aircraft. Lt. John Patton had somehow managed to squeeze the aircraft into the manicured but tiny grounds of the Val-de-Grace Hospital. Both Major Carpenter and Lt. Franklin had also landed beside him in their battle-scarred Nieuport 28 Biplanes, creating quite a stir. They managed to rush him into the hospital on their shoulders.

Unknown to the three pilots at the time was that this was the first aeromedical evacuation ever accomplished and would later lead to timely life-saving intervention.

Duke underwent immediate lifesaving surgery, including the removal of his left kidney, but his intestines were spared injury. The pain in his chest was from the Colt .45 round that hit his Alexander the Great oversized coin and was deflected from his heart, leaving a deep swollen bruise over his sternum. This led to a second procedure to drain a hematoma from his pericardium later on the first day he was in the hospital.

It required a delicate touch and skill which was only available in Paris. Juliette had recruited the famous physician and family friend, Alexis Carrel, MD, to take over Duke's care and perform this surgery to save his life.

Duke's appetite was immense, and he began walking around his hospital room and ward, regaining his strength each day as spring blossomed around the beautiful grounds of the hospital.

The warm late spring sunshine of May 1918 and the encouraging reports from Dr. Carrel charged Duke's spirit as he began feeling human again.

Then, two weeks to the day after his arrival, an unexpected entourage of brass arrived and politely asked Juliette for some privacy with Colonel Thomas.

Duke barely had time to prop himself on his pillow and pull his bathrobe around his neck before General "JJ" Grant arrived and told all but his chief of staff to leave the room.

"Colonel, I know you killed my nephew. I want to hear why it happened from your own lips!" said the General with a grim snarl on his face.

Duke slowly but accurately related the events of what seemed a lifetime ago. The General seemed unmoved and coldly determined. He had obviously heard these events before from Duke's junior officers.

"We didn't think you were going to survive. But now that you have and because of your status as a war hero who claimed to have killed the Red Baron and has more confirmed enemy aerial victories than anyone else in our Air Service, I will give you a choice," said the General sternly.

"You can take an immediate medical discharge and retain your rank and current honors, but you must leave France and this war permanently and return to private life. You will not receive the medal of honor nor any other further recognition for your service as long as I am in command. The story that will be published for morale purposes is that you were badly wounded during your final aerial engagement, during which you brought down twelve enemy aircraft. My nephew was later killed by a German sniper after he saved your life and will be given a posthumous Silver Star for valor and elevation in rank to Lieutenant for his service.

"We have discussed this with your squadron executive officer and the men who flew you here against all Army regulations. I have agreed not to pursue court martials against them in return for their silence, but they have refused to agree until they speak with you. So, they are now outside after being released from custody by the MPs this morning to come here.

"Or, you can repeat that outrageous story you just told me and face court-martials with your men for ordering them to break Army regulations and fly you here. You will all be found guilty, demoted in rank to enlisted privates, and sent immediately to the front!

"But if you agree, they will return to the 94th squadron, of which your executive officer will be given command and continue to serve with full honors with the new SPAD XIII aircraft. I will give you five minutes with your men to decide, and if everyone agrees, sign this statement confirming the events we just discussed as well as your medical discharge papers.

"Oh! By the way, your victory over the bloody Red Baron is being contested by the Australians who now claim he was shot down by one of their anti-aircraft gunners from the 24th machine gun company, a Sergeant Cedric Popkin, who claims to have fired the .303 round that killed him. An autopsy of Captain von Richthofen by the British flight surgeon in their sector showed a single .303 round through the chest brought him down and killed him, so this story is feasible."

"However, the RAF also credited Canadian Captain Brown who was flying a black Sopwith Camel, which was also firing .303 Vickers machine guns in the same sector with the victory.

"You were not available to present your claim for shooting down the Red Baron in his Fokker DR1 425/17 Triplane. Neither were your officers who were in custody here, so I already agreed to allow the victory to go to RAF Captain Brown," scowled the General as he and his aide de camp walked out.

The MPs immediately ushered Duke's men in. The room was deathly silent.

"Gentlemen, I want to thank you for saving my life!" said Duke.

The men relaxed and smiled at their commander. They vigorously shook his hand and filled him in on the events of the past two weeks while they languished in military police custody.

"We didn't think you would pull through!" said Major Carpenter with tears in his eyes.

The friendship of these brothers at arms who had all stared death in the face together, including Jimmy and John, both of whom Duke had personally saved on more than one occasion in aerial combat, was so deep, it even equaled the bonds of family. They seemed to have an innate and unbreakable understanding of each other.

Duke then knew what he had to do and said, "General Grant has agreed to allow you all to return to our 'Hat in the Ring' 94th squadron. Keith, you will take over as commander with new SPAD aircraft to re-equip our worn-out Nieuports, promised immediately. Until that time, I hope you will take care of *The Reaper* for me and keep her and Junior safe. If possible, I would like Junior after the end of this conflict.

"I have been ordered to take a forced medical discharge and return to private life. My home, family, and support will always be there for any of you at any time," said Duke as he choked back tears.

"We must sign this statement regarding recent events and never discuss it again," frowned Duke.

He angrily scratched his name on the untruthful statement, followed by his loyal lieutenants and Executive Officer. *The lives of my men are the most important thing,* he thought, and he knew karma would resolve things in time.

"My heart and prayers will be with each of you and the wonderful 94th," said Duke as he shook each man's hand and looked knowingly into their eyes. He wondered if any of them would ever see the other again, but as they all knew, fate was a vicious and unpredictable hunter.

The men came to rigid attention and briskly saluted their commander for the last time with tears in their eyes and said in unison, "Colonel, it has been the honor and highlight of our lives to have served under your command!"

They filed out the door as the General's aide de camp, Colonel Sanders, came in.

He looked at the documents and said, "Very wise, Colonel. Dr. Carrel has agreed under protest to move up your hospital discharge to tomorrow. I suggest you leave the continent immediately."

As Colonel Sanders closed the door, he turned and said, "Oh, by the way, that Hun you escorted back to your base and saved is on the next ward under guard. He will face a military court for his crimes and surprisingly seems to have pulled through as well. You two have some kind of luck! But he will have a tough time in the POW camp as Spanish influenza has broken out there, so his days are surely numbered."

Duke collapsed back on the bed. He was physically, emotionally, and spiritually exhausted at the turn of events and fell into a deep, troubled sleep. When he awoke to the gentle hand of Juliette, he felt refreshed, yet his sixth Alexander sense warned him that he needed to move quickly and leave the hospital.

"Darling, I have resigned my commission and been issued an immediate medical discharge, but we need to leave the hospital and Paris immediately," said Duke.

He admired the beauty of his wife's Parisian skin and her now clearly visible pregnant belly, which he rubbed affectionately.

Suddenly, he received a kick from his unborn for the first time, which brought a fatherly smile to his face and a giggle from Juliette.

"He is going to be a warrior just like his father," she said warmly and knowingly.

"We need to telegraph Captain Jones and tell him we need *The Wolf* sooner than we expected. Have him meet us at Le Havre as soon as possible with as much as he can stock in supplies," Duke said.

"Please go home and pack all you need and see if you can arrange private river transport on the Seine to Le Havre, leaving tonight! I will rest and await your arrival, and we will slip out of the hospital at dark. Darling, I know this is sudden, but you must trust me. I don't have time to explain yet," exclaimed Duke with a serious tone to his voice.

Juliette didn't hesitate and said, "Of course, mon amour!" and vanished after a deep kiss.

Duke looked around the room for a weapon or civilian clothing, but there was nothing, and before he could gather the strength to stand up, he once again fell into a deep, troubled sleep. When he woke, late afternoon shadows were stretching across his private, antiseptic-smelling hospital room from the tall glass window, which looked west from the Baroque-style hospital.

He felt stronger and stood up, pulling on the single private garment in the room, his blue silk bathrobe, which Juliette had specially monogrammed for him with his initials: DT.

He quickly made his way into the hall and across to the next ward looking for Max.

He picked up a scalpel from a wound care and debridement tray and slipped it into the palm of his hand.

Finally, he found Max at the far end of the large open ward with dozens of wounded soldiers surrounding him. They had amputated limbs, disfigured faces and bodies, and many moaned and smelled of antiseptics or worse, all separated by white sheets serving as non-acoustic walls.

Duke was exhausted from the short search and sat briefly on the bench beside the ward door waiting for Max's guard to look the other way.

When he did, Duke quietly slipped unseen past the guard who was thankfully ogling a French nurse and yawning with boredom.

Max was propped up in bed and looked much better than their previous meeting at the airfield. He had a tight white bandage around his chest with only a trace of old blood.

His ankles were strapped tightly to the bed with cloth shackles, but his hands were free. His eyes were closed in light sleep.

Duke leaned over and whispered, "Hello, my friend."

Max's eyes opened slowly like a mongoose looking for his prey.

"I only have a moment, and we must be quiet so as not to alert the guard," mouthed Duke.

Then he quietly filled Max in on the details, including the deadly Spanish flu sweeping the POW camps.

Duke watched Max's eyes, which seemed to be hostile. However, when he quietly spoke with his rich Oxford accent and said, "Thank you, my friend," he seemed to be himself again, or did he?

Duke hesitated; should he give Max the scalpel which he would surely use for escape into downtown Paris, perhaps killing another guard? He would blend in with his Oxford accent and excellent French and then quickly return to battle on the German front. He seemed more distant and reserved.

262

Maybe it was the chest wound, or was it more? Had he decided after their last combat that it was every man for himself and first come, first take at Alexander's tomb filled with treasure? Were he and Max now enemies even outside of the war-torn sky? Would he fulfill their blood oath of secrecy they made together at Alexander's tomb just a few months ago? Would he be convicted at his military trial for killing two soldiers during his last escape?

Duke's honor and code of chivalry toward his friends were at odds with his nagging gut instinct to pocket the scalpel and walk away. The cold look in Max's eyes helped him make the difficult decision. He had warned Max, and that was more than he should have done. He realized Max was no longer the friend he thought he was due to his actions and the spine-tingling sixth sense.

Duke quietly stood up and kept the scalpel in his pocket. Max didn't even say goodbye. He silently disappeared into the ward, once again avoiding being seen by the guard who was now talking with an attractive nurse in the corner.

It was almost dark as Duke slipped silently back toward his room. The shadows of twilight deepened the eeriness of the ancient hospital, and the moans of the sick and dying seemed much louder than ever. The intense smell of antiseptic and rubbing alcohol penetrated the hall, as did the terrible sweet smell of gas gangrene that thrived in the wounds of these war-torn men and led to constant amputations and miserable death.

Duke was about to push open the door when he hesitated, listening to the now familiar sixth sense of Alexander, which warned him to stop. He backtracked and flattened himself against the shadowy wall and listened to the faint whispering coming from his room. It was Arabic, and they were angry!

Like a wounded leopard, Duke slipped back to the stairwell and watched the door. Then, like ghosts, he saw two white-cloaked Arabs in tight white turbans and flowing white gowns with bejeweled daggers hanging on their hips quietly emerge from the room.

They looked in both directions before walking toward the nurse's station. One exclaimed, "Nurse, our friend, no in room!"

Visions of Juliette flew through Duke's head as he immediately fled down the stairs in his blue silk gown toward the main entrance. He knew the Arabs would kidnap and kill her if they found her first. He prayed he was in time. The love of his life was walking straight into this trap. His legs felt like noodles and shook with weakness from two weeks in bed as he took stair after stair from the 3rd floor.

He finally pushed open the door to the main floor of the hospital. Duke dropped onto a dark wooden bench inside the entrance of the tall cathedral-like main doors of the hospital, watching intensely for his love.

Soldiers of all allied services, civilians, priests, nuns, children, and vendors came and went through the doors. It was almost total darkness outside as the candles of the chandeliers and torches by the doors shed light on the passersby.

Finally, like an angel, she appeared out of the darkness wearing her traveling khaki pants with polished black riding boots and her flowing white silk shirt, which showed her generous cleavage, or was he dreaming?

He lifted himself in what felt like slow motion and went to her, mouthing her name, but his lips were so dry with tension that nothing came out. She saw him and embraced him with eyes of passion and confusion, tightly and strongly supporting him out the door.

"We must leave now, my love!" Duke finally eked out of his dry mouth.

Despite her confusion, she turned with him on her arm, and they disappeared through the hospital entrance to the dark streets of Paris, where Juliette had a coach and driver awaiting them.

The torches were flaming on the coach as it disappeared

down the cobblestone deserted evening byways of Paris, making for the waiting river transport Juliette had arranged. She helped Duke into his travel clothing as they thundered down the empty streets and handed him Raj's Khukuri blade, which he tucked into his loose black buffalo belt. Then, he leaned back fully into the cool black leather of the empty private coach as his head buzzed with fatigue.

Juliette leaned out and yelled, "Plus vite!" to the coachman.

He snapped his whip over the chargers as they reached a gallop down the dark blacked-out streets of Paris.

Ten minutes later, the coachman yelled, "Ho!" as he pulled the lathered chargers to a stop beside the private dock on the Seine river. A sleek river barge was barely visible, with only a small anchor torch showing on the stern. The coachman jumped on the roof, manhandling the two large travel trunks and tossing them to the waiting boatman, who quickly loaded them with other smaller bags onto the river barge. He then released the lines from the dock while Juliette handsomely paid off the coachman and told him, "C'est secret!"

He nodded obediently and disappeared into the dark of the night, as did the barge. Juliette quickly jumped aboard and took Duke below to their private quarters. The barge churned silently into the midst of the Seine and disappeared with the current past the ancient sentinel Notre Dame and into the eerie silence of the night.

They were the only passengers, and Juliette had pulled family strings to arrange for this sudden private passage to Le Havre, which was a three-day, non-stop journey. Unfortunately, she was not familiar with the boatman, nor was her family.

Their travel time would coincide with the arrival of *The Wolf*, which had been itching to get back to sea for another long voyage, according to Captain Jones' telegraph from that afternoon.

But first, Juliette turned into a nurse again as she helped Duke out of his leather jacket, white silk shirt, khaki travel pants with his large black belt, Khukuri blade, and calfskin boots. He collapsed on the bed, barely visible under the glow of the whale oil lamp burning on low beside the door. He pulled her to his aching chest and planted a deep wet kiss on her moist red lips in the process.

"Merci, mon amour," Duke whispered and fell immediately into a deep healing sleep.

Juliette unpacked the essentials in their room and then made her way to pay the first half of the King's ransom for this sudden journey. She then discussed more details of the trip with the smiling boatman, Paul Lafitte.

Paul was pleased to receive half of the payment he had requested without negotiations as he calculated his profits and considered what he would do with the balance.

He wondered the reason for his good fortune as the gentleman looked injured, and the lady was ravishing. Maybe he should send word of his journey to a friend who could investigate and perhaps turn up more profits. He smiled happily at his brilliant idea and silently lit a cheroot to celebrate. But the lady would not leave the pilot cabin, and when she did, she was watching his every move.

Juliette listened to her gut feelings and realized they were in danger but didn't understand why. Instead of returning immediately to the cabin, she decided to keep watch on their progress until they were well clear of Paris. She paced the deck and watched the boatman. Her instincts told her she couldn't trust him as the nautical clock in the small deckhouse passed midnight, and they left the dim lights of Paris and shadow of the Eiffel tower well behind.

Monsieur Lafitte had repeatedly asked to stop for the night.

Juliette calmly said, "No!" She reminded him this was a

non-stop journey for which she had paid handsomely. She reached into her waistcoat, feeling for the small Derringer pistol that she had learned to carry while in the war-torn capital of France, and made sure it was ready, just in case.

Paul became agitated as his idea to capitalize on his good fortune was blocked by this mysterious lady. He decided they must be wanted; eventually, she would fall asleep, and then he would pull ashore. But for the whole night, Juliette Thomas remained on deck, only making quick trips below to check on Duke, who was snoring deeply while warmly encased in a wool blanket with his head snuggled into his favorite goose-down pillow, which she had wisely brought from their Parisian home.

She brewed up coffee, which she shared liberally with the boatman, who realized his patience was necessary. But like a cobra, he thought, he would wait for his time to strike. Then he smiled and accepted the strong Turkish brew which Juliette now always made for Duke.

The late spring morning dawned bright and fresh. The earthy smell from the tree-lined bank and spring flowers filled the air with the glorious scents of the French countryside as small villages gently passed the river barge steamer. After her third cup of coffee disappeared, Juliette made her way to the small onboard kitchen galley and began making fresh bacon and eggs with croissants and cheese, one of Duke's favorite morning meals.

As the aroma of bacon and coffee filled the galley and wafted into Duke's room, he awoke, pulling on his light leather jacket over his dry dressings and khaki pants. He was drawn like a moth to the flame of the galley stove. Quietly, he sneaked in behind Juliette and engulfed her with both arms.

To her surprise and delight, he gently squeezed her enormous breasts, which seemed to become fuller with each day of her pregnancy. She giggled with love and turned around, engulfing the love of her short life with a tight hug and a wet kiss.

They both were smiling as they settled in for a hearty breakfast at a battered wooden table with chairs on the deck behind the pilot's wheelhouse. They enjoyed the fresh, light scented breeze and warm late spring sun while Duke downed two full helpings of the nourishment he needed so badly to replace the 20 lbs of muscle weight he had lost in his fight for survival.

He spoke quietly, watching the smoke waft from the steam engine's tiny smokestack at the back of the barge while they churned steadily toward Le Havre and sanctuary in *The Wolf*.

Duke filled Juliette in on the events of the last 24 hours and their need to leave quickly from Paris and the continent, including the Arab visitors that had made a surprise visit to his hospital room. She stared at her husband in awe and with love as she likewise filled Duke in on the events of the night and her suspicions of the boatman, Paul. She made him promise to never hide anything from her, and he promised to always be honest, no matter how much he wanted to protect her.

"Darling, you are a true warrior and savant. I promise to never hide or sugarcoat anything from you again. I'm so proud of your courage and planning everything so quickly, but you and our unborn need sleep, so let me get you below while I watch this rascal and absorb some badly needed Vitamin D from the sun," said Duke.

He engulfed Juliette in a deep hug and walked her down to their stateroom. She immediately fell into a deep rejuvenating sleep until the evening.

They continued this routine for the next two days. Unfortunately, Duke never saw the boatman pass a message to a friend on a passing river barge headed to Paris as they drifted slowly past the small village of Vernon while he dozed on deck in the warm spring sun later that first day.

However, Duke felt rejuvenated as he continued to gain

weight and strength with each meal and moment on deck. Even the booming thunderstorm which rocked the boat and lit up the night sky on the last evening on the boat failed to dampen the couple's spirits.

They dined below deck on veal, fresh new potatoes, asparagus, and a spring mix salad with olive oil and an oaky Chardonnay that Juliette had collected from a local barge family they passed earlier that morning. Duke marveled at her beauty, courage, and knowledge of the local delicacies as he absorbed her historical narration of this famous Norman region of France.

The Celts had populated the region until conquered by the Romans in 98AD. Then after the fall of Rome in the mid-fifth century, the Franks became the majority ethnic group, building monasteries and civilizing the area before the Vikings devastated the region with raids and then intermixed with the diverse population.

It was an area that had been at constant war, but the food and beauty of the region were mesmerizing, and Duke absorbed the earthiness and health with every mile that passed. He began to feel like a man again, but now a free man. He reflected on the famous conflict that engulfed the region as he thought of his own life.

Since leaving his beloved Georgia and family, the last year and a half had been an endless war with Germany. He felt at the time that by volunteering to fight against tyranny and injustice while pursuing his flying passion as a Lafayette Escadrille fighter pilot, he could make the world a better place. After all, hadn't his family always stood up for freedom, independence, and justice, despite all the risks and dangers?

He wanted to make them proud and continue the traditions of duty, honor, and country, which General Robert E. Lee had always told his troops even when the odds were against them. But now, with the Arabic bounty hunters and even his own country turning on him and discarding him like yesterday's trash because of a General who would stop at nothing to protect his family name, Duke realized he was fighting on many fronts and could trust no one except the love of his life and his family.

Duke had achieved more aerial success, awards, and victories than any other American pilot. But now, because of the relations of the reigning General whose nephew had almost killed him, he was a persona non-grata and felt like a panther being ruthlessly hunted for doing his duty. The dogs of death had been loosed against Duke, and if they treed him, it was over.

He began to feel that the power of Alexander was needed more than ever to survive these ruthless hunters and rid the world of these political and military leaders who ignored the truth and mercilessly killed anyone that got in their way. Duke would need all of Alexander's power in the upcoming struggles.

The morning of the third day broke clear and scenic. It looked like one of Duke's favorite artist's paintings, Claude Monet's *Sunrise*, an impressionist painting of the port of Le Havre with the sun rising like an orb through the mist and haze, as they approached the Port.

By lunch, they had arrived at the Outer Harbor of Le Havre with the French tricolor flag flapping in the freshening breeze. The wharf was crowded with men of all nations mixed with allied soldiers, naval officers, and ruffins wandering in the midst.

The boatman would go no further and quickly offloaded their trunks and gear after Juliette paid the other half of the exorbitant fare. He snarled and immediately departed, leaving them both with an unsettled feeling.

They made their way to the harbor master's office and found out *The Wolf* had arrived earlier that morning and was still anchored in the middle harbor. Duke negotiated for a message to be sent to *The Wolf* for transport while Juliette sent a telegram to her family, letting them know she was departing for a long sea voyage.

We made it

Duke was feeling much stronger but still not himself. The bandages were off, but his surgical wound was fresh and bright red where the sutures had recently been removed from his left flank, and his chest was still deeply bruised and sore.

He wore his light leather flying jacket in the breezy harbor with his lucky cavalry saber, his Khukuri blade on his thick black American buffalo belt, and a leather brimmed safari hat. This would be their last afternoon onshore for quite a while, so Duke proposed a quick drink at the Le Havre Harbour cafe. They rushed to the cafe as the inner harbor transport pulled out to notify *The Wolf* of their arrival, loaded with their gear.

There was just enough time for a quick celebration of their escape from Paris and his improving health, so they ordered Juliette's favorite, a 1905 Dom Perignon Champagne. Duke carefully chose a table in the back of the cafe with his back to the wall facing the entrance. He felt a growing sense of unease and wanted to watch the cafe entrance just in case.

The Normans are a proud people; many descended from the Vikings who controlled these waters almost a thousand years ago. They even contributed to naming the harbor, not officially founded until 1517. One of the first international trades involved slaves but had since expanded to all areas, especially wartime munitions and weapons. Many nationalities were present and all languages spoken; it sounded like the tower of Babel. Smuggling was a lucrative trade, and the men out of uniform were armed and had a frontier look in their dress and eyes.

The champagne quickly arrived, and the couple proposed a toast to themselves for a "lifetime of love and happiness!" as they downed the blanc de blanc from the wonderful white grapes of Chardonnay. The tiny bubbles of the Moet & Chandon Dom Perignon teased their palates and relaxed Duke's tension. They drew together and shared deep longing kisses as they anticipated being together in their excellent stateroom on *The Wolf*.

After the second bottle, Duke understood why this had been Napoleon's favorite champagne and why he shipped it directly from Epernay to Paris on the Marne River to supply his Imperial House. Of course, Juliette loved it since her family name graced the bottle, and the profits afforded her family a life of luxury and decadence, which she chose to ignore, except for the family Parisian home she used and enjoyed.

Just as they paid the waiter, Duke felt the all too familiar Sixth Alexander sensation of danger. He loosened his saber and eased his chair back. He whispered for Juliette to leave from the back of the cafe and meet him at the inner harbor transport dock where he hoped *The Wolf's* transport tinder would arrive at any moment.

She looked into his eyes, questioning, as they stood up together.

At that moment, Paul, the boatman, walked in the entrance of the cafe and pointed toward them, showing a group of Arabs in white turbans where the couple sat.

The Arabs smiled, flashing their ivory white teeth, and moved toward the couple with the grace of warriors. They removed their white robes and revealed curved swords and jeweled daggers. *These were not ordinary soldiers,* Duke thought.

Duke didn't hesitate. He pulled out his saber while pushing Juliette behind him, just as the first warrior ran directly at him, yelling, "Allah Akbar!"

The other drinkers and cafe customers scattered in confusion.

Duke clashed with their blades in mid-air. He parried and brought his blade high while pushing his body against his agile opponent, who briefly withdrew, allowing Duke to disengage. Then, with a stroke like lightning, Duke slashed the Arab above his Adam's apple. Blood exploded from both carotid arteries, and the Arab dropped his blade, collapsed to the floor holding both hands over the profuse blood flow, but to no avail.

The next two Arabs approached side by side and were briefly confused, lowering their guard as they watched their comrade hold his throat, mouthing words for help as his lifeblood soaked the floor.

Duke sprang like a lion to impale the Arab on his right. He twisted and withdrew his sword while spinning his body in a 360 arc. His sword arm flashed the singing blade through the exposed wide-eyed body of the third attacker. He was cleaved in half and dropped to the floor, screaming, "Allah!"

Duke was breathing heavily and knew his strength was almost at its end as he locked eyes with the obvious leader of the group who yelled, "You're mine!" and lunged directly at Duke.

Their blades crashed together like thunder. Duke held the blades together as long as possible, but as stroke after stroke from his attacker exhausted his sword arm, he began to shake. He gave way to the powerful sword strokes and backpedaled.

Now with a gleam in his eye, the Arab attacker, whose awful breath smelled like a hyena as it fumigated Duke's face with the fetid aroma, pushed to conclude his deadly attack. Sweat dripped from his forehead, mingling with Duke's as their faces were only inches apart. The two great blades remained locked, and the smiling Arab pushed Duke back, feeling his growing weakness like a jackal on the prowl.

Finally, Duke was bent backward over the cafe bar with the blade only an inch from cutting his throat. Duke desperately reached with his free left hand and pulled Raj's Khukuri blade from his buffalo belt. With his last ounce of energy, he plunged it under the sternum and up into his attacker's exposed chest. He felt the attacker's strength evaporate as he twisted it into his heart, and the Arab's curved sword loudly dropped to the floor, followed by his limp body. Duke was breathing so hard he could barely hold his weapons. He sheathed his knife and collapsed back onto the bar as stars danced in his eyes.

A pistol shot rang out. The wood beside Duke's head on the bar splintered, and as he turned, he saw the boatman, Paul Lafitte, moving toward him with a German Luger pistol pointed at his head for the kill. Duke reached down, grabbing the Arab's bejeweled sword in his left hand while holding the Confederate cavalry sword in his right and began a desperate rush at his opponent. He would not die on his knees or on his back, even though he knew he had little chance to survive. Even if it took all his dwindling strength and life, he would protect the love of his life, Juliette!

Then, two quick pops like firecrackers echoed around the room. The boatman looked down at his chest as blood formed around each of the small bullet holes from the Derringer, which Juliette, who now stood beside Duke, had fired into the evil man.

He dropped to the floor like a sack of flour while Juliette rushed forward and kneeled down, grabbing the Luger pistol and his filthy black hair. She jerked his face to hers to get answers before he took his last breath. She was livid with anger at this villain who ruthlessly tried to kill the father of her unborn and the man she loved more than life itself.

She spoke in quick French to the dying boatman, who answered hoarsely as she mercilessly pulled his head to her ear, and the cafe patrons began forming around the dying man. He spoke his last mysterious words that only she could hear.

Duke reached out, grabbing Juliette's arm as the villain's eyes took on the vacant look of the dead with dilated pupils gazing into hell. They pushed their way through the crowd of onlookers to the door, running into Captain Jones, who, with the giant cook and first mate Black George, cleared a path directly to *The Wolf's* tender. Two other Arab bodies lay inert on the ground, and Duke saw blood dripping from the Captain's British saber, which he quickly sheathed with a knowing wink and said, "Don't like the scum either."

They departed the dock to the sound of police whistles, which were now swarming into the cafe. They were barely out of earshot by the time the police rushed to the dock, wildly gesturing for their attention. No one looked back, and the crew knowingly pulled for all they were worth for *The Wolf*, whose second mate was wisely already pulling anchor.

Before the French customs and police boat could be launched, *The Wolf* was under full sail. She disappeared out of the harbor and into the wind-frothed English Channel, heading for the North Atlantic and safety. No other schooner or launch could ever hope to catch *The Wolf* under full sail on a fast beam reach. Captain Jones turned the schooner over to his capable new second mate, Jim Downing, and went below to check on his passengers.

They gathered in the mess hall while Black George filled four large mugs with dark Caribbean 1703 Mt. Gay rum as they all caught their breath, especially Duke, who was still pale and shaking after the mortal combat. His fresh wound had reopened, and Juliette had just finished binding it, stopping the bleeding.

"Good to see you, Captain," said Duke with a grimace and pain in his eyes. "Please accept my compliments on you and your crew's timely arrival. Thanks for clearing our escape route with your nice blade work!"

The Captain smiled and said, "You are handy with the sword as well, Colonel, and ma'am, I have never seen cleaner shooting. I never liked those ragheads anyway, much less competing boatmen! Where are we off to?"

"The Caribbean to start with, and then we will decide from there," said Duke and Juliette together with a knowing smile between them.

"Anything I need to know about? We are provisioned for eight weeks," said the Captain.

"Well, I think we should avoid Germans, French, Americans, and especially Arabs!" laughed Duke as the rum began to circulate through his body, easing the pain.

"Yes, sir, Colonel!" responded the Captain with a smile.

He and George joined in with deep laughter, and the rum flowed freely. They quickly drained the last of their drinks and headed back on deck to trim the ship for top speed through these contested waters.

Duke leaned back and pulled the Arab's bejeweled sword from his belt and said to Juliette, "This is the same style as the

276

Sheikh's son I killed in the desert. His father, Abdul Muhamed, who started the uprising, is the one who has placed a large bounty of gold on my head. He has called for a blood feud, and with his immense wealth, he will stop at nothing."

Juliette looked deeply into Duke's eyes and began, "The boatman said whoever killed you was entitled to a bounty of 12,000 pieces of gold. The Arabs had been tipped off by him while en route to Le Havre. He also said right before he took his last breath that an American had already tried to kill you for the bounty, and a German had told the Arabs of your presence in the hospital for a share of the bounty!"

Juliette looked at Duke wide-eyed and added with a smile, "But we showed them, didn't we, darling?"

"Yes, my love!" Duke said.

He absorbed these facts and realized the long odds he had just survived were due to his wonderful wingwoman, Juliette.

She had not only saved his life but had solved some of the strange events of the past several weeks. The American she spoke of was the pathetic alcoholic medic who was General Grant's nephew, but how could he ever prove that? Duke wondered if the General also was involved.

His instincts were right. Max had changed and wasn't the friend who translated the mysterious treasure map and shared in the discovery of Alexander's tomb in the desert. He had turned on him like a lion trying to take over the pride from the wounded and scarred leader. There was a fine line between love and hate, friend and foe, and now Duke saw it firsthand and had survived the mortal threat—this time.

"Mon amour, together we can defeat any enemy. You saved my life today, and you are my lioness. Now we will embrace our freedom, have our first child, and build a life of love and happiness in a better place!" said Duke with conviction.

Juliette jumped into his arms with an infectious smile of pure adoration. They embraced in a passionate, wet, lingering kiss of happiness and love before walking out on deck together.

The freshening breeze promised a fast voyage as it blew their hair toward the wake. Arm in arm, they looked together toward the yellow, orange, and bronze reflected rays of the setting sun just off the bow as they raced toward sanctuary in the healing waters of the Caribbean.

The crashing bow of the schooner threw a shower of salt spray that covered them in a mist of refreshing cool water. It seemed to be baptizing them with a new life and washing away the horror of death and destruction, which now lay behind them in another continent as they flew with the wind to peace, freedom, and safety.

Duke now knew who some of his enemies were. As the ancient Chinese General Sun Tzu said in *The Art of War* from the 6th century BC, "Know your enemy and know yourself and you can fight a hundred battles without defeat."

How many more battles are awaited? Duke smiled as he reached for his now deeply dented but powerful talisman, Alexander's coin. He had already won over forty-eight aerial battles and countless ground conflicts. He knew with control of Alexander the Great's armor, body, and tomb and with its powerful protective prophecy, but most importantly, with Juliette at his side, he could win them all!

THE END

DISCLAIMER

This is a work of historical fiction. The main characters are fictional personalities that reflect some of the events/aircraft/archaeological facts of the time and are not based on characters living then. Some of the pivotal leaders and pilots are based on true historical facts and actions. Any resemblance of the main characters to any actual people is unintentional. Any references to historical events, real people, real places, air battle victories or defeats are used fictitiously.

ABOUT THE AUTHOR

Thomas Upson, MD, FACS, is a U.S. Air Force veteran with a special interest in antique aircraft and aviation history. He is retired from the surgical practice of medicine.

He has traveled extensively throughout the world personally, while working as an MD with the USA Unlimited Aerobatic Team, NASA, and also while volunteering his medical skills for expeditions to Mt. Everest and Patagonia. He has a keen interest in ancient military history which began while he attended the United States Air Force Academy.

He is also a Commercial Pilot and Certified Flight Instructor, hunter, master falconer, sailor, scuba diver, explorer, and enologist.

This is his first novel, with a sequel currently in the works. He is a Georgia native and resides in the beautiful Florida Keys aboard a sailing vessel.

Learn more, or contact the author at:

Legendaryflying.com

THE WOLF RISING

By Thomas Upson

Colonel Duke Thomas, VC (Victoria Cross), crept silently through the dusty body-strewn streets of Tripoli with his lethal companion, Junior, now a full-grown African lion. He made his way to Sheikh Abdul Muhamed's massive walled compound in the darkest part of the moonless night. The past years of being ruthlessly hunted by the Sheik's agents and assassins had turned Duke's body into a killing machine. His mind reeled at the body count these villains had left behind among his friends and family. He had lost count of the number of assassins he had dispatched. Duke knew the only solution was to cut off the head of the Snake/Sheik who sponsored these agents of death before his luck and the power of Alexander the Great might disappear.

He knew his one-time friend and now arch-enemy, Captain Max von Wagner, would soon mount an expedition to retrieve the treasure, body, and power of Alexander for his new master, the emerging Nazi Third Reich. Little did he know the surprises that Duke had wisely left behind at Alexander's secret tomb.

Duke had cruised the Mediterranean in *The Wolf*, fending off pirates, Germans, and assassins. He was hunting for the ultimate prize Alexander had discovered in the treasure house of Babylon shortly before his death at the hands of his most trusted

Generals on June 10th, 323BC. They feared the prize and power Alexander had just discovered and was pursuing would prevent any chance of his removal or death.

It opened a map to a whole new world, which Alexander would surely attempt to conquer, along with its promise of immortality.

Made in the USA
Columbia, SC
18 June 2024

36794165R00163